Street by Street

SOUTHAMPTON

EASTLEIGH, HYTHE, LYNDHURST, ROMSEY

Cadnam, Chandler's Ford, Fawley, Hamble-le-Rice, Hedge End, Netley, North Baddesley, Totton, Warsash, West End

Ist edition May 2001

© Automobile Association Developments Limited 2001

This product includes map data licensed from Ordnance Survey® with the permission of the Controller of Her Majesty's Stationery Office. © Crown copyright 2000. All rights reserved. Licence No: 399221.

Published by AA Publishing (a trading name of Automobile Association Developments Limited, whose registered office is Norfolk House, Priestley Road, Basingstoke, Hampshire, RG24 9NY. Registered number 1878835).

Mapping produced by the Cartographic Department of The Automobile Association.

ISBN 0 7495 2617 3

A CIP Catalogue record for this book is available from the British Library.

Printed by Edicoes ASA, Oporto, Portugal

The contents of this atlas are believed to be correct at the time of the latest revision. However, the publishers cannot be held responsible for loss occasioned to any person acting or refraining from action as a result of any material in this atlas, nor for any errors, omissions or changes in such material. The publishers would welcome information to correct any errors or omissions and to keep this atlas up to date. Please write to Publishing, The Automobile Association, Fanum House, Basing View, Basingstoke, Hampshire, RG21 4EA.

Ref: ML004

Key to map pages — ii-iii

Key to map symbols — iv-1

Enlarged scale pages — 2-3

Street by Street — 4-73

Index – towns & villages — 74

Index – streets — 75-88

Index – featured places — 88-90

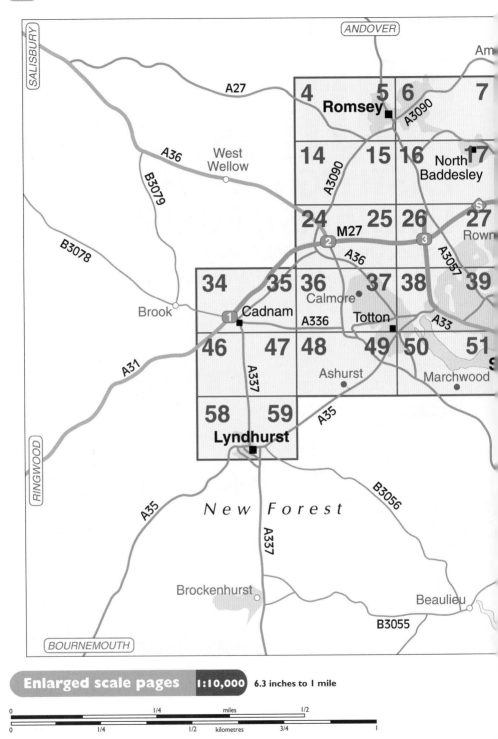

Enlarged scale pages 1:10,000 6.3 inches to 1 mile

miles

kilometres

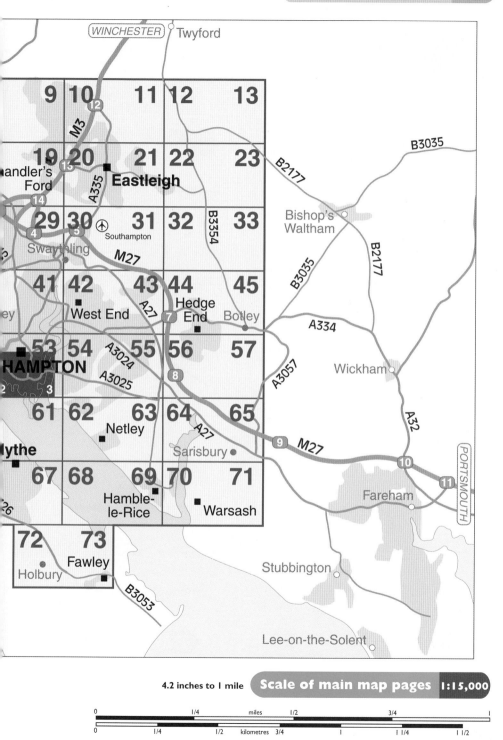

WINCHESTER — Twyford

9 | 10 | 11 | 12 | 13

M3

19 | 20 | 21 | 22 | 23
andler's Ford — Eastleigh
A335

B3035

B2177

29 | 30 | 31 | 32 | 33
Southampton
Swaythling
M27
B3354
Bishop's Waltham
B3035
B2177

41 | 42 | 43 | 44 | 45
West End — Hedge End — Botley
A27
A334

53 | 54 | 55 | 56 | 57
HAMPTON
A3024
A3025
Wickham
A3057
A32

61 | 62 | 63 | 64 | 65
Netley
Sarisbury
M27
PORTSMOUTH

67 | 68 | 69 | 70 | 71
Hamble-le-Rice — Warsash
Fareham

72 | 73
Holbury — Fawley
B3053
Stubbington

Lee-on-the-Solent

4.2 inches to 1 mile — **Scale of main map pages** — **1:15,000**

miles: 0 — 1/4 — 1/2 — 3/4 — 1
kilometres: 0 — 1/4 — 1/2 — 3/4 — 1 — 1 1/4 — 1 1/2

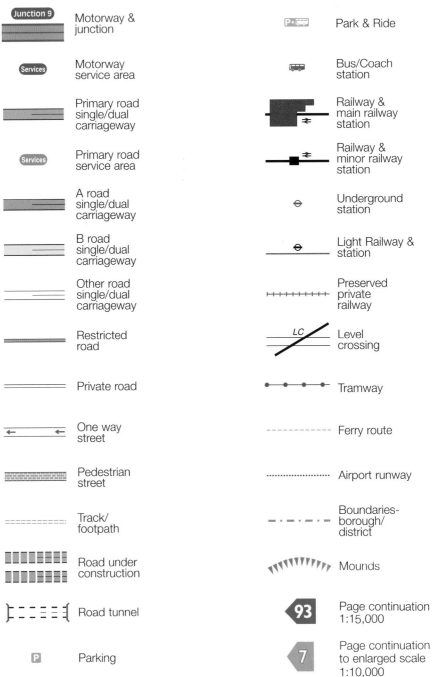

Junction 9	Motorway & junction
Services	Motorway service area
	Primary road single/dual carriageway
Services	Primary road service area
	A road single/dual carriageway
	B road single/dual carriageway
	Other road single/dual carriageway
	Restricted road
	Private road
	One way street
	Pedestrian street
	Track/footpath
	Road under construction
	Road tunnel
P	Parking

P+	Park & Ride
	Bus/Coach station
	Railway & main railway station
	Railway & minor railway station
	Underground station
	Light Railway & station
+++++++	Preserved private railway
LC	Level crossing
	Tramway
- - - - -	Ferry route
....	Airport runway
	Boundaries-borough/district
	Mounds
93	Page continuation 1:15,000
7	Page continuation to enlarged scale 1:10,000

	River/canal, lake, pier	♿	Toilet with disabled facilities
	Aqueduct, lock, weir	🔋	Petrol station
465 ▲ Winter Hill	Peak (with height in metres)	PH	Public house
	Beach	PO	Post Office
	Coniferous woodland	📖	Public library
	Broadleaved woodland	*i*	Tourist Information Centre
	Mixed woodland	♜	Castle
	Park		Historic house/ building
	Cemetery	Wakehurst Place NT	National Trust property
	Built-up area	Ⓜ	Museum/ art gallery
	Featured building	†	Church/chapel
⊓⊔⊓⊔⊓⊔⊓	City wall	⛲	Country park
A&E	Accident & Emergency hospital	🎭	Theatre/ performing arts
	Toilet		Cinema

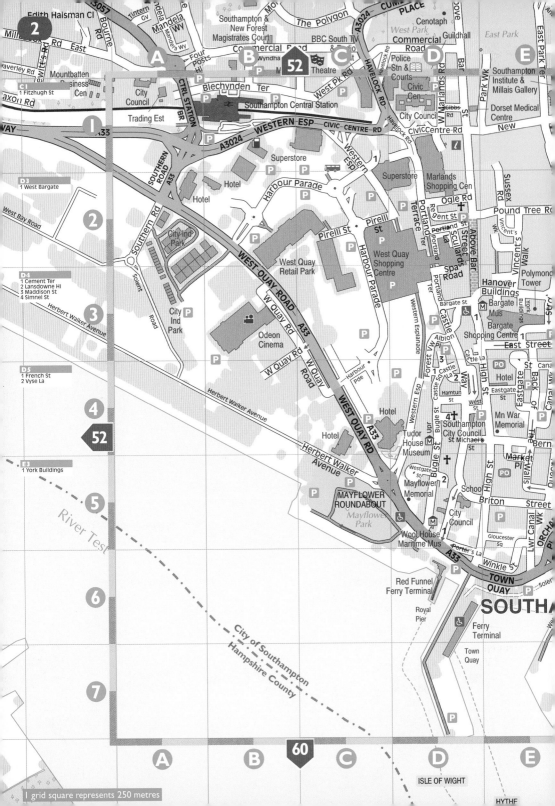

4

Lower Ratley

A   B   C   Stanbridge Earls School   D

Awbridge Danes

Danes Road

Coombe

Roke Manor F

1

Old Salisbury Lane

Test way

Shootash

Roke Manor

2   Stanbridge Ranvilles Fm

Tanners Lane

Squabb Wood

3   A27

4

Embley Lane

Spursholt Ho

5   Embley Park School   A27

A   B   **14**   C   D

Hall Copse   Gardeners Lane   Burnt Grove

1 grid square represents 500 metres

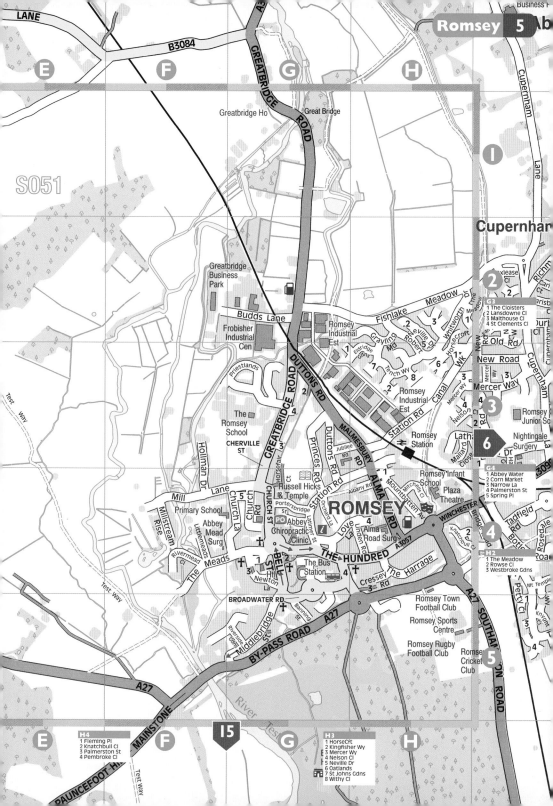

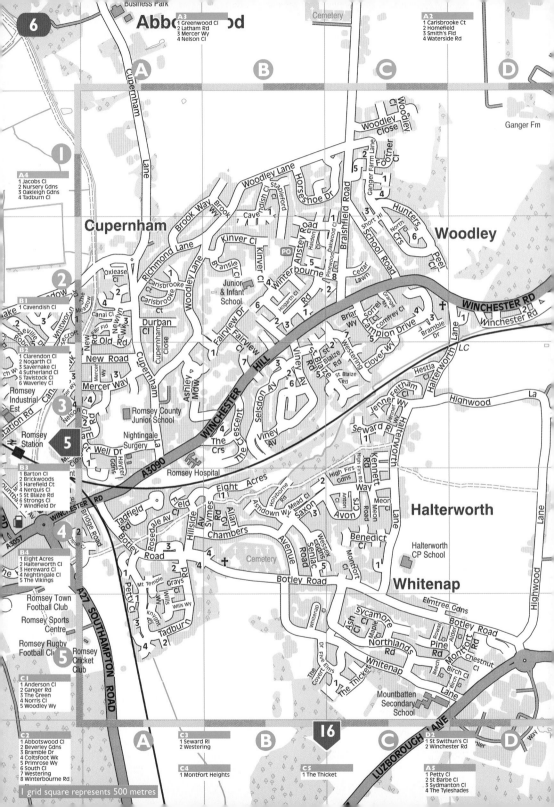

E F G H

I

Gosport

2

Crampmoor

3

8

4

5

Warren Fm

Baddesley
Common

Grovely Wy

pmoor Lane

Green Lane

Crampmoor Lane

LC

Pound Lane

Pound Lane

STRAIGHT MILE

A3090

uth
olmes
Copse

ROAD A27

BOTLEY ROAD

17

West Lane

Broad La

Andrews Cl

Rownhams La

Dunnings

Hillcrest Cl

Ringwo

Orchar Cl

Juniper Cr

Cedar

Poplar

Linden Wk

Emer Cl

Whitebeam

grove Wy

Nutburn Road

Nutburn La

St End

Sandy La

S052

E F G H

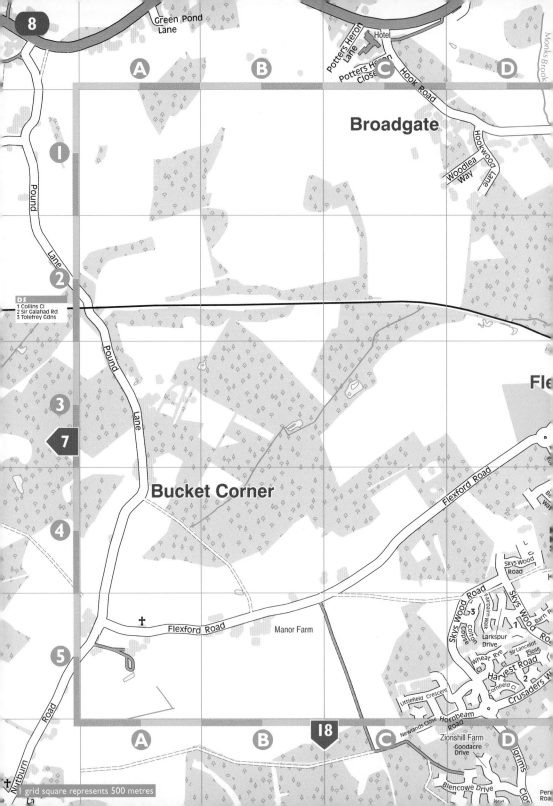

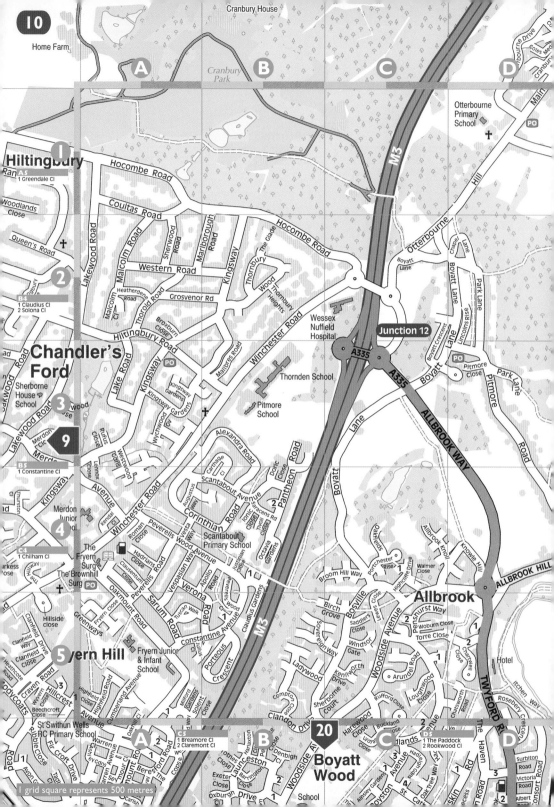

E F G H

B3

HIGHBRIDGE ROAD

B3354

I

MAIN ROAD

PO

Kiln Lane

Brooklyn Cl

Itchen Way

The Itchen Navigation

Brambridge House

Itchen Way

The Itchen Navigation

Fleming Pl

Moors Road

Orchard Close

New Road

Springfield Close

House Close

Boyes

2

Moors Close

Spring Lane

Lower Moors

Frampton Close

Chestnut Avenue

Hazel Cl

Upper Moors Road

Spring

Twyford Surgery

PO

St vigor Way

Hill La

Ash Close

Colden Common Primary School

Moors Rd

PO

Oak Tree Cl

Burr Close

Setters Close

Brickmakers Road

Whitebeam Close

Alder Close

Lime Close

Year's La

3

Church

Pennington Close

Upper Piping Road

Piping Close

Hack Drive

Hawthorn Close

I2

Lane

Grays Close

Valley Close

Church Lane

Nob's

Cro

4

Brambridge

Wardle Road

Lordswood

Bishopstoke Lane

HIGHBRIDGE ROAD

Itchen Way

B3335

Highbridge

5

E F G H

Stoke Common

2I

Road

Stoke Com Way

Pedula Way

Church

Bishops Court

Sheffield Close

Wilmot

Stoke Park Farm

PH

E F G H

I

2

Lower Baybridge Lane

Lower Farm

Whaddon Farm

Whaddon Lane

3

Marwell Zoological Park

Marwell House

Hotel

Thompson's Lane

Hurst Farm

4

Mo

Roug

Hurst Lane

Hatchley Lane

5

Marwell Manor

PORTSMOUTH

ROAD B2177

E F G H

23

Low Hill Farm

14

Embley
Park
School

A   B   **4**   C   D

Gardeners Lane

I

Hall
Copse

Burnt
Grove

2

Gardeners Lane

Kentford
Lake

3

Embley
Wood

Ranvilles Fm

Hammonds Fm

4

A3090

Semple Ho

Shelley
Lane

5

Ridge Lane

A   B   **24**   C   D

1 grid square represents 500 metres

7

EY ROAD A27

E **F** **G** **H** **I**

BOTLEY ROAD

West Lane
Broad La
St
Andrews Cl
Willow Gdns
Orcha Cl
Baddesley
Baddesley

Linden Wk
Poplar
Cedar
Emer Cl
Crs Cl
Whitebeam
Sycamore
Juniper
Firgrove Road
Camelia
Laburnum
Six

S052

Nutburn Rd
St End
Sandy La
Sandy Lane

Nutburn

Ringwood
Dunnings La
Hillcrest Cl
The Birches
Amberley Cl
Fores Cl
Woodlands Way
Ash La
Crescent
Spring Gdns
Merry Gdns
Middle Rd
Oaks
Rd
Edwina Close
PO
Baddesley Park
Industrial Est

Ringwood Drive
Cerne Cl
Hollywood Close
Copse
Ringwood Dr
Seymour La
Gap
Wynyards
Upper Crs Rd
Rosslyn
Firgrove
North Baddesley
The Vineyards
Church Cl
Willis Av
County Infants School
North Baddesley Junior School
Castle Lane
A27

BOTLEY ROAD

Queen's Ride
Tornay Gv
Sylvan
Hulles Wy
Langham Cl
Fielden
Drive
Rownhams Lane
St Christopher's Cl
Thomas Rd
Ennel Copse
Rownhams
Brownhill Road
Church Cl
Brownhill Rd
Avenue
Norton Welch Close
Health Centre

Hoe Fm
Torteval Cl
Renaie Cl
Sylvan
Drive
Launcelyn Cl
Lavington Gdns
Mortimer Way
Proctor Dr
Dibble Dr
Winston Cres
Meadow
Heath Road
Brook
Bracken Lane
Tanners Rd
Fleming
Bracken Road

2
E1
1 Broad La
2 Highlands Cl
3 Overbrook Wy

18
F1
1 Heatherview Cl
2 Pine Cl

3

Telegraph Wood

Toothill

Tanner's Brook

Lane
Rownhams Lane
Packridge

Upper
Toothill Road
Greentile
Greentile Lane

4
F2
1 Heathrbr Gdns
2 Northerwood Cl
3 Tutland Rd
4 Woodside Rd

CH
Ol

5

27
ms Service

E **F** **G** **H**
H1
1 Sandy La
G1
1 Emer Cl

M27

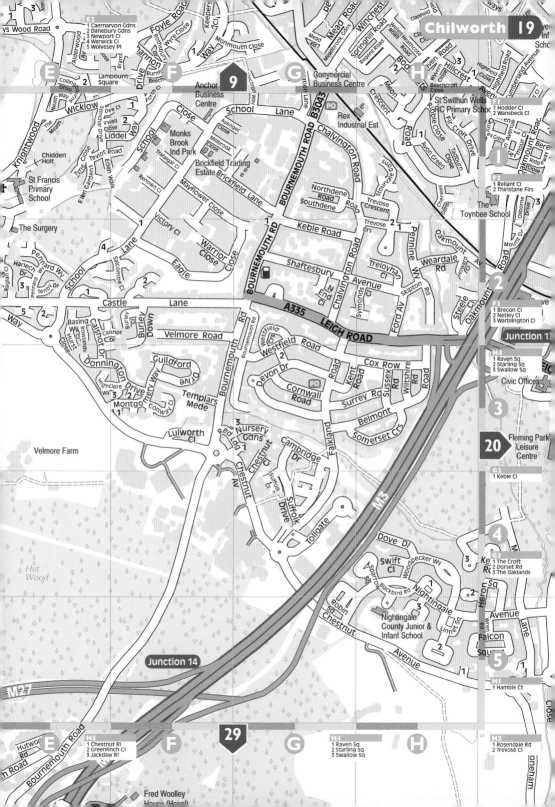

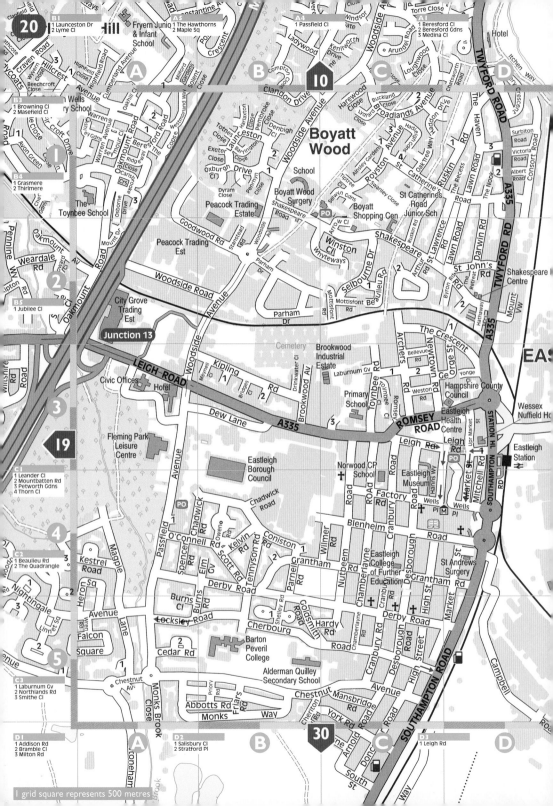

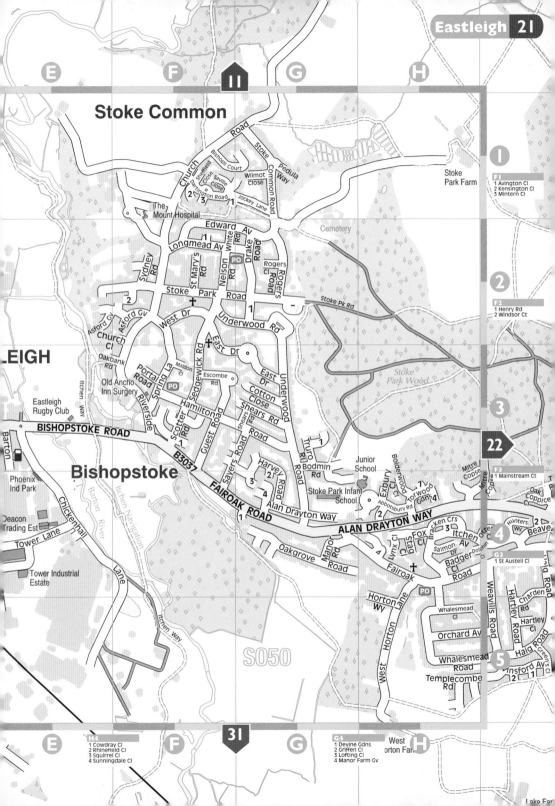

Stoke Common

Stoke Park Farm

LEIGH

Bishopstoke

22

I

2

3

4

5

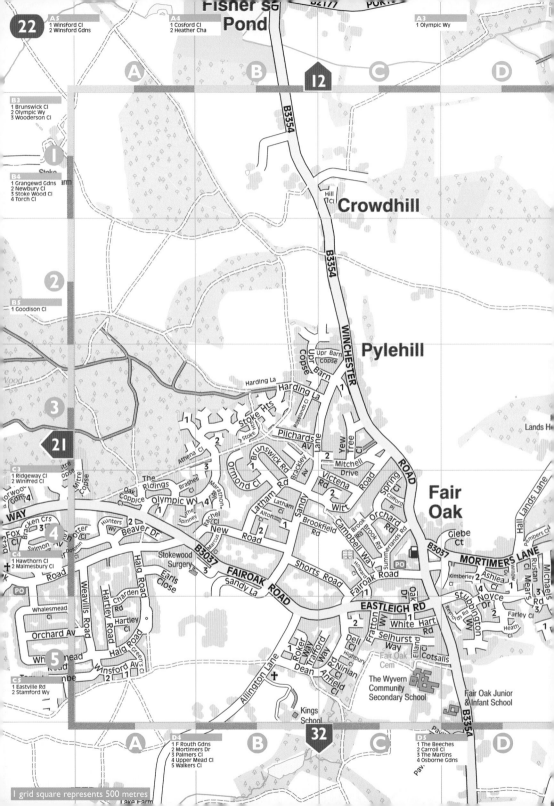

Marwell Manor

PORTSMOUTH

E F **13** G H

ROAD

B2177

Low
Hill Farm

I

*Park
Hills
Wood*

PORTSMOUTH ROAD

Stroudwood Farm

Stroudwood Lane

2

E4
1 Bradshaw Cl

B3037

3

Stroudwood
Dairy Farm

LANE

Alma Lane

Camelia Gv
High Trees
Glenwood
Court
Mimosa Dr
Magnolia
Gv
Cedar Wd
Close

MORTIMERS

Mortimers Farm

The Crescent

4

1

tland Cl

borne

Durley

5

Hall

Du
Ha

East
Horton Farm

Knowle Lane

Greenwood Lane

E F **33** G H

Greenwood Farm

24

A   B   **14**   C   D

1

2

Lane

Shelley Fm

Old Salisbury Rd

Hotel

ROAD

A36(T)

River Blackwater

3

A36 ROMSEY

Mortimers Farm
Industrial
Estate

Ower

Wade
Park Fm

Junction 2

4

Romsey Road

A326

Hi

ROMSEY ROAD   A31

**Brooke's
Hill**

5

Whitemoor Lane

Stonyford

Lopewc

Brookes Hill
Industrial
Estate

Letts

A   B   **36**   C   D

1 grid square represents 500 metres

A   B   **16**   C   D

I

Lee Church Lane

Lee

Lee Lane

Coldharbour   Lane

Nightingale Wood

2

C4
1 Blake Cl
2 Blann Cl
3 Tuffin Cl

est Way

M271

The Atherley School

Upton

Upton Cr

Upton Lane

Lymer La

Nutfield Rd

Greenwood Rd

Balmoral

Betteridge Drive

3

25

D4
1 Westways Cl

Church   Lane

ırsling Ho

Upton La

Paulet Lacave Av

Lukin Dr

Standen

Testlands Av

Broadmead Rd

Rufus Cl

Westway

Winfrith

ROME

4

Test Way

Station Rd

Junction 3

Nursling   Street

Home Fld Dr

Crawford Cl

Mill Cl

Wy

1

1

PO

Winstanley

Shepherds Wy

C of E Primary School

Nursling

Wilks Cl

Cranmer

Watley Close

2
3

Dairy   Lane

Nursling Industrial Estate

Canberra Rd

Chambers Close

Drive

5

Mauretania Rd

Oriana

Station Road

Weston La

Majestic Rd

Redbridge Lane

Manor Ho Fm

Hillyfields

A   B   **38**   C   D

Nursling Industrial Est

Andes Rd

Yewtree Lane

Redbridge Lane

Danebury Wy

Frogmore

Hightrees

Brownhil

28

University

Manor

Venture Road

Chilworth

Enterprise Rdo

A

B

Southampton University

18

Roman Road

C

ROAD

Green Lan

D

Heatherlands Road

M27

Junction 4

Pinelands Rd

Chilworth Drove

1

Chilworth Common

Pine Way

2

A5
1 Bransbury Cl
2 Lyburn Cl
3 Purbrook Cl

Dene Cl

Pine Walk

Ling Pl

Lingwood Cl

1

Fitzroy Cl

A33

Heath Way

Roman Dr

Julian Rd

The Ring Cl

2

Bassett Heath Av

Bassett Dale

Links Vw

Wy

Saxholm

Saxholm Way

Saxholm

Saxholm Dl

3

Road

11

Widgeon

27

C5
1 Shawford Cl
2 Underwood Cl
3 Wykeham Cl

Golf Course Road

Bassett Row

Greenbank Crs

Ridgemount Av

Bassett Ms

Bassett +

1

Beechmou Rd

Griffin Rd

Woburn Rd

Dunvegan Drive

Dunvegan Dr

Dunster

Melville Close

Oakwood Dr

Junior School

Curlew Cl

4

Fulmar Rd

D2
1 Lingwood Wk
2 Pinehurst Rd

Balmoral Cl

Oakwood DR

Oakwood Drive

Prunus Cl

Robinia Cl

Grafton Gdns

Southampton City Council

Holly Dell

Holly Hl Cl

Holly Hill

Holly Ltl Oak

Holly Hi

Chetwynd Dr

Beaulieu Cl

Petworth Gdns

Abbotsfield

Petworth Gdns

Lord's Hill Way

Salerno Road

Waltham

3

Taranto Rd

Aldermoor

Vermont School

Red Lodge School

The Firs

Talbot Rd

Vermont Close

Denbigh Gdns

Bas

Longleat Gdns

Cowdray Close

Road

5

ringford Cl

Jex Blake Cl

Springford Gdns

Preshaw Cl

Bradley Gn

Wonston Rd

Springford Rd

Aldermoor Rd

PO

Shaldon

Greywell Av

Coxford Road

Aldermoor Health Centre

Dunkirk Rd

Falaise Rd

Dunkirk Rd

Arnhem Cl

Lordswood Gdns

Lordswood Road

Lordswood

Southampton Sports Centre

Redhill Close

Red Hill Crs

Redhill Wy

Underwood Rd

Boldrewood Rd

Overcliff Rd

Bassington Dr

3

Winchester Rd

2

Bassett Crescent West

Bassett Meadow

Oakland Way

BASSETT AV

2

Bas

Springford Crs

Hollybrook Gallery

A

D4
1 Gables Ct

Valley Rd

Linford Crescent

Oakwood Avenue

Seagarth Lane

School

B

Highcliffe Road

Rockleigh Road

40

Hill La

A35

Pointout Rd

Pointout Rd

C

CHESTER ROAD

6

D5
1 The Mount
2 Tudor Wood Cl

Carron Road

Carron (WY)

M

Butt

Bassett

Bas

Crescent

D

Univers Southam

Pointout

The Winchester Gallery

cess Anne spital

1 grid square represents 500 metres

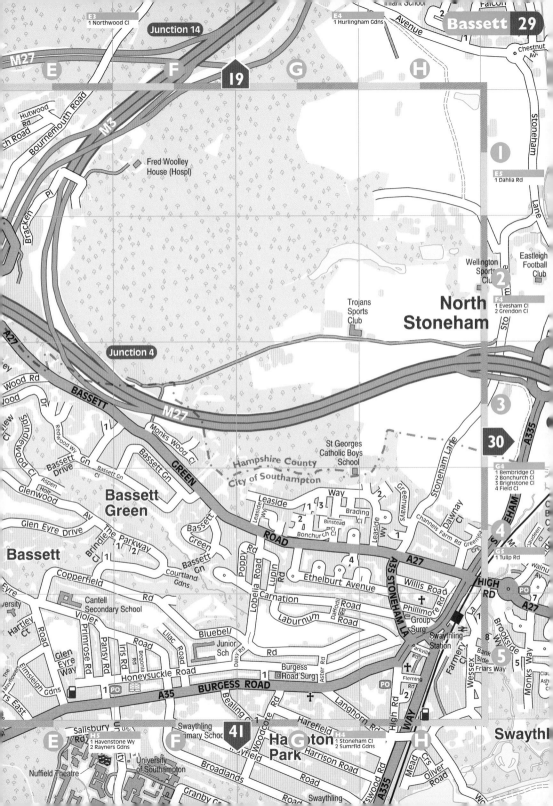

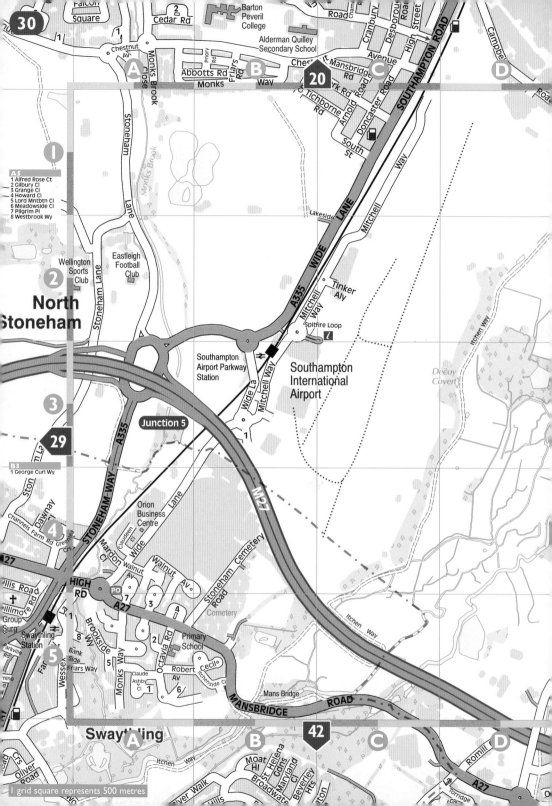

E   F   G   H

Orchard Av

West Horton Farm

I

Lake F

West Horton Rd

Templecombe Rd
2   1

Allington Manor
Business Centre

Allington Manor Farm

2

River Itchen

Hogwood Lane

3

32

Itchen Valley
Country Park

Allington Lane

4

Oaklands House

Winslowe House

5

Lane

Moorgreen Farm

Quob

Cemetery

Lime C

Moorgreen

32

ORCHARD AV
Halesmead Road
Haig Road
Winsford Av
Templecombe Rd

22

Allington Lane
Dean
Roker Way
Trafford Way
Anfield Cl
Ninian Cl
Highbury Cl
Dell Cl
Selhurst Way
Elland
Cotsalls

Fair Oak Cem
The Wyvern Community Secondary School
Fair Oak Junior & Infant S

School

Pavilion Way
Pavilion Close
B3354

BOTLEY
Knowle Lane

Lake Farm

Firtree Farm

Anson Rd
Chapel Dro
Fir Tree
York Cl
Ascot Road

I

Fir Tree Lane

Angelica Gdns
Burnetts Gdns
Burnetts Flds
Centaury Gdns
Westfield Cl
Dumpers Dro
ROAD

Horto Heath
Oakmo Sch

2

PO

1

Burnetts Lane
Crispin Cl
Meadowsweet Wy
Avens Cl
St Andrews Pk
The Dro

3

Chalcroft Farm

Cherry Drove

31

4

Blind Lane

B3342

Bubb Lane

Jacksons Farm

5

green Farm

Burnetts Lane

Lane

North Lane

44

B3342
Bubb

Marlborough
Peppercorn Wy
Adams Cl
Wainwright Gdns
Nelsons Gdns
Gardens

A **B** **C** **D**

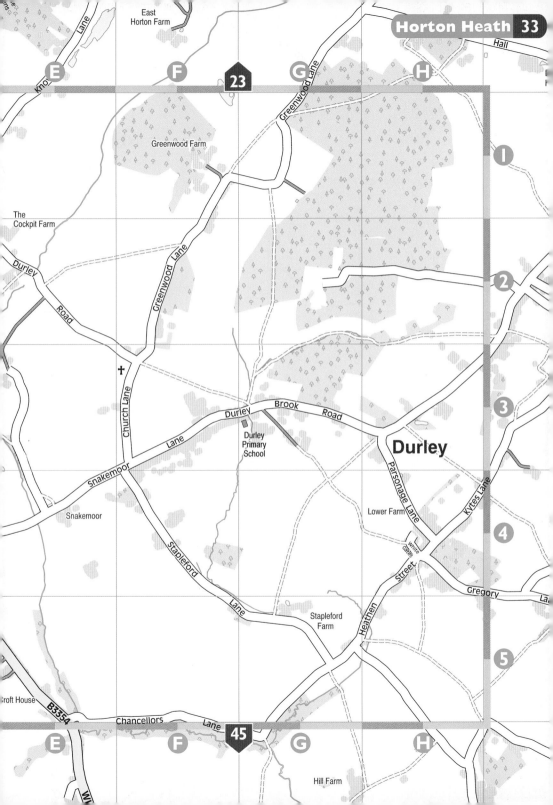

East
Horton Farm

Hall

E F **23** G H

I

Greenwood Lane

Greenwood Farm

Greenwood Lane

The
Cockpit Farm

2

Durley

Road

Church Lane

Snakemoor

Lane

Durley Brook Road

Durley

Durley
Primary
School

3

Parsonage Lane

Kytes Lane

Snakemoor

Lower Farm

4

Stapleford

White Cross

Street

Gregory

La

Lane

Stapleford
Farm

Heathen

5

Croft House

B3354

Chancellors Lane **45**

E F G H

Hill Farm

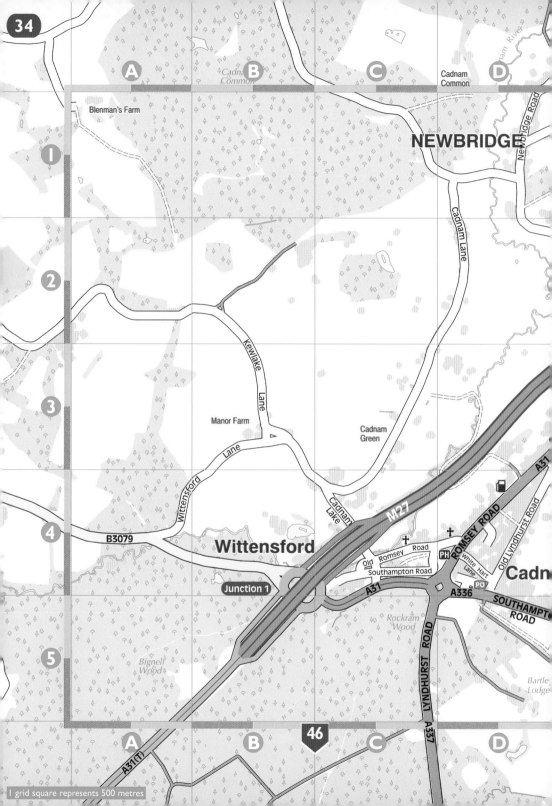

A B C D

I

Blenman's Farm

Cadna Common

Cadnam Common

NEWBRIDGE

Cadnam Lane

New Bridge Road

2

Kewlake Lane

3

Manor Farm

Cadnam Green

Wittensford Lane

Cadnam Lake

M27

A31

4

B3079

Wittensford

Old Romsey Road

Southampton Road

PH

White Hart Lane

Romsey Road

Old Lyndhurst Road

Cadn

Junction 1

A31

A336

PO

SOUTHAMPT ROAD

Rockram Wood

5

Bignell Wood

LYNDHURST ROAD

A337

Bartle Lodge

A B C D

A31(T)

1 grid square represents 500 metres

ROMSEY ROAD

Whitemoor Lane

E   F   G   H

I

Copythorne Common

Barrow Hill Road

M27

Copythorne Crs

Bunker's Hill

Copythorne

Barrow Hill

Copythorne First School

Barrow Hill Road

2

Newbridge

Pound Lane

Rd

A31

Pollards

Vicarage Lane

PO

†

Pollards Moor

Winsor Road

Winsor

3

Newbridge Road

Moor

36

Road

Winsor Lane

4

The Brickyard

Winsor Road

Cadnam Surgery

Barneyhayes La

Kennington La

Bartley C of E Middle School

Eadens Lane

5

Bartley Grange

SOUTHAMPTON ROAD A336

Rockram

New Inn Road

Oakfield Rd

Bartley

Abbot

New Inn La

PO

47

Chinham   Road

H

E   F   G

Shepherds Road

Shepherds

Riverside Cl

Parag

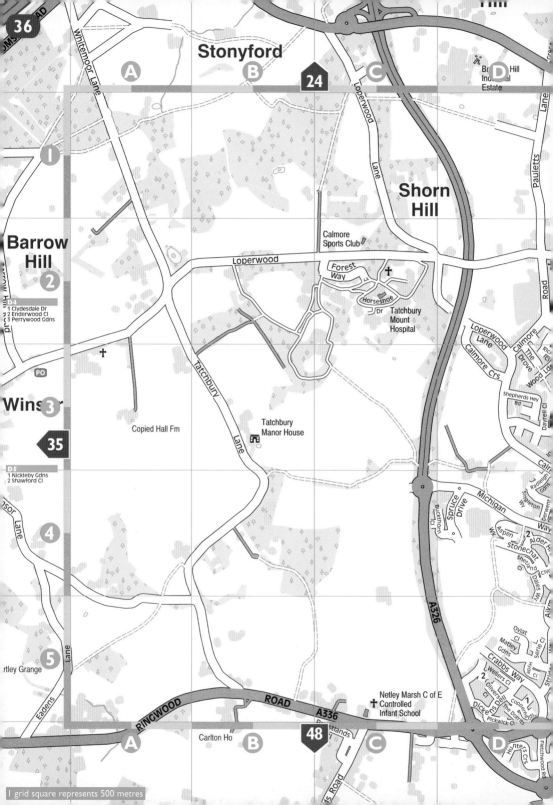

36

Whitemoor Lane

A

Stonyford

B

24

C

D

Br Hill Industrial Estate

I

Loperwood Lane

Paulletts Lane

Shorn Hill

Barrow Hill

2

D4
1 Clydesdale Dr
2 Enderwood Cl
3 Perrywood Gdns

Calmore Sports Club

Loperwood

Forest Way

Horseshoe
Dr

Tatchbury Mount Hospital

Loperwood Lane

The Wood Ldg

Calmore Crs

Calmore

Rich

Dayrell Rd

Shepherds Hey Rd

PO

†

Tatchbury Lane

Wins

3

35

Copied Hall Fm

Tatchbury Manor House

D5
1 Nickleby Gdns
2 Shawford Cl

Calr

Radleigh

Singleton

Derwent

Way

Michigan

Spruce Drive

Buckthorn Cl

Aspen Wk

Stonechat Cl

Shetland Dales Wy

Aldern

2

4

sor Lane

Oviat Cl

Matley Gdns

L Serle Cl

Hr Oak

Alkm

5

rtley Grange

Eadens Lane

Crabbs Way

Wellers Cl

Oliver Sd

Dicke

Pickwick Cl

Huntess Crs

Fleetwood Rd

Netley Marsh C of E Controlled Infant School

A

RINGWOOD ROAD

B

Carlton Ho

48

A336

C

Woodlands

D

s Road

I grid square represents 500 metres

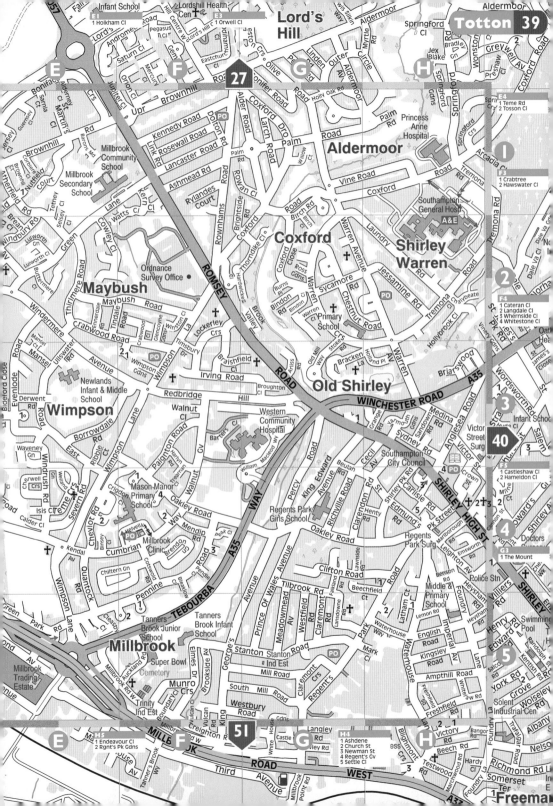

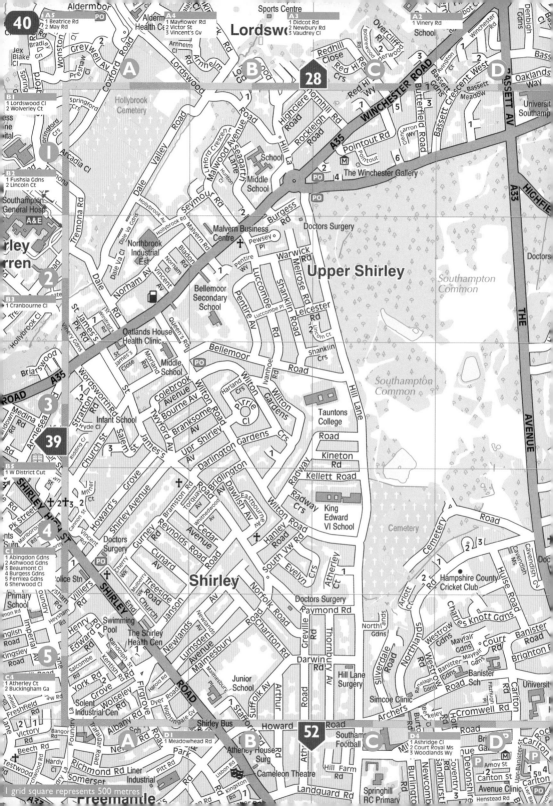

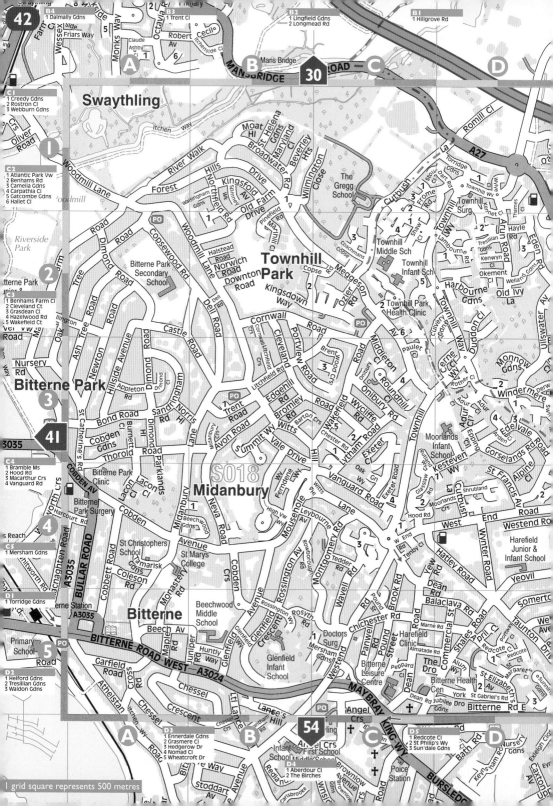

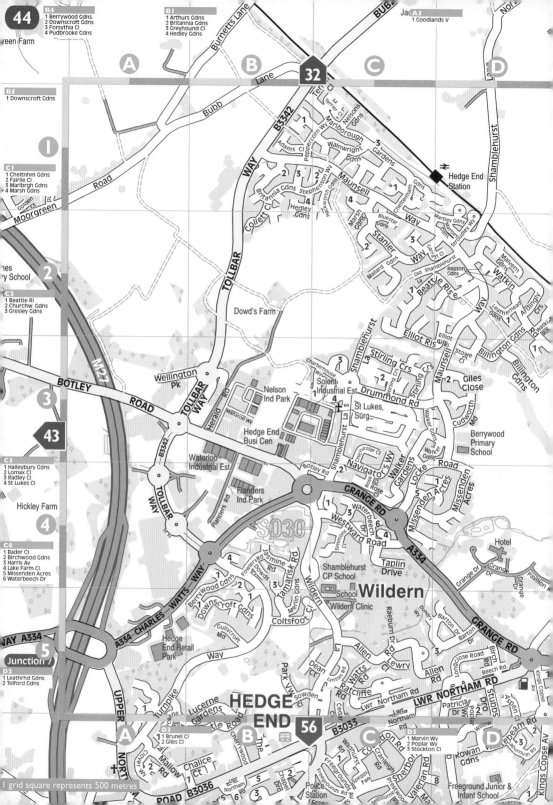

1 grid square represents 500 metres

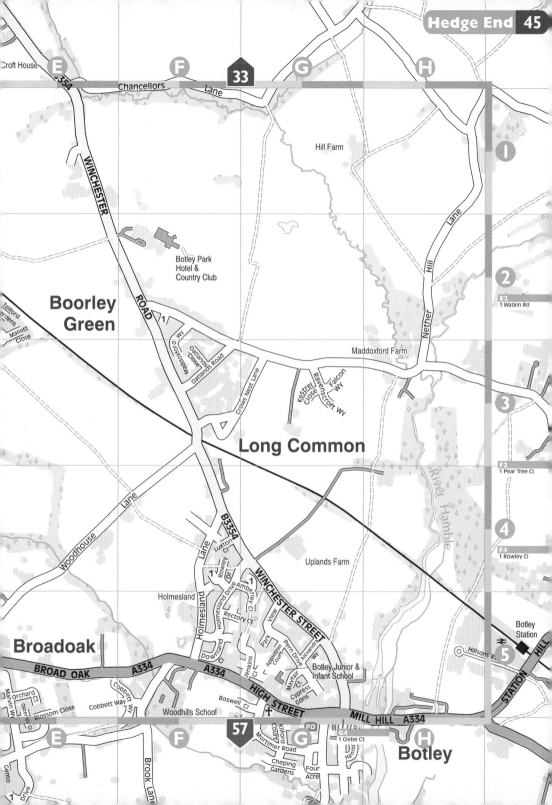

E **354** Croft House

F

33

G

H

I

Chancellors Lane

WINCHESTER ROAD

Hill Farm

Nether Hill

Hill Lane

2

E2
1 Watkin Rd

Boorley Green

Botley Park Hotel & Country Club

Telford Gardens

Mallett Close

1

Maddoxford Wy

Oatlands Close

Oatlands Road

Crows Nest Lane

Maddoxford Farm

3

E2
1 Pear Tree Cl

Kestrel Close

Ravenscroft Wy

Falcon Wy

Long Common

River Hamble

4

F4
1 Rowley Cl

Woodhouse Lane

B3354

Luxton Ct

Rowley Dr

1

Amberley Cl

WINCHESTER STREET

Uplands Farm

Holmesland

Holmesland Lane

Holmesland Drive

Rectory Ct

Park View

Fern Drive

Alexandra Wy

Botley Station

Hillsons Rd

5

Broadoak

BROAD OAK A334

Cobbett Ct

Marvin Wy

Orchard Ct

Osterley Ct

Blossom Close

Cobbett Way

Cobbett Wy

Woodhills School

A334

Dowland

Jenkins Cl

Appletree Ct

Mayfair Ct

Cypress Gdns

Botley Junior & Infant School

STATION HILL

Boswell Cl

HIGH STREET

MILL HILL A334

57

Mortimer Road

Kilford Court

Cheping Gardens

PO

Four Acre

G4
1 Glebe Ct

Hamble

Botley

E

F

G

H

Brook Lane

Gento Drive

A   B   34   C   D

Bignell
Wood

*Bartley
Lodge*

LYNDHURST RD

A31(T)

A337

I

Shave
Green
Inclosure

Beechwood Road

2

Shave
Wood

A337

3

Seaman's

**London
Minstead**

Brockishill Road

*Brockis
Hill*

Minstead
Lodge

Lane

4

Bull Lane

Minstead

Congleton Close

Football Green

PH

PO

Newtown

5

Mill Lane

043

A   B   58   C   D

A337

*Manor
Wood*

The

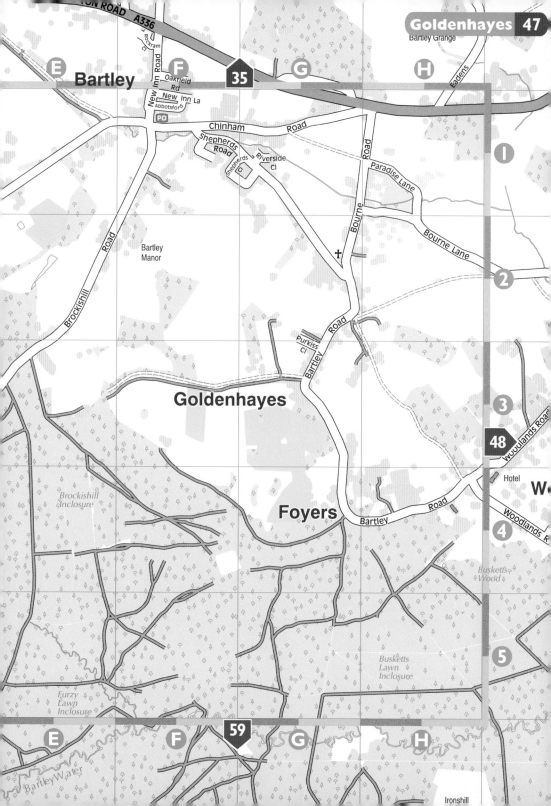

48
rtley Grange

Eadens Lane

A RINGWOOD **B** ROAD **36** **C** Netley Marsh C of E controlled Infant School **D**

Carlton Ho

Priestlands Cl

Matley Gdns

Crabbs Way

Wellers Cl

Pickwick Cl

I

Woodlands Road

NETLEY MARSH

Bourne Lane

Willswood Fm

2

Lanesbridge Cl

Green Cl

Minvina Cl

PH

3

Woodlands Road

47

Great Fletchwood Fm

Bartley Wate

Hotel

Woodlands

Woodlands Road

4

Alpine Road

The Crs

Hazel Gv

Woodlands Drove

Busketts Wood

Fletchwood Rd

Fletchwood Copse

Elm Tree Cl

Fir Road

Ash

5

Beech Rd

Princess Rd

Holly Rd

Busketts Wy

Perterscroft Av

Ash Rd

LYNDHURST

A **B** **C** **D**

PO

Ashurst Hospital

Ironshill

E1
1 Ashwood Gdns
2 Chillenden Ct
3 Copinger Cl
4 Driftwood Gdns
5 Maple Gdns
6 Peregrine Cl
7 Timson Cl

RINGWOOD

37

E F G H

RINGWOOD ROAD

First School
Forest Gate
burg

Larchwood Rd
Harold

Briarwood Road
Deerhurst Cl Rowan

Ashurst Bridge Road

Ashurst Bridge

Monkton La

A326

Denbigh
Reynolds

Surrey
Durley Cl
Ibbotson Way
Birchlands
Pentridge Wy
Mill Way

Blenheim
Pemvale
Rosleigh
Lynton
Amberley Ct

Cocklydown Lane

Rockleigh
Kenmore
Wy
Fairmead

Foxhills
Lane

Kneliers
Lane

Foxhills Cl

Wharton's

Foxhills
County
First School

Foxhills

S040

Rye
Dr

Copsewood
Rd
Cooper
Road

Lakewood Road

Chestnut
Av

Woodside
Gdns

Dene Way

Dene Rd

Cecil Av

ROAD A35

Ashurst

Colbury

Hunters
Inn Hill

Longdown
Dairy Fm

Deerleap Lane

HUNTERS HILL

Pound Lane

BartleyWater

Lackford
Avenue

Culford Avenue

Manor

Rushington
Av

Frampton
Wy

Bartley Av
Oakleigh Crs

Hemming

Lane

Spicer's Hill

Rushington Cl

Players
Crs

SPICER'S WY

Loose
Lane

Spicer's
Hill

Totten
Coll

Chapel
Lane

Rushington
Business Park

MAIN ROAD

Jacob's
Wk
Moorcross
Wy

Jacob's
Gutter

Hampshire
Co Council

LC

Hounsdown

Hounsdown
School

Rushington

RUMBRIDGE STREET

TOTTON

PO

I

E4
1 Wingrove Rd

Down's Pa

A326

The Drive

Roberts
Rd

Hounsdown
Av

Powell
Crs

Orchard
Meadow

Valley Rd

Brookside

Riverview

Kirk
Gdns

The
Retr
The
Retreat

Lane

BY-PASS

2

E5
1 Boakes Pl

3

50

F1
1 Chillenden Ct
2 Hudson Ct
3 Thomas Cl

Colbury Fm

A326

4

F2
1 Chiltern Cl
2 Highgrove Cl

Durley Fm

5

E F G H

G2
1 Elldene Ct
2 Falstaff Wy
3 Hambert Wy
4 Trevone Cl

G1
1 Springfield Dr

50 📵

Maynard Road

Totton Station

HIGH STREET

BY-PASS

River Test

A **B** **38** **C** **D**

Osbor.

PO

A

Winsor Rd

Rose Rd

TOTTON

Eling County
Infant School

School Lane

Fisher's Rd

Bartram Rd

Brokenford Lane

Jackie Wigg Gdns

Treeside AV

Mill St

Junction Rd

Cross Rd

Avenue

1 ⛽

Rushington

Roberts Rd

Drive

A326

Parkside

MARCHWOOD

Down's Park Avenue

Milverton Rd

Down's Pk Rd

Down's PK Crs

Down's PK

Lexby Rd

Eling Hill

The Heritage Centre & Museum
Tide Mill

✝

Eling

Cemetery

2

Brookside

1 Boothby Cl

Powell Crs

Meadow AV

Riverview

Kirk Gdns

The Retreat

The Retreat Lane

Gutter

LC

BY-PASS

Bury Lane

Marchwood Road

Hounsdown Sch

3

49

A326

A326

Durley Fm

4

Trotts Lane

Trotts

Bury

Bury

5

LC

LC

MARCHWOOD

Pooksgree

Park

Pooksgreen

Bohinton

Park Lane

BY-PASS

rshfield Cl

A **B** **C** **D**

Langley
Lodge

Staplewood Lane

Long

I grid square represents 500 metres

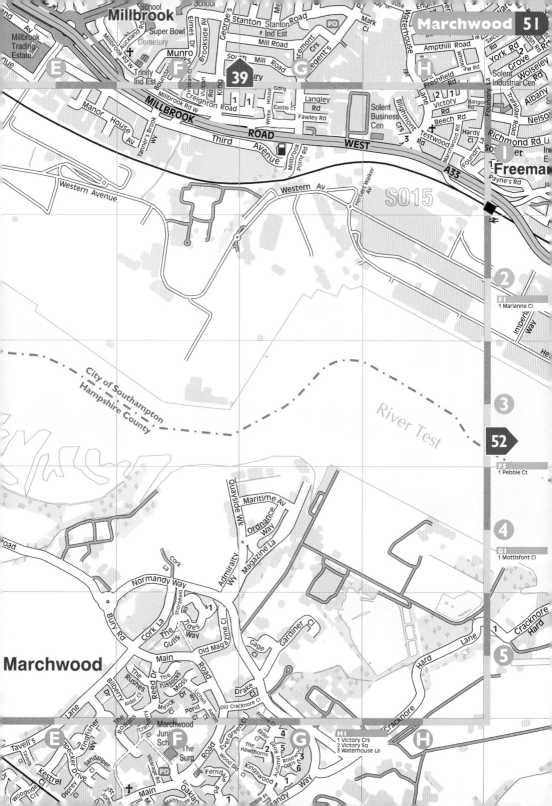

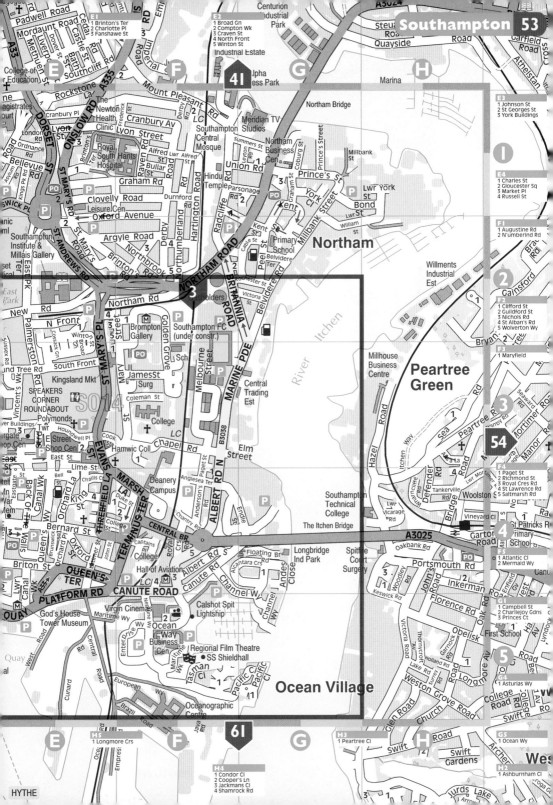

E
Padwell Road
Mordaunt Road
Liverpool St
Methuen St
Cranbury Pl

E1
1 Brinton's Ter
2 Charlotte Pl
3 Fanshawe St

E2
1 Broad Gn
2 Compton Wk
3 Craven St
4 North Front
5 Winton St

Centurion Industrial Park

Steuart Road
Quayside

Garfield Road
Athelstan

Marina

E3
1 Johnson St
2 St Georges St
3 York Buildings

I

College of Education
Rockstone La A335
Mount Pleasant Rd

Northam Bridge

E4
1 Charles St
2 Gloucester Sq
3 Market Pl
4 Russell St

The Newton Health Clinic
Cranbury Av
Frederick St
Lyon Street
Meridian TV Studios
Southampton Central Mosque

F1
1 Augustine St
2 N'umberind Rd

Royal South Hants Hospital
Alfred St
Lwr Alfred St
Hindu Temple
Union Rd
Prince's St
Coburg St
Prince's Street
Millbank St

Clovelly Road
Durnford Rd
Parsonage
York
Graham St
Lwr York St
Bond
Millbank Street

2
Gainsford

Leisure Cen
Oxford Avenue
Kent
Lwr
William
St

Argyle Road
Northbrook Rd
Derby Rd
Radcliffe Rd
Hartington Road
Kent St
Cable St
Primary School
Belvidere
St

Northam

Willments Industrial Est

F2
1 Clifford St
2 Guildford St
3 Nichols Rd
4 St Alban's Rd
5 Wolverton Wy

Bryan
F3
1 Maryfield

East Park
Palmerston Rd
N Front
Winton
St
Brompton Gallery
Golden Grove
Southampton FC (under constr.)
Rochester St
Victoria St
Belvidere Rd

Millhouse Business Centre

Peartree Green

3
Mortimer Rd

South Front
Kingsland Mkt
Mary St
James St
Surg
Melbourne Street
River Itchen

Hazel Road
Peartree Rd
Seaward Rd

54

SPEAKERS CORNER ROUNDABOUT
S014
Coleman St
College
LC

F4
1 Paget St
2 Richmond Rd
3 Royal Cres Rd
4 St Lawrence Rd
5 Saltmarsh Rd

Polymonds
Houndwell
E Street Shop Cen
Hamwic Coll
Chapel Rd
Elm Street
B3038

Manor
Defender Rd

St Patricks
Primary
School

4

Deanery Campus
Anglesea Ter
Paget St
Anderson's Rd

Southampton Technical College
The Itchen Bridge

Lwr Vicarage Rd
Woolston
Garton Rd

F5
1 Atlantic Cl
2 Mermaid Wy

Bernard St
Orchard Pl
Oxford St
Central Br
Albert Rd N
Chantry Rd
Endle St

A3025
Portsmouth Road
Oakbank Rd
Florence Rd
Woodley
Keswick Rd

G1
1 Campbell St
2 Charlejoy Gdns
3 Princes Ct

QUEEN'S TER
PLATFORM RD
CANUTE ROAD
Albert Rd S
Canute Road
Channel Wy
Longbridge Ind Park
Spitfire Court Surgery

First School

God's House Tower Museum
Virgin Cinemas
Maritime Wy
Ocean
Calshot Spit Lightship
Andes Cl
Close

Obelisk
Victoria Road
John St
Inkerman Rd
Enfield

5

Quay
West Quay Rd
Enterprise
Way
Business Cen
Regional Film Theatre
SS Shieldhall
Tasman Cl
Pacific Cl

Weston Grove Road
Church
Glen Road
College Road
Swift

G4
1 Asturias Wy

Oceanographic Centre
Brazil Road
Java Rd

Ocean Village

E
H1
1 Longmore Crs

F
61

G
H1
1 Peartree Cl

Swift
Road
Swift Gardens

H
G5
1 Ocean Wy
Archery

West

H2
1 Ashburnham Rd

HYTHE
H4
1 Condor Cl
2 Cooper's Ln
3 Jackmans Cl
4 Shamrock Rd

Jurds Lake

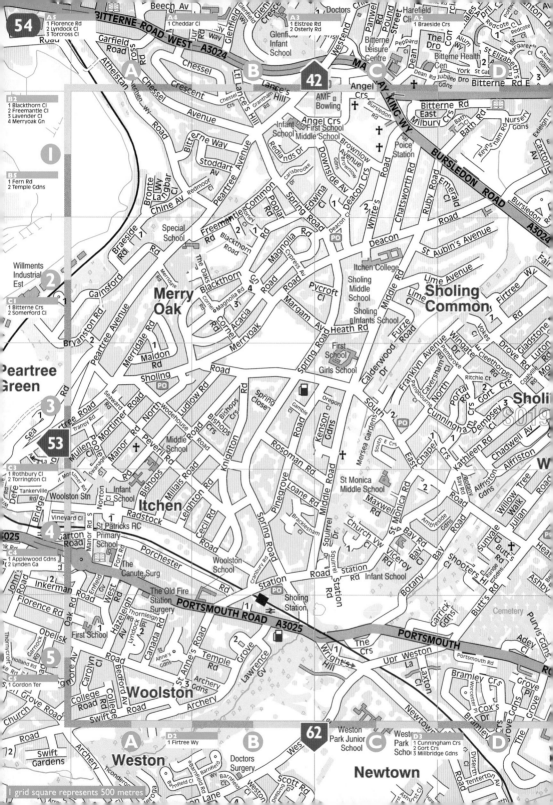

1 grid square represents 500 metres

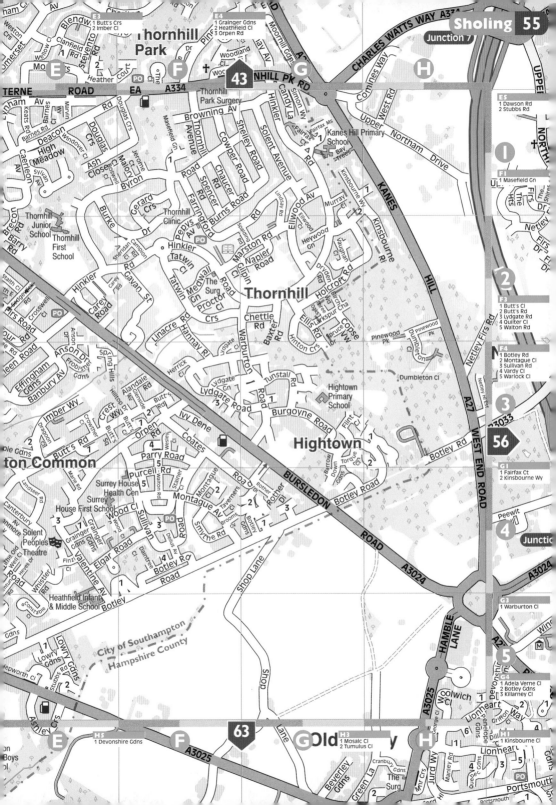

Broadoak

Station

Broadoak

BROAD OAK A334

HIGH STREET

MILL HILL A334

E **F** **45** **G** **H**

Woodhills School

Botley Junior & Infant School

PO

Balley Cl

Kilford Court

Mortimer Road

Cheping Gardens

Four Acre

Downland

Jenkins Cl

Park

Appletree Court

Pern Drive

Mayfair Cl

Alexandra Wy

Halfpenny Dwn

Cobbett Way

Cobbett Wy

Orchard Cl

Osterley Cl

Blossom Close

Marlin Wy

Gento

Sovereign Drive

1

Tickner Close

Brook Lane

Brook Lane

Church Lane

Steeple Court

Manor Farm

Botley

I

2

E1
1 Montrose Cl

3

4

River Hamble

Burridge Farm

Burridge

Burridge Social & Sports Club

Eyers Down Farm

A3051

BOTLEY ROAD

RO

5

E **F** **65** **G** **H**

Green Lane

Burridge

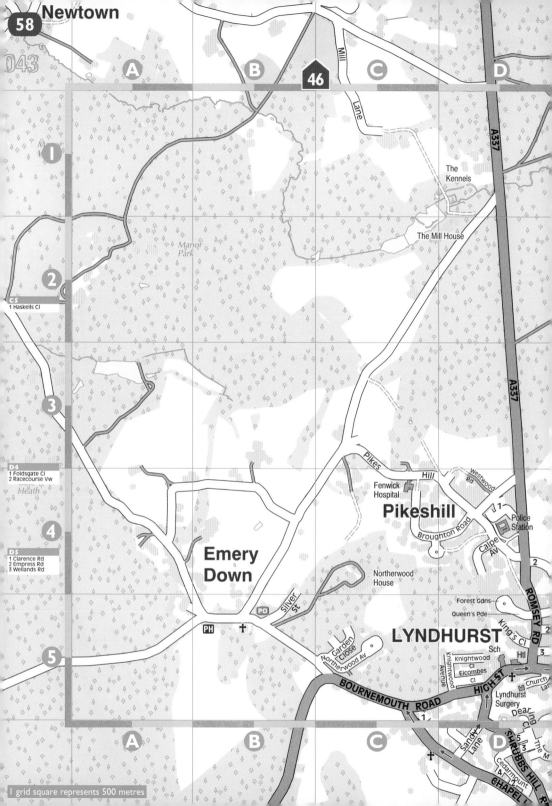

46

A B C D

I

2
CS
1 Haskells Cl

3

D4
1 Foldsgate Cl
2 Racecourse Vw

Heath

4

D5
1 Clarence Rd
2 Empress Rd
3 Wellands Rd

Manor Park

The Kennels

The Mill House

Mill Lane

A337

Pikes Hill

Fenwick Hospital

Pikeshill

Westwood Rd

Broughton Road

Police Station

Calpe Av

Emery Down

Northerwood House

Silver St

PO

PH †

Garden Close

Northerwood Av

Forest Gdns

Queen's Pde

LYNDHURST

King's Cl

ROMSEY RD

Sch

Htl

Knightwood Cl
Elcombes Cl

Knightwood Avenue

HIGH ST

Lyndhurst Surgery

Dear

Church

BOURNEMOUTH ROAD

Sandy Lane

†

SHRUBBS HILL Rd

CHAPEL

Cedarmount

The M

1 grid square represents 500 metres

Busketts
Lawn
Inclosure

E

F

47

G

H

Curzy
Lawn
Inclosure

BartleyWater

I

Ironshill
Lodge

Rushpole
Wood

Ironshill
Inclosure

2

Lodgehill
Cottage

A35

3

Mallard
Wood

ROAD

New
Forest
Golf Club

4

Dunces Arch

White
Moor

SOUTHAMPTON

Princes Cresent

Hotel

5

umberton Rd

Wellands Rd

Custards

PO

HIGH ST A35

Cemetery

Hotel

ew Forest Museum
Visitors Centre

1995
adow

GOSPORT LANE A35

E

F

BEAULIEU

G

H

ds Rd

City of Southam...
Hampshire County

Old Netley

E F 55 G H

Lowry Gdns
Lowry Gdns
...worth Cl

Ashley Crs

A3025

Beverley Gdns
Green La
Cranbur...
The
Surg
Lowford
Ravenscroft
Elm... Gdns
Reeves
Cl
Pallot Cl
Reeves
Wy
Larch Wy
Woodland Vw
The
Oaks
Silver B...
Boundary Rd
Oak Rd
Hamble La
Pound Rd
Pound
Rd
Oak Rd
B3397

Woolwich
Cl
Lionheart
penelope
Gdns
pilligen
Way
Lionheart
Way
Portsmouth
Gt.George Cl
Mnr Crs
Jurd Wy
Manley Rd
Quebe... Gdns
Griffon
Wy
Devonshire
Gdns
PROVIDE

PROVIDE

I PO Portsmouth

1 Calbourne
2 Carisbrooke
3 Culver
4 Kingston
5 Nettlestone
6 Shorewell
7 Whitwell
8 Wootton

Estri...
Estridge

Bursledon
C of E Jun
Infant Scho

2

E4
1 Arreton
2 The Badgers
3 Newbridge
4 Oakhurst Cl

Nightingale Rd
Rowan
Sycamore
Cl
Mallards Road
Woodlands Wy
The Acorns
Cedar Cl
Kew
Hungerford

3

64

E5
1 Latelie Cl
2 Waverley Ct

Grange Road

Butlocks Heath

Cranmore
Rookley
Ingleside
Catcombe
Stenbury Wy
Heath Gdns
Bowcombe
Chillerton
Chillerton
Woolston
The Grove
Shalcombe

4

F3
1 Old School Cl

PO
Yaverland
Bembridge
Abbeyfields
Abbots
Rd Wy
Hound
Way
Hound
Road
Hound
Rd
Hound Cl
Hound Gdns Rd

Kelvin
Cv
Sellwood
Road
Hunt avenue

Hound

Hamble County
Secondary
School

Broad Wy

5

Avenue
Victoria Gld
...tley Ldg Cl
Station Rd
Waverley Av
St Wood...
Oakhurst Rd
St Mary's
Netley
Station
Sidings
Industrial
Est
The Sidings

Hamble
Station

Satchell Lane

Albert
Cl
Night...
Wk

Royal
Victoria
Country Park

H2
1 Ash Cl
2 Chamberlayne Rd
3 Pllands Wood Rd

H1
1 Grace Dieu Gdns
2 Kevlyn Crs
3 Manor Cl
4 Quebec Gdns
5 Reeves Wy
6 Seaford Cl

BLE
LANE
HAMBLE LANE

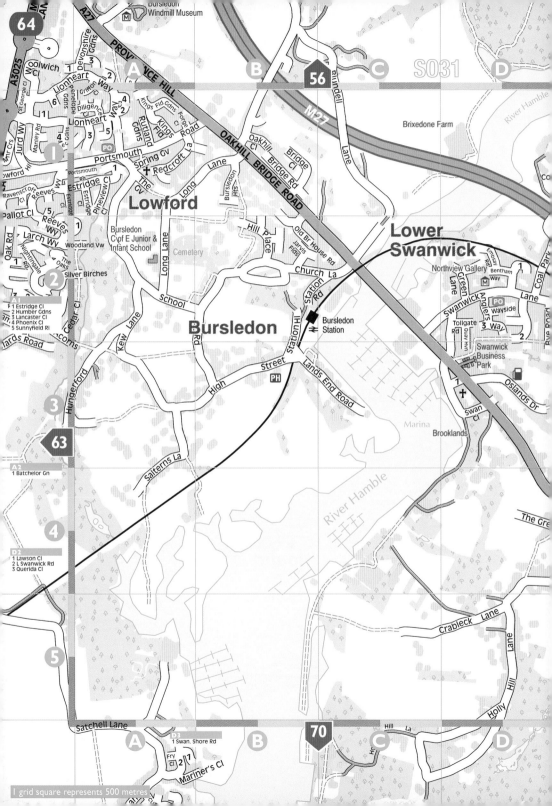

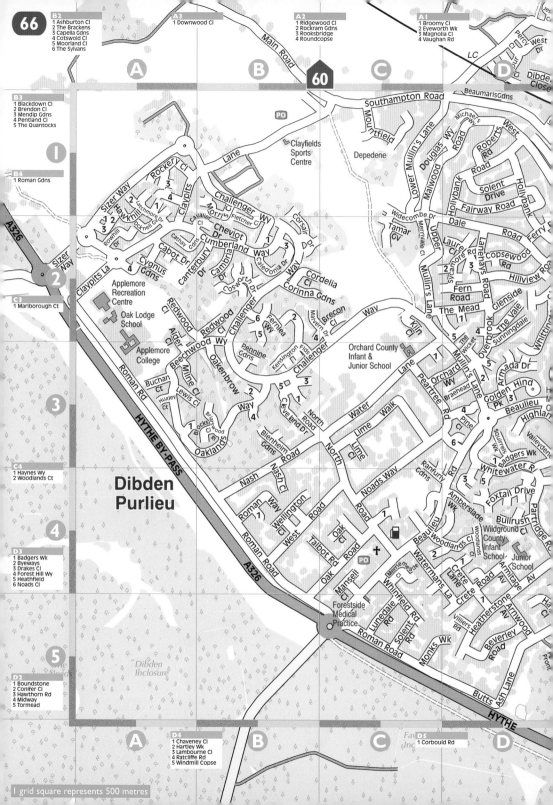

E1
1 Alexandra Cl
2 Carpenter Cl
3 Court House Cl
4 Drummond Rd
5 Fairfield Cl
6 Green Cl
7 Mariners Ms
8 Pylewell Rd

E2
1 Abbey Cl
2 Coat Gdns
3 Freedom Ct

E3
1 Frayslea
2 Greatwood Cl
3 Knightstone Gra
4 Langdown Ln Cl
5 Rose Cl

E4
1 Andrew Cl
2 Buttercup Cl
3 Butts Ash La
4 Chaloner Crs
5 Hartley Cl
6 Ingle Gln
7 Northbourne Cl
8 Silvers End

E5
1 Devonshire Gdns
2 Stokesay Cl

F1
1 Sir Christopher Cl

F3
1 Pinewood Crs
2 Spinney Gdns
3 Tates Rd

F5
1 Tates Rd

E5
1 Laburnum Crs
2 Maple Rd

F4
1 Furzedown Ms
2 Hamilton Ms

HYTHE

Langdown

Frostlane

Buttsash

A

B

62

C

D

I

2

3

67

4

5

Southamptor

First Street

Av C

Second St

Av D

Avenue E

Road

AV
C

A

B

73

C

D

Cadland
Creek

School

Road

Secondary School

Hamble Station

63

LANE

Royal Victoria Country Park

Nightingale Wk.

Albert Cl

E

F

HAMBLE

G

Satchell Lane

H

I

LANE

Cerdic M

Satchell

Hamble County Primary School

Hamblecliff House

Solent Way

B3397

Verdon Av

Tutor

Kings Av

PO

Sydney Avenue

Flowers Cl

Gardens

Astral

Baron

Cl

**HAMBLE-
LE-RICE**

2

F3
1 Westfield Common

Yorke Wy

Chalmers Wy

Cliffe Av

Way

2

1

Coach

Road

Grantham Av

Norbury Gdns

South Ct

Westfield Cl

Beech Gdns

Beech Cl

Beech

Cl

Deanfield

Barton

Aquila Wy

Dr

Spitfire Wy

1

2

Cirrus Gdns

The Bartletts

Meadow

La

1

Riv Gn

3

Cl

Copse La

70

G2
1 Coronation Pde
2 Hardwicke Wy

Emmons Cl

Solent Way

Ensign Way

School

La

4

H2
1 Acorn Ct

5

ater

E

F

G

H3
1 College Cl
2 Pegasus Cl

H

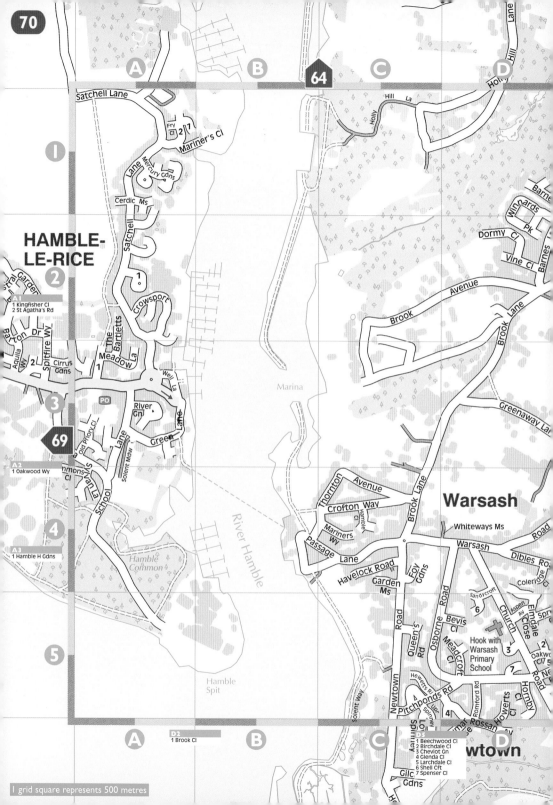

64

Satchell Lane

Fry Cl

Mariner's Cl

Mercury Gdns

Lane

Cerdic Ms

Satchell

HAMBLE-LE-RICE

2

A1
1 Kingfisher Cl
2 St Agatha's Rd

Crowsport

Garden

Spitfire Wy

Aquila Vw

Barton Dr

Cirrus Gdns

The Bartletts

Meadow La

3

PO

69

Old Priory Cl

Sivell Cl

Commons La

River Grn

Green Lane

Well La

Solent Mdw

School Lane

A2
1 Oakwood Wy

4

A3
1 Hamble H Gdns

Hamble Common

5

River Hamble

Hamble Spit

Marina

Holly Hill Lane

Hill La

Holly

Barnes

Winnards Pk

Dormy Cl

Vine Cl

Barnes

Avenue

Brook

Brook Lane

Greenaway Lan

Brook Lane

Warsash

Thornton Avenue

Crofton Way

Hamble Cl

Mariners Wy

Whiteways Ms

Passage Lane

Warsash Road

Dibles Road

Coleridge

Havelock Road

Garden Ms

Foy Gdns

Sandycroft

Aspen Av

Church Close

Elmdale Close

Oakwood Cl

Queen's Rd

Bevis Cl

Osborne Road

Meadcroft Rd

Hook with Warsash Primary School

Shell Cft

6

3

7

2

Newtown Road

Newtown Road

Hewetts Rd

Pitchponds Rd

Upr Spinney

Romford Rd

Rossan Av

Howerts Cl

Hornby Cl

Spinney

4

Solent Way

Queen's

Lomar

Gilc Gdns

Ntown

D2
1 Brook Cl

B

C

D

D1
1 Beechwood Cl
2 Birchdale Cl
3 Cheviot Grn
4 Glenda Cl
5 Larchdale Cl
6 Shell Cft
7 Spenser Cl

1 grid square represents 500 metres

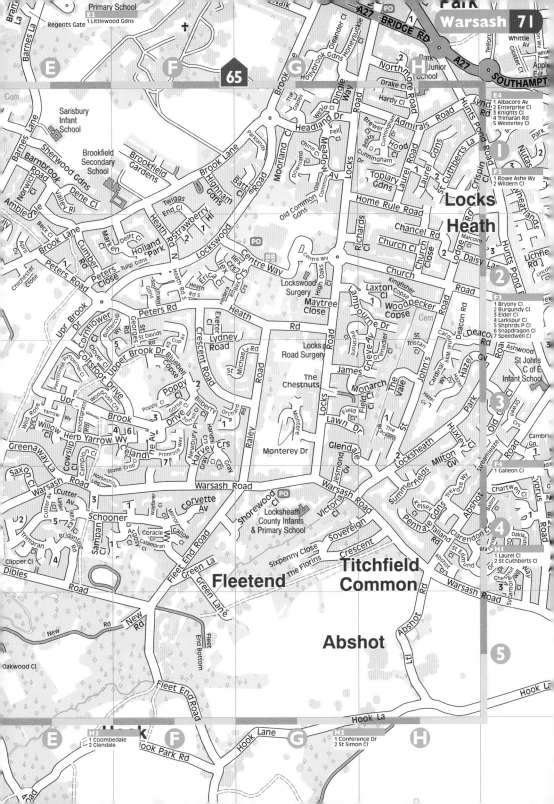

67

Hardley

Little Holbury

Holbury

New Road

LYTHE

BY-PASS

Solent Way

A326

Forest Front

Ash Lane

Forest Meadow

Sash Avenue

Hamilton Rd

Laburnum

Holly Close

Cedar

Elm Crs

Fawley Rd

Fawley Road

Hardley La

Cadland Road

Lime Kiln Lane

Roman Rd

Chevron Business Park

Old School Cl

Harrier Wy

Falconer Ct

The Mill Pond

Main Rd

A326

Cadlands Pk Est

LONG

Long Lane

LANE

13th Street

14th Street

12th Avenue

Avenue 11

D Avenue

C Avenue

B Avenue

A Avenue

10th

9th

Lane

Larch Av

Sycamore Dr

Hardley School

The Warren

Lime Kiln

Lime Kiln La

Holbury Purlieu

Manor Infant School

Larkspur Gdns

Wedgewood Cl

Mulberry Cl

Albany Rd

Manor Road

Southbourne Avenue

Westbourne Rd

Ivor Close

Drove

Renda

Ruxley Cl

Oakley Cl

Watton Rd

Watton Road

Nelson

Burbush

Springfield Rd

Springfield

Stanley Cl

Waltons Avenue

PO

Holbury

Depedene Cl

Bower Cl

Studley Av

Broadoak

School

Beechwood Rd

Park Hl

William Cl

Winters Cl

Raymond Cl

The Close

Long Lane Close

May Close

Park Lane

Whyte Cl

Moat

Foxcroft Dr

Eastcot Cl

Redrise

Gt Elms

Stonymoor

Whitefield

Perrywood

Fenley Cl

Faircross

Roewood Rd

Bramble

Myvern Cl

Rollestone Road

Crawte Avenue

Page Cl

Rollstone

Rollesto arm

Alum Cl

May Crs

May Copse

GV

1 grid square represents 500 metres

68

E F G H

I

Cadland Creek

2

Foreshore

North

South

North

HS
1 Admirals Cl
2 Churchfields
3 Denny Cl
4 The Lane
5 Linda Rd
6 Meadow Wy
7 The Paddocks
8 Rhyme Hall Ms
9 The Square
10 Whites La

Foreshore

P.L.P.H.

Burmah

Road

South

3

Cadland

Road

Old

Agritor Road

Saps

4

Flume

J Av

H Avenue

Avenue

G

6th St

F

Avenue

5th Street

7th Street

E Avenue

E Avenue

Jetty Road

D Av

7th Street

6th Street

5th Street

Street

8th

6th

Street

4th Street

3rd Street

2nd St

1st Street

Oil Refinery

Marsh Lane

Saltern's La

7th Street

South Avenue

Marsh Lane

Rye Paddock La

Copthorne

Lane

Copthorne Lane

Sheringham Cl

Church

Orchard Cl

Wooville

Coleville Av

Rd

Falcon

Rds

Nett

5

S045

Fawley County First School

Forest

Edge

7

6

School Rd

10

9

4

The Coast Clinic

Ashle

Fawley Business Centre

PO

School Rd

8

3

Calshot Rd

FAWLEY →

ROAD

Ashdown

B3053

Fawley

FAWLEY BY-PASS

Copse

E F G H

Newlands Road

Ashdown Road

Slades Hill

Blackfield Rd

The Pentagon

Chapel La

Fry Cl

Bevis Cl

Road

Toomer

Priest Cl

Abshot	71 C5	Dibden Purlieu	66 A4	Locks Heath	71 H1	Rownhams	27 F2
Aldermoor	39 G1	Durley	33 H3	London Minstead	46 A3	Rushington	49 H1
Allbrook	10 C5	Eastleigh	20 D3	Long Common	45 F3	St Denys	41 G4
Ashfield	16 B2	Eling	50 B2	Lord's Hill	27 G5	Sarisbury	65 E5
Ashurst	49 E5	Emery Down	58 B4	Lordswood	28 B5	Shirley	40 B4
Ashurst Bridge	49 E2	Fair Oak	22 C4	Lower Swanwick	64 C2	Shirley Warren	39 H2
Barrow Hill	35 H2	Fisher's Pond	12 B5	Lowford	64 A1	Sholing	54 D3
Bartley	35 E5	Fleetend	71 F4	Lyndhurst	58 C5	Sholing Common	54 C2
Bassett	29 E4	Flexford	8 D3	Marchwood	51 E5	Shorn Hill	36 C1
Bassett Green	29 E4	Foxhills	49 F4	Maybush	39 E2	Southampton	2 D6
Bishopstoke	21 E4	Foyers	47 G4	Merry Oak	54 A2	Stoke Common	21 E1
Bitterne	42 A5	Freemantle	52 A1	Midanbury	42 B4	Stonyford	24 B5
Bitterne Park	41 H3	Frostlane	67 G3	Millbrook	39 E5	Swanwick	65 G3
Boorley Green	45 E2	Fryern Hill	9 H5	Moorcourt	25 E2	Swaythling	42 A1
Botley	57 H1	Goldenhayes	47 F3	Moorgreen	43 H1	Testwood	37 G2
Boyatt Wood	20 B1	Gosport	7 G1	Netley	62 D4	Thornhill	55 G2
Brambridge	11 F3	Halterworth	6 C4	Netley Hill	56 A3	Thornhill Park	43 F5
Broadgate	8 C1	Hamble-le-Rice	69 H2	Netley Marsh	48 C1	Titchfield Common	71 G4
Broadoak	45 E5	Hampton Park	41 G1	New Town	62 C1	Toothill	17 E5
Brooke's Hill	24 D5	Hardley	72 C2	Newbridge	34 C1	Totton	38 A4
Bucket Corner	8 A4	Harefield	43 E5	Nob's Crook	12 A4	Townhill Park	42 B2
Bunker's Hill	35 E2	Hatch Bottom	43 F2	North Baddesley	17 G2	Trotts	50 C4
Burridge	65 H1	Hedge End	44 B5	North Stoneham	29 H2	Upper Shirley	40 B2
Bursledon	64 A2	Hensting	12 D2	Northam	53 G2	Upton	26 D2
Butlocks Heath	63 F3	Highbridge	11 F4	Nursling	26 C4	Warsash	70 D4
Buttsash	67 F5	Highfield	41 E2	Nutburn	17 H1	West End	43 G4
Cadnam	34 D4	Hightown	55 G3	Ocean Village	3 H6	Weston	62 A1
Calmore	37 E3	Hillstreet	24 D4	Old Netley	63 G1	Weston Common	54 D3
Chilworth	18 B5	Hillyfields	26 C5	Old Shirley	39 G3	Whitenap	6 C4
Chilworth Old Village	18 A4	Hiltingbury	9 H1	Ower	24 A3	Wildern	44 C5
Colbury	49 F5	Holbury	72 C5	Park Gate	65 H5	Wimpson	39 E3
Colden Common	12 A2	Horton Heath	32 D2	Peartree Green	53 H3	Winsor	35 H3
Copythorne	35 G2	Hound	63 G4	Pikeshill	58 C4	Wittensford	34 B4
Coxford	39 G2	Hounsdown	49 G3	Pooksgreen	50 D5	Woodlands	48 A4
Crampmoor	7 E2	Hythe	67 F1	Portswood	41 F3	Woodley	6 C2
Crowdhill	22 C1	Itchen	54 A4	Pylehill	22 C3	Woolston	54 A5
Cupernham	6 A2	Langdown	67 F2	Redbridge	38 C4		
Custards	59 E5	Lee	26 A1	Ridge	15 E5		
Dibden	60 B5	Little Holbury	72 B3	Romsey	5 G4		

USING THE STREET INDEX

Street names are listed alphabetically. Each street name is followed by its postal town or area locality, the Postcode District, the page number, and the reference to the square in which the name is found.

Example: **Abbey Cl** *FAWY* SO45..............**67** E2 🔟

Some entries are followed by a number in a blue box. This number indicates the location of the street within the referenced grid square. The full street name is listed at the side of the map page.

GENERAL ABBREVIATIONS

ACC	ACCESS	CSWY	CAUSEWAY	GND	GROUND	MEM	MEMORIAL
ALY	ALLEY	CT	COURT	GRA	GRANGE	MKT	MARKET
AP	APPROACH	CTRL	CENTRAL	GRG	GARAGE	MKTS	MARKETS
AR	ARCADE	CTS	COURTS	GT	GREAT	ML	MALL
ASS	ASSOCIATION	CTYD	COURTYARD	GTWY	GATEWAY	ML	MILL
AV	AVENUE	CUTT	CUTTINGS	GV	GROVE	MNR	MANOR
BCH	BEACH	CV	COVE	HGR	HIGHER	MS	MEWS
BLDS	BUILDINGS	CYN	CANYON	HL	HILL	MSN	MISSION
BND	BEND	DEPT	DEPARTMENT	HLS	HILLS	MT	MOUNT
BNK	BANK	DL	DALE	HO	HOUSE	MTN	MOUNTAIN
BR	BRIDGE	DM	DAM	HOL	HOLLOW	MTS	MOUNTAINS
BRK	BROOK	DR	DRIVE	HOSP	HOSPITAL	MUS	MUSEUM
BTM	BOTTOM	DRO	DROVE	HRB	HARBOUR	MWY	MOTORWAY
BUS	BUSINESS	DRY	DRIVEWAY	HTH	HEATH	N	NORTH
BVD	BOULEVARD	DWGS	DWELLINGS	HTS	HEIGHTS	NE	NORTH EAST
BY	BYPASS	E	EAST	HVN	HAVEN	NW	NORTH WEST
CATH	CATHEDRAL	EMB	EMBANKMENT	HWY	HIGHWAY	O/P	OVERPASS
CEM	CEMETERY	EMBY	EMBASSY	IMP	IMPERIAL	OFF	OFFICE
CEN	CENTRE	ESP	ESPLANADE	IN	INLET	ORCH	ORCHARD
CFT	CROFT	EST	ESTATE	IND EST	INDUSTRIAL ESTATE	OV	OVAL
CH	CHURCH	EX	EXCHANGE	INF	INFIRMARY	PAL	PALACE
CHA	CHASE	EXPY	EXPRESSWAY	INFO	INFORMATION	PAS	PASSAGE
CHYD	CHURCHYARD	EXT	EXTENSION	INT	INTERCHANGE	PAV	PAVILION
CIR	CIRCLE	F/O	FLYOVER	IS	ISLAND	PDE	PARADE
CIRC	CIRCUS	FC	FOOTBALL CLUB	JCT	JUNCTION	PH	PUBLIC HOUSE
CL	CLOSE	FK	FORK	JTY	JETTY	PK	PARK
CLFS	CLIFFS	FLD	FIELD	KG	KING	PKWY	PARKWAY
CMP	CAMP	FLDS	FIELDS	KNL	KNOLL	PL	PLACE
CNR	CORNER	FLS	FALLS	L	LAKE	PLN	PLAIN
CO	COUNTY	FLS	FLATS	LA	LANE	PLNS	PLAINS
COLL	COLLEGE	FM	FARM	LDG	LODGE	PLZ	PLAZA
COM	COMMON	FT	FORT	LGT	LIGHT	POL	POLICE STATION
COMM	COMMISSION	FWY	FREEWAY	LK	LOCK	PR	PRINCE
CON	CONVENT	FY	FERRY	LKS	LAKES	PREC	PRECINCT
COT	COTTAGE	GA	GATE	LNDG	LANDING	PREP	PREPARATORY
COTS	COTTAGES	GAL	GALLERY	LTL	LITTLE	PRIM	PRIMARY
CP	CAPE	GDN	GARDEN	LWR	LOWER	PROM	PROMENADE
CPS	COPSE	GDNS	GARDENS	MAG	MAGISTRATE	PRS	PRINCESS
CR	CREEK	GLD	GLADE	MAN	MANSIONS	PRT	PORT
CREM	CREMATORIUM	GLN	GLEN	MD	MEAD	PT	POINT
CRS	CRESCENT	GN	GREEN	MDW	MEADOWS	PTH	PATH

PZ PIAZZA
QD QUADRANT
QU QUEEN
QY QUAY
R RIVER
RBT ROUNDABOUT
RD ROAD
RDG RIDGE
REP REPUBLIC
RES RESERVOIR
RFC RUGBY FOOTBALL CLUB
RI RISE
RP RAMP
RW ROW
S SOUTH
SCH SCHOOL
SE SOUTH EAST
SER SERVICE AREA
SH SHORE
SHOP SHOPPING
SKWY SKYWAY
SMT SUMMIT
SOC SOCIETY
SP SPUR
SPR SPRING
SQ SQUARE
ST STREET
STN STATION
STR STREAM
STRD STRAND
SW SOUTH WEST
TDG TRADING
TER TERRACE
THWY THROUGHWAY
TNL TUNNEL
TOLL TOLLWAY
TPK TURNPIKE
TR TRACK
TRL TRAIL
TWR TOWER
U/P UNDERPASS
UNI UNIVERSITY
UPR UPPER
V VALE
VA VALLEY
VIAD VIADUCT
VIL VILLA
VIS VISTA
VLG VILLAGE
VLS VILLAS
VW VIEW
W WEST
WD WOOD
WHF WHARF
WK WALK
WKS WALKS
WLS WELLS
WY WAY
YD YARD
YHA YOUTH HOSTEL

POSTCODE TOWNS AND AREA ABBREVIATIONS

BPWT Bishop's Waltham
BROC Brockenhurst
CHFD Chandler's Ford
ELGH Eastleigh
FAWY Fawley/Hythe
FHAM Fareham
FHAM/STUB Fareham/Stubbington
HEND Hedge End
HLER Hamble-le-Rice
ITCH Itchen
LYND Lyndhurst
NBAD North Baddesley
PTSW Portswood
ROMY Romsey
ROWN Rownhams
RWIN Rural Winchester
SHAM Southampton
TOTT Totton
WEND West End
WSHM Southampton west

10th St *FAWY* SO45 72 D4
11th St *FAWY* SO45 72 D3
12th St *FAWY* SO45 72 D3
13th St *FAWY* SO45 72 D2
14th St *FAWY* SO45 72 C3
1st St *FAWY* SO45 73 G5
2nd St *FAWY* SO45 73 G3
3rd St *FAWY* SO45 73 F4
4th St *FAWY* SO45 73 F4
5th St *FAWY* SO45 73 F3
6th St *FAWY* SO45 73 E4
7th St *FAWY* SO45 73 E5
8th St *FAWY* SO45 73 E4
9th St *FAWY* SO45 72 D4

A

Aaron Ct *TOTT* SO40 51 F5
A Av *FAWY* SO45 72 D3
Abbey Cl *FAWY* SO45 67 E2 1
Abbeyfields Cl *HLER* SO31 63 F4
Abbey Hl *ITCH* SO19 62 A2
Abbey Water *ROMY* SO51 5 G4 1
Abbotsbury Rd *ELGH* SO50 21 H4
Abbotsfield *TOTT* SO40 37 G5
Abbotsfield Cl *ROWN* SO16 28 A4
Abbotsford *TOTT* SO40 47 F1
Abbots Wy *HLER* SO31 63 F4
Abbotswood Cl *ROMY* SO51 6 C2 1
Abbotts Rd *ELGH* SO50 20 A5
Abbotts Wy *PTSW* SO17 41 F3
Abercrombie Gdns *ROWN* SO16 27 G5
Aberdeen Rd *PTSW* SO17 41 G3
Aberdour Cl *WEND* SO18 42 D4 1
Abingdon Gdns *ROWN* SO16 40 C1 1
Above Bar St *SHAM* SO14 2 D2
Abraham Cl *HEND* SO30 56 D2
Abshot Cl *FHAM/STUB* PO14 71 H4
Abshot Rd *FHAM/STUB* PO14 71 H4
Acacia Rd *ITCH* SO19 54 B2
Acorn Ct *HLER* SO31 69 H2 1
Acorn Dr *ROWN* SO16 27 E2
Acorn Gv *NBAD* SO52 18 D2
The Acorns *HLER* SO31 63 H2
Adams Cl *HEND* SO30 44 B1
Adamson Cl *CHFD* SO53 9 H3
Adams Rd *FAWY* SO45 67 E3
Addison Rd *ELGH* SO50 20 D1 1
HLER SO31 65 F4
Adelaide Rd *PTSW* SO17 41 G4
Adela Verne Cl *ITCH* SO19 55 G4 1
Adey Cl *ITCH* SO19 54 D5
Admirals Cl *FAWY* SO45 73 H5 1
Admirals Rd *HLER* SO31 71 H1
Admiralty Wy *TOTT* SO40 51 F4
Adur Cl *WEND* SO18 42 D3
Aikman La *TOTT* SO40 36 D5
Ailsa La *ITCH* SO19 53 H3
Ainsley Gdns *ELGH* SO50 20 C1
Aintree Cl *ELGH* SO50 32 D2 1
Aintree Rd *TOTT* SO40 37 E3
Alandale Rd *ITCH* SO19 55 F3
Alan Drayton Wy *ELGH* SO50 21 G4
Albacore Av *HLER* SO31 71 E4 1
Albany Rd *FAWY* SO45 72 C4
ROMY SO51 5 G4
WSHM SO15 52 A1
Albert Cl *HLER* SO31 63 E5
Albert Rd *ELGH* SO50 20 D1
HEND SO30 56 B2
Albert Rd North *SHAM* SO14 3 H4
Albert Rd South *SHAM* SO14 3 H5
Albion Pl *SHAM* SO14 2 D3
Albury Pl *CHFD* SO53 9 F2 1
Alcantara Crs *SHAM* SO14 3 H5
Alder Cl *FAWY* SO45 66 A2
ROMY SO51 6 D5
RWIN SO21 12 A3
TOTT SO40 51 F5
Alder Hill Dr *TOTT* SO40 36 D4
Aldermoor Av *ROWN* SO16 27 G5
Aldermoor Cl *ROWN* SO16 28 A5
Aldermoor Rd *ROWN* SO16 27 H5
Alderney Cl *ROWN* SO16 27 E5
Alder Rd *ROWN* SO16 39 F1
Alderwood Av *CHFD* SO53 9 E5
Alexander Cl *TOTT* SO40 37 F4
Alexandra Cl *FAWY* SO45 67 E1 1
Alexandra Rd *CHFD* SO53 10 B3
FAWY SO45 67 E1
HEND SO30 56 B2
WSHM SO15 52 B1
Alexandra Wy *HEND* SO30 45 G5
Alfred Cl *TOTT* SO40 37 E4 1
Alfred Rose Ct *WEND* SO18 30 A5 1
Alfred St *SHAM* SO14 53 F1
Alfriston Gdns *ITCH* SO19 54 D4
Allan Gv *ROMY* SO51 6 B4
Allbrook Hl *ELGH* SO50 10 D4
Allbrook Knoll *ELGH* SO50 10 C4
Allbrook Wy *ELGH* SO50 10 C3
Allen Rd *HEND* SO30 44 C5
Allerton Cl *TOTT* SO40 37 F3
Allington La *HEND* SO30 31 G4
Allington Rd *WSHM* SO15 38 D5
Allotment Rd *HLER* SO31 65 E5
Alma La *BPWT* SO32 23 H4
Alma Rd *ROMY* SO51 5 H4
SHAM SO14 41 E4
Almatade Rd *WEND* SO18 42 C5
Almond Rd *WSHM* SO15 52 A2
Alpine Cl *WEND* SO18 42 D4
Alpine Rd *TOTT* SO40 48 B4
Alton Cl *ELGH* SO50 22 B4
Alum Cl *FAWY* SO45 72 D5
Alum Wy *WEND* SO18 42 D5
Amberley Cl *HEND* SO30 45 F4
NBAD SO52 17 E1
Amberley Ct *TOTT* SO40 49 G1
Amberslade Wk *FAWY* SO45 66 D4
Amberwood Cl *TOTT* SO40 37 E2
Ambledale *HLER* SO31 71 E1
Ambleside *HEND* SO30 56 D2
Ambleside Gdns *ITCH* SO19 54 C4
Amoy St *WSHM* SO15 52 D1
Ampthill Rd *WSHM* SO15 39 H5
Ancasta Rd *SHAM* SO14 41 F5 1
Andalusian Gdns *HLER* SO31 65 H2
Anderby Rd *ROWN* SO16 38 D2
Anderson Cl *ROMY* SO51 6 C1 1
Anderson's Rd *SHAM* SO14 3 H4
Andes Cl *SHAM* SO14 3 J5
Andes Rd *ROWN* SO16 38 B1
Andover Rd *WSHM* SO15 52 B1
Andrew Cl *FAWY* SO45 67 E4 1
TOTT SO40 37 F5
Andromeda Rd *ROWN* SO16 27 E5
Anfield Cl *ELGH* SO50 22 C5
Angel Crs *ITCH* SO19 42 C5
Angelica Gdns *ELGH* SO50 32 C2
Anglers Wy *HLER* SO31 64 D2
Anglesea Rd *WSHM* SO15 39 H3
Anglesea Ter *SHAM* SO14 3 H4
Anson Dr *ITCH* SO19 55 E3
Anson Rd *ELGH* SO50 32 C2
Anstey Rd *ROMY* SO51 6 B2
Anton Cl *ROMY* SO51 6 C4
Apollo Rd *CHFD* SO53 10 B4
Appleton Rd *WEND* SO18 42 A3
Appletree Cl *TOTT* SO40 37 E4
Appletree Ct *HEND* SO30 45 G5
Applewood Gdns *ITCH* SO19 54 C4 1
Applewood Pl *TOTT* SO40 49 E1
April Cl *WEND* SO18 42 D5
April Gv *HLER* SO31 71 E2
Apsley Pl *CHFD* SO53 9 F2 2
Aquila Wy *HLER* SO31 69 H3
Arcadia Cl *ROWN* SO16 39 H1
Archers Cl *TOTT* SO40 37 E2
Archers Rd *ELGH* SO50 20 C2
WSHM SO15 52 C1
Archery Gdns *ITCH* SO19 54 B5
Archery Gv *ITCH* SO19 54 A5
Archery Rd *ITCH* SO19 62 A1
Arden Cl *WEND* SO18 42 D3
Ardingly Crs *HEND* SO30 44 D2
Argosy Cl *HLER* SO31 71 F4
Argyle Rd *SHAM* SO14 53 E2
Arliss Rd *ROWN* SO16 39 G3
Arlott Ct *WSHM* SO15 40 C5
Armada Cl *ROWN* SO16 27 E2
Armada Dr *FAWY* SO45 66 D3
Armitage Av *FAWY* SO45 66 D4
Armstrong Ct *ROWN* SO16 27 F4 1
Arnheim Cl *ROWN* SO16 28 A5
Arnheim Rd *ROWN* SO16 28 B5
Arnold Rd *ELGH* SO50 30 C1
PTSW SO17 41 G2
Arnwood Av *FAWY* SO45 66 D5
Arreton *HLER* SO31 63 E4 1
Arrow Cl *ELGH* SO50 20 C2
ITCH SO19 61 H1
Arthur Rd *ELGH* SO50 20 C2
WSHM SO15 40 B5
Arthurs Gdns *HEND* SO30 44 B1 1
Arundel Rd *ELGH* SO50 10 C5
TOTT SO40 38 A4
Arun Rd *WEND* SO18 42 D2
Ascot Rd *ELGH* SO50 32 D2
Ascupart St *SHAM* SO14 3 G2
Asford Gv *ELGH* SO50 21 F2
Ashbridge Ri *CHFD* SO53 9 E2
Ashburnham Cl *ITCH* SO19 53 H2 1
Ashburton Cl *FAWY* SO45 66 B2 1
Ashby Rd *ITCH* SO19 54 D4
TOTT SO40 37 F5
Ash Cl *FAWY* SO45 67 E5
HLER SO31 63 H2 1
ITCH SO19 55 E1
NBAD SO52 17 F1
ROMY SO51 6 C5
RWIN SO21 11 H3
Ashdene *WSHM* SO15 39 H4 1
Ashdene Rd *TOTT* SO40 48 D5
Ashdown *FAWY* SO45 73 F5
Ashdown Cl *CHFD* SO53 9 G1
Ashdown Dr *CHFD* SO53 9 G1
Ashdown Rd *CHFD* SO53 9 G2
Ashdown Wy *ROMY* SO51 6 B4
Ashen Cl *CHFD* SO53 9 G3
Ashford Crs *FAWY* SO45 67 F2
Ash Gv *TOTT* SO40 49 E5
Ashlea Cl *ELGH* SO50 22 D4
Ashleigh Cl *FAWY* SO45 67 E5
Ashley Cl *HLER* SO31 65 H3
Ashley Ct *HLER* SO31 56 A5 1
Ashley Crs *ITCH* SO19 55 E5
Ashleycross Cl *FAWY* SO45 72 D5 1
Ashley Gdns *CHFD* SO53 20 A1
Ashley Mdw *ROMY* SO51 6 A3
Ashmead Rd *ROWN* SO16 39 F1
Ashridge Cl *WSHM* SO15 40 D4 1
Ash Rd *TOTT* SO40 48 D5
Ash Tree Rd *WEND* SO18 42 A3
Ashurst Bridge Rd *TOTT* SO40 49 E1
Ashurst Cl *ITCH* SO19 62 C1
TOTT SO40 48 D5
Ashwood Gdns *ROWN* SO16 40 C1 2
TOTT SO40 49 E1 1
Aspen Av *HLER* SO31 70 D5
Aspen Cl *HEND* SO30 44 D5
RWIN SO21 12 A3
Aspen Holt *ROWN* SO16 29 E4
Aspen Wk *TOTT* SO40 36 D4
Aster Rd *ROWN* SO16 29 G5
Astra Ct *FAWY* SO45 61 E5
Astral Gdns *HLER* SO31 69 H2
Asturias Wy *SHAM* SO14 3 J5
Asylum Rd *WSHM* SO15 53 E1
Atheling Rd *FAWY* SO45 67 E1
Athelstan Rd *ITCH* SO19 42 A5
Athena Cl *ELGH* SO50 22 A3
Atherfield Rd *ROWN* SO16 39 E1
Atherley Ct *WSHM* SO15 40 C4 1
Atherley Rd *WSHM* SO15 52 B1
Atlantic Cl *SHAM* SO14 3 H7
Atlantic Park Vw *WEND* SO18 42 C2 1
Auckland Rd *WSHM* SO15 39 F5
Augustine Rd *SHAM* SO14 53 F1 1
Augustus Wy *CHFD* SO53 10 A4
Austen Cl *TOTT* SO40 49 F1
Avebury Gdns *CHFD* SO53 9 E2
Avenger Cl *CHFD* SO53 19 F1
Avens Cl *ELGH* SO50 32 C3
Avenue C *FAWY* SO45 68 A5
Avenue D *FAWY* SO45 68 A5
Avenue E *FAWY* SO45 68 A5
Avenue Rd *SHAM* SO14 41 E4
The Avenue *PTSW* SO17 40 D2
Avington Cl *ELGH* SO50 21 F1 1
Avington Ct *ROWN* SO16 28 D5
Avonborne Wy *CHFD* SO53 9 F3
Avon Crs *ROMY* SO51 6 C4
Avon Gn *CHFD* SO53 19 H1
Avon Rd *WEND* SO18 42 B3
Avon Wy *HEND* SO30 43 G2

B

Back of the Walls *SHAM* SO14 ...... 2 E4
Bacon Cl *ITCH* SO19 .... 62 B1
Baddesley Cl *NBAD* SO52 .... 17 F1
Baddesley Rd *CHFD* SO53 ...... 9 E2
Bader Cl *HEND* SO30 .... 44 C4
Badger Cl *ELGH* SO50 .... 21 H4
Badgers Run *ROWN* SO16 .... 65 E4
The Badgers *HLER* SO31 .... 63 E4
Badgers Wk *FAWY* SO45 .... 66 D3
Bagber Rd *TOTT* SO40 .... 37 H5
Bailey Cl *HEND* SO30 .... 57 F1
Bakers Dro *ROWN* SO16 .... 27 E4
Balaclava Rd *WEND* SO18 .... 42 C5
Balfour Rd *ITCH* SO19 .... 54 D2
Ballard Cl *ROWN* SO16 .... 38 C3
Balmoral Cl *CHFD* SO53 ...... 9 F3
 ROWN SO16 .... 28 A4
Balmoral Wy *ROWN* SO16 .... 26 D3
Baltic Rd *HEND* SO30 .... 43 C2
Banbury Av *ITCH* SO19 .... 55 E3
Bangor Rd *WSHM* SO15 .... 51 H1
Banister Gdns *WSHM* SO15 .... 40 D5
Banister Rd *WSHM* SO15 .... 40 D5
Bank Side *WEND* SO18 .... 29 H5
Banning St *ROMY* SO51 .... 5 G5
Barbe Baker Av *HEND* SO30 ...... 43 E2
Barford Cl *CHFD* SO53 .... 9 F3
Bargate St *SHAM* SO14 2
Barker Mill Cl *ROWN* SO16 .... 27 E3
Barle Cl *WEND* SO18 .... 42 D3
Barnbrook Rd *HLER* SO31 .... 71 E1
Barnes Cl *HLER* SO31 .... 70 D1
 ITCH SO19 .... 55 E1
Barnes La *HLER* SO31 .... 65 E5
 HLER SO31 .... 70 D2
Barnes Rd *ITCH* SO19 .... 55 E1
Barneyhayes La *TOTT* SO40 ...... 35 E4
Barnfield Cl *ITCH* SO19 .... 62 A1
Barnfield Ct *ITCH* SO19 .... 62 B1
Barnfield Rd *ITCH* SO19 .... 62 A1
Barnfield Wy *ITCH* SO19 .... 62 B1
Barn Piece *NBAD* SO52 .... 8 D3
Barnsfield Crs *TOTT* SO40 .... 37 E5
Barnsland *HEND* SO30 .... 43 E2
Baron Rd *HLER* SO31 .... 69 H2
Barons Md *ROWN* SO16 .... 39 E1
Barrington Cl *ELGH* SO50 .... 20 B3
Barrow Down Gdns *ITCH* SO19 ... 55 G4
Barrow Hill Rd *TOTT* SO40 .... 35 H1
Barry Rd *ITCH* SO19 .... 54 D2
Barters Cl *ROWN* SO16 .... 39 F3
The Bartletts *HLER* SO31 .... 70 A3
Bartley Av *TOTT* SO40 .... 49 G1
Bartley Rd *TOTT* SO40 .... 47 C4
Barton Cl *ROMY* SO51 .... 6 B3
Barton Crs *WEND* SO18 .... 42 B3
Barton Dr *HEND* SO30 .... 44 D5
 HLER SO31 .... 69 H2
Barton Rd *ELGH* SO50 .... 21 E3
Bartram Rd *TOTT* SO40 .... 50 A1
Basing Wy *CHFD* SO53 .... 19 E2
Bassett Av *ROWN* SO16 .... 28 D4
Bassett Cl *ROWN* SO16 .... 28 D5
Bassett Crs East *ROWN* SO16 .... 28 D5
Bassett Crs West *ROWN* SO16 .... 40 D1
Bassett Dl *ROWN* SO16 .... 28 D5
Bassett Gdns *ROWN* SO16 .... 28 C5
Bassett Gn *ROWN* SO16 .... 29 F4
Bassett Green Cl *ROWN* SO16 .... 29 E4
Bassett Green Dr *ROWN* SO16 .... 29 E4
Bassett Green Rd *ROWN* SO16 .... 29 E4
Bassett Heath Av *ROWN* SO16 .... 28 D2
Bassett Meadow *ROWN* SO16 .... 40 D1
Bassett Ms *ROWN* SO16 .... 28 D4
Bassett Rw *ROWN* SO16 .... 28 D3
Bassett Wood Dr *ROWN* SO16 .... 28 D3
Bassett Wood Rd *ROWN* SO16 .... 28 D3
Batchelor Gn *HLER* SO31 ...... 64 A2
Bath Cl *ITCH* SO19 .... 54 D1
Bath Rd *ITCH* SO19 .... 54 D1
Bath St *SHAM* SO14 .... 41 E5
Battle Cl *HLER* SO31 .... 71 F1
B Av *FAWY* SO45 .... 72 D3
Baxter Rd *ITCH* SO19 .... 55 C3
Bay Cl *ITCH* SO19 .... 54 C4
Bay Rd *ITCH* SO19 .... 54 C4
Bay Trees *ITCH* SO19 .... 55 C1
Beacon Bottom *HLER* SO31 ...... 65 G4
Beacon Cl *HLER* SO31 .... 65 G4
Beacon Mt *HLER* SO31 .... 65 G4
Beacon Rd *HEND* SO30 .... 43 F4
Beacon Wy *HLER* SO31 .... 65 G4
Bealing Cl *ROWN* SO16 .... 29 F5
Bearslane Cl *TOTT* SO40 .... 37 F3

Beatrice Rd *WSHM* SO15 ...... 40 A5
Beattie Ri *HEND* SO30 .... 44 C2
Beatty Cl *HLER* SO31 .... 71 E1
Beaulieu Cl *ROWN* SO16 .... 27 H4
Beaulieu Rd *ELGH* SO50 .... 20 C2
 FAWY SO45 .... 66 C4
Beaumaris Gdns *FAWY* SO45 .... 66 D1
Beaumont Cl *ROWN* SO16 .... 40 C1
Beaumont Rd *TOTT* SO40 .... 38 A5
Beauworth Av *WEND* SO18 .... 43 E4
Beaver Dr *ELGH* SO50 .... 22 A4
Beck Cl *HLER* SO31 .... 71 E2
Bedford Av *ITCH* SO19 .... 54 A5
Bedford Cl *HEND* SO30 .... 56 D1
Bedford Pl *WSHM* SO15 .... 52 D1
Bedwell Cl *ROWN* SO16 .... 27 F4
Beech Av *WEND* SO18 .... 42 A5
Beech Cl *CHFD* SO53 .... 9 H3
 HLER SO31 .... 69 C3
 ROMY SO51 .... 6 C5
Beech Crs *FAWY* SO45 .... 67 E5
Beechcroft Cl *CHFD* SO53 ...... 19 H1
Beechcroft Wy *CHFD* SO53 ...... 9 H5
Beechdale Cl *TOTT* SO40 .... 37 E2
The Beeches *ELGH* SO50 .... 22 D5
Beechfield Ct *WSHM* SO15 ...... 39 G4
Beech Gdns *HLER* SO31 .... 69 C3
Beechmount Rd *ROWN* SO16 .... 28 D4
Beech Rd *CHFD* SO53 .... 9 H3
 HEND SO30
 TOTT SO40 .... 48 D5
 WSHM SO15 .... 51 H1
Beechwood Cl *CHFD* SO53 .... 9 E2
 HLER SO31 .... 70 D5
Beechwood Crs *CHFD* SO53 ...... 9 E1
Beechwood Gdns *WEND* SO18 .... 42 A4
Beechwood Ri *WEND* SO18 .... 43 E3
Beechwood Rd *FAWY* SO45 ...... 72 C5
 TOTT SO40 .... 46 D2
Beechwood Wy *FAWY* SO45 ...... 66 A3
Begonia Rd *ROWN* SO16 .... 29 F5
Belgrave Rd *PTSW* SO17 .... 41 G2
Bellemoor Rd *WSHM* SO15 .... 40 B3
Bellevue Rd *ELGH* SO50 .... 20 C3
 WSHM SO15 .... 53 E1
Bellflower Wy *NBAD* SO52 .... 8 D4
Bell St *ROMY* SO51 .... 5 G4
 SHAM SO14 .... 3 F4
Belmont Cl *FAWY* SO45 .... 67 E3
Belmont Rd *CHFD* SO53 .... 19 H3
 PTSW SO17 .... 41 E3
Belstone Rd *TOTT* SO40 .... 37 G5
Belton Rd *ITCH* SO19 .... 54 D4
Belvedere Rd *FAWY* SO45 .... 67 E3
Belvidere Rd *SHAM* SO14 .... 3 J1
Belvidere Ter *SHAM* SO14 .... 53 G2
Bembridge *HLER* SO31 .... 63 E4
Bembridge Cl *ROWN* SO16 .... 29 G4
Benedict Cl *ROMY* SO51 .... 6 C4
Benhams Farm Cl *WEND* SO18 .. 42 C3
Benhams Rd *WEND* SO18 ...... 42 C2
Benmore Gdns *CHFD* SO53 .... 9 F3
Benson Rd *WSHM* SO15 .... 39 H4
Bentham Wy *HLER* SO31 .... 64 D2
Bentley Cl *WEND* SO18 .... 43 E4
Bere Cl *CHFD* SO53 .... 9 F5
Beresford Cl *CHFD* SO53 ...... 20 A1
Beresford Gdns *CHFD* SO53 .... 20 A1
Beresford Rd *CHFD* SO53 .... 20 A1
 ITCH SO19 .... 54 A5
Bergen Crs *HEND* SO30 .... 56 C2
Berkeley Cl *WSHM* SO15 .... 40 C5
Berkeley Gdns *HEND* SO30 .... 56 C2
Bernard St *SHAM* SO14 .... 3 F6
Berry Cl *HEND* SO30 .... 56 D1
Berrywood Gdns *HEND* SO30 .... 44 B4
Betteridge Dr *ROWN* SO16 .... 26 D3
Beulah Rd *ROWN* SO16 .... 39 G3
Bevan Cl *ITCH* SO19 .... 62 A1
Beverley Gdns *HLER* SO31 ...... 63 C1
 ROMY SO51 .... 6 C2
Beverley Hts *WEND* SO18 .... 42 B2
Beverley Rd *FAWY* SO45 .... 66 D5
Bevis Cl *HLER* SO31 .... 70 D5
Bevois Gdns *SHAM* SO14 .... 41 E5
Bevois Hl *PTSW* SO17 .... 41 F4
Bevois Valley Rd *SHAM* SO14 .... 41 F5
Bideford Cl *ROWN* SO16 .... 39 E3
Bilberry Cl *HLER* SO31 .... 71 F3
Bilberry Dr *TOTT* SO40 .... 51 E5
Billington Gdns *HEND* SO30 ...... 44 D3
Bindon Cl *ROWN* SO16 .... 39 G2
Bindon Rd *ROWN* SO16 .... 39 G2
Binsey Cl *ROWN* SO16 .... 39 E4
Binstead Cl *ROWN* SO16 .... 29 G4
Birch Cl *ROMY* SO51 .... 6 C5
 ROWN SO16 .... 29 E1
Birch Dl *FAWY* SO45 .... 67 E5
Birchdale Cl *HLER* SO31 ...... 70 D5

The Birches Cl *NBAD* SO52 ...... 17 F1
The Birches *WEND* SO18 ...... 42 D4
Birch Gv *ELGH* SO50 .... 10 B5
Birchlands *TOTT* SO40 .... 49 F2
Birch Rd *HEND* SO30 .... 44 D5
 ROWN SO16 .... 29 E1
 ROWN SO16 .... 39 C2
Birch Wd *ITCH* SO19 .... 55 G2
Birchwood Gdns *HEND* SO30 .... 44 C4
Bishops Cl *TOTT* SO40 .... 37 G4
Bishops Ct *ELGH* SO50 .... 21 F1
Bishops Crs *ITCH* SO19 .... 54 B3
Bishops Rd *ITCH* SO19 .... 54 A4
Bishopstoke La *ELGH* SO50 .... 11 C5
Bishopstoke Rd *ELGH* SO50 .... 21 E3
Bitterne Crs *ITCH* SO19 .... 54 C1
Bitterne Rd East *WEND* SO18 .... 42 B5
Bitterne Rd West *WEND* SO18 .... 42 A5
Bitterne Wy *ITCH* SO19 .... 54 A1
Blackberry Ter *SHAM* SO14 ...... 41 F5
Blackbird Rd *ELGH* SO50 .... 19 H4
Blackbushe Cl *ROWN* SO16 .... 27 F4
Blackdown Cl *FAWY* SO45 ...... 66 B3
Blackthorn Cl *ITCH* SO19 .... 54 B2
Blackthorn Gn *RWIN* SO21 .... 12 A3
Blackthorn Rd *ITCH* SO19 .... 54 B2
Blackwater Dr *TOTT* SO40 .... 37 F3
Blackwater Ms *TOTT* SO40 .... 37 F3
Bladon Rd *ROWN* SO16 .... 40 A2
Blake Cl *ROWN* SO16 .... 26 C4
Blakeney Rd *ROWN* SO16 .... 38 D2
Blann Cl *ROWN* SO16 .... 26 C4
Bleaklow Cl *ROWN* SO16 .... 39 F4
Blechynden Ter *WSHM* SO15 .... 2 B1
Blencowe Dr *NBAD* SO52 .... 18 C1
Blendworth La *WEND* SO18 .... 43 E5
Blenheim Av *PTSW* SO17 .... 41 E3
Blenheim Cl *NBAD* SO52 .... 18 D2
 TOTT SO40 .... 49 F1
Blenheim Gdns *FAWY* SO45 .... 66 B3
 PTSW SO17 .... 41 F2
Blenheim Rd *ELGH* SO50 .... 20 C4
Blighmont Crs *WSHM* SO15 .... 51 H1
Blind La *BPWT* SO32 .... 32 C4
Blossom Cl *HEND* SO30 .... 57 E1
Bluebell Copse *HLER* SO31 ...... 71 F3
Bluebell Rd *ROWN* SO16 .... 29 F5
Bluestar Gdns *HEND* SO30 .... 44 C4
Blundell La *HLER* SO31 .... 56 C5
Blyth Cl *ROWN* SO16 .... 38 D2
Boakes Pl *TOTT* SO40 .... 49 E5
Bodmin Rd *ELGH* SO50 .... 21 C3
Bodycoats Rd *CHFD* SO53 .... 9 H5
Bolderwood Cl *ELGH* SO50 .... 21 H3
Boldrewood Rd *ROWN* SO16 .... 28 C5
Bonchurch Cl *ROWN* SO16 .... 29 G4
Bond Rd *WEND* SO18 .... 42 A3
Bond St *SHAM* SO14 .... 53 C1
Boniface Cl *TOTT* SO40 .... 37 F4
Boniface Crs *ROWN* SO16 .... 39 E1
Boothby Cl *TOTT* SO40 .... 50 A1
Borrowdale Rd *ROWN* SO16 .... 39 E3
Bossington Cl *ROWN* SO16 .... 27 E4
Bosville *ELGH* SO50 .... 10 C5
Boswell Cl *HEND* SO30 .... 45 F5
 ITCH SO19 .... 55 E1
Botany Bay Rd *ITCH* SO19 .... 54 C5
Botley Gdns *ITCH* SO19 .... 55 G4
Botley Rd *ELGH* SO50 .... 32 D1
 HEND SO30 .... 43 H3
 HLER SO31 .... 65 H1
 ITCH SO19 .... 55 E5
 NBAD SO52 .... 18 A3
 ROMY SO51 .... 6 A4
Boundary Cl *WSHM* SO15 ...... 51 F1
Boundary Rd *HLER* SO31 ...... 63 H2
Boundstone *FAWY* SO45 ...... 66 D2
Bourne Av *WSHM* SO15 .... 40 A3
Bourne La *TOTT* SO40 .... 47 H2
Bournemouth Rd *CHFD* SO53 .... 19 F3
 LYND SO43 .... 58 C5
 ROWN SO16 .... 29 E1
Bourne Rd *TOTT* SO40 .... 47 C2
 WSHM SO15 .... 52 B2
Bowater Cl *TOTT* SO40 .... 37 E3
Bowater Wy *TOTT* SO40 .... 37 E3
Bowcombe *HLER* SO31 .... 63 E3
Bowden La *PTSW* SO17 .... 41 C2
Bower Cl *FAWY* SO45 .... 72 C5
 ITCH SO19 .... 62 B1
Bowland Ri *CHFD* SO53 .... 9 E4
Boyatt Crs *ELGH* SO50 .... 10 C3
Boyatt La *CHFD* SO53 .... 10 C2
 ELGH SO50 .... 10 C4
Boyes La *RWIN* SO21 .... 12 A2
Boynton Cl *CHFD* SO53 .... 9 F3
Brabant Cl *HLER* SO31 .... 65 H3
Bracken Cl *NBAD* SO52 .... 17 G3

Bracken Crs *ELGH* SO50 .... 21 H4
Bracken La *ROWN* SO16 .... 39 C3
Bracken Pl *ELGH* SO50 .... 29 E2
Bracken Rd *NBAD* SO52 .... 17 G3
The Brackens *FAWY* SO45 ...... 66 B2
 HLER SO31 .... 71 H3
Brackenway Rd *CHFD* SO53 .... 9 G3
Bracklesham Cl *ITCH* SO19 .... 54 B4
Brackley Av *ELGH* SO50 .... 22 B4
Brackley Wy *TOTT* SO40 .... 37 F4
Brading Cl *ROWN* SO16 .... 29 G4
Bradley Gn *ROWN* SO16 .... 27 H5
Bradshaw Cl *ELGH* SO50 .... 23 E4
Braehead *FAWY* SO45 .... 66 D3
Braeside Crs *ITCH* SO19 .... 54 A2
Braeside Rd *ITCH* SO19 .... 54 A2
Braishfield Cl *ROWN* SO16 .... 39 F3
Braishfield Rd *ROMY* SO51 .... 6 C2
Bramble Cl *ELGH* SO50 .... 20 D1
 FAWY SO45 .... 72 C5
Bramble Dr *ROMY* SO51 .... 6 C2
Bramble Hl *CHFD* SO53 .... 9 F5
Bramble La *HLER* SO31 .... 65 H3
Bramble Ms *WEND* SO18 .... 42 C4
Brambles Cl *RWIN* SO21 .... 12 A3
Brambling Cl *ROWN* SO16 .... 27 H3
The Bramblings *TOTT* SO40 .... 37 E4
Bramdean Rd *WEND* SO18 .... 43 F5
Bramley Crs *ITCH* SO19 .... 54 D5
Bramshott Rd *ITCH* SO19 ...... 62 B1
 ITCH SO19 .... 62 C2
Bramston Rd *WSHM* SO15 .... 40 A4
Branksome Av *WSHM* SO15 .... 40 A3
Bransbury Cl *ROWN* SO16 .... 28 A5
Bransley Cl *ROMY* SO51 .... 6 B2
Brasher Cl *ELGH* SO50 .... 22 A4
Brazil Rd *SHAM* SO14 .... 3 G7
Breamore Cl *ELGH* SO50 .... 10 C5
Breamore Rd *WEND* SO18 .... 43 F5
Brean Cl *ROWN* SO16 .... 39 E1
Brecon Cl *CHFD* SO53 .... 19 F3
 FAWY SO45 .... 66 C2
Brecon Rd *ITCH* SO19 .... 55 E2
Brendon Cl *FAWY* SO45 .... 66 B3
Brendon Gn *ROWN* SO16 .... 39 F4
Brentwood Crs *WEND* SO18 .... 42 C3
Breton Cl *FHAM* PO15 .... 65 H3
Brewer Cl *HLER* SO31 .... 71 H1
Briardene Ct *TOTT* SO40 ...... 37 G5
Briarswood *ROWN* SO16 .... 39 H3
Briarswood Ri *FAWY* SO45 ...... 66 B3
Briar Wy *ROMY* SO51 .... 6 C2
Briarwood Rd *TOTT* SO40 .... 49 E1
Brickfield La *CHFD* SO53 ...... 19 F1
Brickfield Rd *PTSW* SO17 .... 41 G2
Brickmakers Rd *RWIN* SO21 ...... 11 H3
Brickwoods *ROMY* SO51 .... 6 B2
The Brickyard *TOTT* SO40 .... 35 F4
Bridge Cl *HLER* SO31 .... 64 B1
Bridge Rd *HLER* SO31 .... 64 B1
 HLER SO31 .... 65 E4
 ITCH SO19 .... 53 H4
 ROMY SO51 .... 5 H4
Bridgers Cl *ROWN* SO16 .... 27 E4
Bridges Cl *ELGH* SO50 .... 20 B3
Bridgwater Ct *WSHM* SO15 .... 52 B2
Bridlington Av *WSHM* SO15 .... 40 B4
Brigantine Rd *HLER* SO31 ...... 71 E4
Brighstone Cl *ROWN* SO16 .... 29 G4
Brighton Rd *WSHM* SO15 ...... 40 D5
Brightside Rd *ROWN* SO16 .... 39 F2
Brindle Cl *ROWN* SO16 .... 29 E4
Brinton La *FAWY* SO45 .... 61 E5
Brinton's Rd *SHAM* SO14 .... 53 E2
Brinton's Ter *SHAM* SO14 .... 53 E1
Britannia Gdns *HEND* SO30 .... 44 B1
Britannia Rd *SHAM* SO14 .... 53 F2
Briton St *SHAM* SO14 .... 2 D5
Broadbent Cl *ROWN* SO16 .... 26 D3
Broad Gn *SHAM* SO14 .... 3 F1
Broadlands Av *ELGH* SO50 .... 20 C1
Broadlands Rd *PTSW* SO17 ...... 41 F1
Broad La *NBAD* SO52 .... 17 E1
Bradley Cl *FAWY* SO45 .... 72 C4
Broadmeadow Cl *TOTT* SO40 .. 37 G5
Broadmead Rd *ROWN* SO16 .... 26 D3
Broad Oak *HEND* SO30 .... 45 E5
Broadoak Cl *FAWY* SO45 ...... 72 C5
Broadwater Rd *ROMY* SO51 .... 5 G5
 WEND SO18 .... 42 B1
Broad Wy *HLER* SO31 .... 65 E4
Brockishill Rd *LYND* SO43 ...... 46 D3
 TOTT SO40 .... 47 E2
Brocks Cl *FAWY* SO45 .... 66 B3
Brokenford Av *TOTT* SO40 .... 38 A5
Brokenford La *TOTT* SO40 ...... 37 H5
Bromley Rd *WEND* SO18 .... 42 B3
Bronte Cl *TOTT* SO40 .... 49 F1

Bronte Wy *ITCH* SO19 .... 54 A1
Brook Av *HLER* SO31 .... 70 C2
Brook Cl *HLER* SO31 .... 70 D2
  NBAD SO52 .... 17 G3
Brookfield Gdns *HLER* SO31 .... 71 F1
Brookfield Rd *ELGH* SO50 .... 22 B4
Brook La *HEND* SO30 .... 57 F1
  HLER SO31 .... 70 C4
Brook Rd *ELGH* SO50 .... 22 C4
  WEND SO18 .... 42 C5
Brookside *TOTT* SO40 .... 49 H2
Brookside Av *WSHM* SO15 .... 39 F5
Brookside Wy *HEND* SO30 .... 43 G1
  WEND SO18 .... 30 A5
Brookvale Rd *PTSW* SO17 .... 41 E3
Brook Va *ROWN* SO16 .... 39 G2
Brook Wy *ROWN* SO16 .... 6 B1
Brookwood Av *ELGH* SO50 .... 20 B3
Brookwood Rd *ROWN* SO16 .... 38 D4
Broom Hill Wy *ELGH* SO50 .... 10 B4
Brooms Gv *ITCH* SO19 .... 55 F4
Broomy Cl *FAWY* SO45 .... 66 A1
Broughton Cl *ROWN* SO16 .... 39 G3
Broughton Rd *LYND* SO43 .... 58 C4
Brownhill Cl *CHFD* SO53 .... 9 G4
Brownhill Ct *ROWN* SO16 .... 39 E1
Brownhill Rd *CHFD* SO53 .... 9 G4
  NBAD SO52 .... 17 H2
Brownhill Wy *ROWN* SO16 .... 38 C1
Browning Av *ITCH* SO19 .... 55 F1
Browning Cl *ELGH* SO50 .... 20 B3
  TOTT SO40 .... 37 F5
Brownlow Av *ITCH* SO19 .... 54 C1
Brownlow Gdns *ITCH* SO19 .... 54 C1
Broxburn Cl *CHFD* SO53 .... 10 A2
Brue Cl *CHFD* SO53 .... 9 F4
Brunel Cl *HEND* SO30 .... 44 D3
Brunel Rd *TOTT* SO40 .... 37 F1
  WSHM SO15 .... 38 C5
Brunswick Pl *WSHM* SO15 .... 2 D3
Brunswick Rd *ELGH* SO50 .... 22 B3
Brunswick Sq *SHAM* SO14 .... 2 E5
Bryanston Rd *ITCH* SO19 .... 53 H3
Bryony Cl *HLER* SO31 .... 71 F3
Bryony Gdns *ELGH* SO50 .... 32 C3
Bubb La *BPWT* SO32 .... 32 C5
  HEND SO30 .... 44 B1
Buchanan Rd *ROWN* SO16 .... 27 F4
Buchan Ct *FAWY* SO45 .... 66 A3
Buckingham Ga *WSHM* SO15 .... 40 C4
Buckland Cl *ELGH* SO50 .... 20 C1
Buckland Gdns *TOTT* SO40 .... 37 E2
Buckthorn Cl *TOTT* SO40 .... 36 C4
Budds La *ROMY* SO51 .... 5 G2
Bugle St *SHAM* SO14 .... 2 D5
Bullar Rd *WEND* SO18 .... 42 A5
Bullar St *SHAM* SO14 .... 53 F1
Bullfinch Cl *TOTT* SO40 .... 37 E5
Bull La *LYND* SO43 .... 46 A4
Bullrush Cl *FAWY* SO45 .... 66 D4
Burbush Cl *FAWY* SO45 .... 72 C5
Burgess Gdns *ROWN* SO16 .... 40 C1
Burgess Rd *PTSW* SO17 .... 29 F5
  WSHM SO15 .... 40 B2
Burghclere Rd *ITCH* SO19 .... 62 B2
Burgoyne Rd *ITCH* SO19 .... 55 G3
Burgundy Cl *HLER* SO31 .... 71 F3
Burke Dr *ITCH* SO19 .... 55 E1
Burley Cl *CHFD* SO53 .... 19 F2
Burley Down *CHFD* SO53 .... 9 H5
Burlington Rd *WSHM* SO15 .... 52 C1
Burmah Rd South *FAWY* SO45 .... 73 H3
Burnbank Gdns *TOTT* SO40 .... 37 F2
  WEND SO18 .... 42 A3
Burnett Cl *FAWY* SO45 .... 67 F3
Burnetts Flds *ELGH* SO50 .... 32 C2
Burnetts Gdns *ELGH* SO50 .... 32 D2
Burnetts La *HEND* SO30 .... 32 B5
Burnham Beeches *CHFD* SO53 .... 9 F5
Burnham Cha *WEND* SO18 .... 42 D5
Burns Cl *ELGH* SO50 .... 20 A5
Burns Pl *ROWN* SO16 .... 39 G2
Burns Rd *ELGH* SO50 .... 20 A5
  ITCH SO19 .... 55 F2
Burr Cl *RWIN* SO21 .... 11 H3
Burridge Rd *HLER* SO31 .... 57 G5
Bursledon Hts *HLER* SO31 .... 64 B1
Bursledon Rd *HEND* SO30 .... 56 B2
  ITCH SO19 .... 54 C1
Burton Rd *WSHM* SO15 .... 40 C5
Bury La *TOTT* SO40 .... 50 B2
Bury Rd *TOTT* SO40 .... 50 D4
Busketts Wy *TOTT* SO40 .... 48 C5
Buttercup Cl *FAWY* SO45 .... 67 E4
  HEND SO30 .... 56 A1
Buttercup Wy *HLER* SO31 .... 71 E2
Butterfield Rd *ROWN* SO16 .... 28 C5
Buttermere Cl *ROWN* SO16 .... 39 E2

Buttsash Av *FAWY* SO45 .... 67 E5
Butts Ash Gdns *FAWY* SO45 .... 67 E4
Butts Ash La *FAWY* SO45 .... 67 E4
Butts Bridge Hl *FAWY* SO45 .... 67 E3
Buttsbridge Rd *FAWY* SO45 .... 67 E4
Butt's Cl *ITCH* SO19 .... 55 E3
Butt's Crs *ITCH* SO19 .... 55 E3
Butt's Rd *ITCH* SO19 .... 55 E3
Butt's Sq *ITCH* SO19 .... 55 E3
Byeways *FAWY* SO45 .... 66 D3
By-pass Rd *ROMY* SO51 .... 5 C5
Byron Rd *ELGH* SO50 .... 20 D2
  ITCH SO19 .... 55 F1

C

Cable St *SHAM* SO14 .... 53 G2
Cabot Dr *FAWY* SO45 .... 66 A2
Cadland Rd *FAWY* SO45 .... 72 D1
Cadlands Park Est *FAWY* SO45 .... 72 C2
Cadnam La *TOTT* SO40 .... 34 D1
Caerleon Av *ITCH* SO19 .... 55 E1
Caerleon Dr *ITCH* SO19 .... 54 D1
Caernarvon Gdns *CHFD* SO53 .... 19 E2
Caistor Cl *ROWN* SO16 .... 27 G5
Calabrese *HLER* SO31 .... 65 H3
Calbourne *HLER* SO31 .... 63 E3
Calder Cl *ROWN* SO16 .... 39 E4
Calderwood Dr *ITCH* SO19 .... 54 C3
Caledonia Dr *FAWY* SO45 .... 66 B2
Calmore Crs *TOTT* SO40 .... 36 D3
Calmore Dr *TOTT* SO40 .... 37 E2
Calmore Gdns *TOTT* SO40 .... 37 E5
Calmore Rd *TOTT* SO40 .... 36 D3
Calpe Av *LYND* SO43 .... 58 D4
Calshot Dr *CHFD* SO53 .... 19 E2
Calshot Rd *FAWY* SO45 .... 73 H5
Camargue Cl *HLER* SO31 .... 65 H2
Cambria Dr *FAWY* SO45 .... 66 B2
Cambrian Cl *HLER* SO31 .... 56 A5
Cambridge Dr *CHFD* SO53 .... 19 G3
Cambridge Rd *SHAM* SO14 .... 41 E4
Camelia Cl *NBAD* SO52 .... 17 G1
Camelia Gdns *WEND* SO18 .... 42 C2
Camelia Gv *ELGH* SO50 .... 23 E4
Camley Cl *ITCH* SO19 .... 62 A1
Campbell Cl *ELGH* SO50 .... 20 D5
Campbell St *SHAM* SO14 .... 53 G1
Campbell Wy *ELGH* SO50 .... 22 C4
Campion Cl *ELGH* SO50 .... 32 C3
  HLER SO31 .... 71 E4
Campion Dr *ROMY* SO51 .... 6 C2
Campion Rd *ITCH* SO19 .... 55 F2
Canada Rd *ITCH* SO19 .... 54 A5
Canal Cl *ROMY* SO51 .... 6 A2
Canal Wk *ROMY* SO51 .... 5 H3
  SHAM SO14 .... 2 E5
Canberra Rd *ROWN* SO16 .... 26 B5
Candy La *WEND* SO18 .... 43 G5
Canford Cl *ROWN* SO16 .... 38 D2
Cannon St *WSHM* SO15 .... 40 A4
Canoe Cl *HLER* SO31 .... 71 F4
Canterbury Av *ITCH* SO19 .... 55 E4
Canterbury Dr *FAWY* SO45 .... 66 A2
Canton St *WSHM* SO15 .... 52 D1
Canute Rd *SHAM* SO14 .... 3 H5
Capella Gdns *FAWY* SO45 .... 66 B2
Captains Pl *SHAM* SO14 .... 3 G5
Cardinal Wy *HLER* SO31 .... 71 H2
Carey Rd *ITCH* SO19 .... 55 E2
Carisbrooke *HLER* SO31 .... 63 E3
Carisbrooke Ct *ROMY* SO51 .... 6 A2
Carisbrooke Crs *CHFD* SO53 .... 20 A1
Carisbrooke Dr *ITCH* SO19 .... 54 B1
Carlisle Rd *ROWN* SO16 .... 39 H4
Carlton Crs *WSHM* SO15 .... 52 D1
Carlton Pl *WSHM* SO15 .... 52 D1
Carlton Rd *WSHM* SO15 .... 40 D5
Carlyn Dr *CHFD* SO53 .... 9 H4
Carnation Rd *ROWN* SO16 .... 29 C5
Carne Cl *CHFD* SO53 .... 9 G3
Carolyn Cl *ITCH* SO19 .... 54 A5
Carpathia Cl *WEND* SO18 .... 42 C2
Carpenter Cl *FAWY* SO45 .... 67 E1
Carroll Cl *ELGH* SO50 .... 22 D5
Carthage Cl *CHFD* SO53 .... 10 B4
Caspian Cl *HLER* SO31 .... 65 H3
Castle Cl *WSHM* SO15 .... 51 C1
Castle La *CHFD* SO53 .... 19 E2
  NBAD SO52 .... 17 H2
  SHAM SO14 .... 2 D3
Castle Rd *HLER* SO31 .... 62 D4
  WEND SO18 .... 42 A4
Castleshaw Cl *ROWN* SO16 .... 39 F5
Castle Sq *SHAM* SO14 .... 2 D4
Castle St *SHAM* SO14 .... 41 E4

Castle Wy *SHAM* SO14 .... 2 D3
Catamaran Cl *HLER* SO31 .... 71 F4
Cateran Cl *ROWN* SO16 .... 39 F4
Cathay Gdns *FAWY* SO45 .... 66 A2
Catherine Cl *HEND* SO30 .... 43 G2
Catherine Gdns *HEND* SO30 .... 43 G2
Causeway Crs *TOTT* SO40 .... 38 A4
Cavalier Cl *FAWY* SO45 .... 66 A2
Cavendish Cl *ROMY* SO51 .... 6 B1
Cavendish Gv *WSHM* SO15 .... 40 D4
Cavendish Ms *WSHM* SO15 .... 40 D4
C Av *FAWY* SO45 .... 72 D3
Caversham Cl *HEND* SO30 .... 43 F3
  ITCH SO19 .... 54 C3
Cawte Rd *WSHM* SO15 .... 52 A1
Caxton Av *ITCH* SO19 .... 54 D1
Cecil Av *ROWN* SO16 .... 39 H3
  TOTT SO40 .... 49 E5
Cecil Rd *ITCH* SO19 .... 54 B4
Cedar Av *WSHM* SO15 .... 40 B4
Cedar Cl *HEND* SO30 .... 43 G2
  HLER SO31 .... 63 H2
Cedar Crs *NBAD* SO52 .... 17 F1
Cedar Lawn *ROMY* SO51 .... 6 C2
Cedar Rd *ELGH* SO50 .... 20 A5
  FAWY SO45 .... 72 A1
  SHAM SO14 .... 41 E5
Cedar Wood Cl *ELGH* SO50 .... 23 E4
  TOTT SO40 .... 37 E4
Celandine Av *HLER* SO31 .... 71 F3
Celandine Cl *NBAD* SO52 .... 18 D1
Cement Ter *SHAM* SO14 .... 2 D4
Cemetery Rd *WSHM* SO15 .... 40 C4
Centaury Gdns *ELGH* SO50 .... 32 C2
Central Br *SHAM* SO14 .... 3 G4
Central Rd *SHAM* SO14 .... 3 F6
Central Station Br *WSHM* SO15 .... 2 A1
  WSHM SO15 .... 52 C2
Centre Wy *HLER* SO31 .... 71 G2
Cerdic Ms *HLER* SO31 .... 70 A1
Cerne Cl *NBAD* SO52 .... 17 E2
  WEND SO18 .... 42 D3
Chadwell Av *ITCH* SO19 .... 54 D3
Chadwick Rd *ELGH* SO50 .... 20 A4
Chafen Rd *WEND* SO18 .... 41 H4
Chaffinch Cl *TOTT* SO40 .... 37 E4
Chalice Ct *HEND* SO30 .... 56 B1
Chalk Hl *WEND* SO18 .... 43 E3
Challenger Wy *FAWY* SO45 .... 66 B1
Challis Ct *SHAM* SO14 .... 3 F4
Chalmers Wy *HLER* SO31 .... 69 G2
Chaloner Crs *FAWY* SO45 .... 67 E4
Chalvington Rd *CHFD* SO53 .... 19 G2
Chalybeate Cl *ROWN* SO16 .... 39 H2
Chamberlain Rd *PTSW* SO17 .... 41 E1
Chamberlayne Rd *ELGH* SO50 .... 20 C5
  HLER SO31 .... 63 H2
Chambers Av *ROMY* SO51 .... 6 B4
Chambers Cl *ROWN* SO16 .... 26 C4
Chancellors La *BPWT* SO32 .... 45 E1
Chancel Rd *HLER* SO31 .... 71 H2
Chandlers Wy *HLER* SO31 .... 65 H4
Chandos Ho *SHAM* SO14 .... 53 E2
Chandos St *SHAM* SO14 .... 3 F4
Channels Farm Rd *ROWN* SO16 .... 29 H4
Channel Wy *SHAM* SO14 .... 3 H5
Chantry Rd *SHAM* SO14 .... 3 H4
Chapel Crs *ITCH* SO19 .... 54 C3
Chapel Dro *ELGH* SO50 .... 32 C2
  HEND SO30 .... 56 B1
Chapel La *ELGH* SO50 .... 10 D2
  FAWY SO45 .... 73 G5
  TOTT SO40 .... 49 G2
Chapel Rd *HEND* SO30 .... 43 G2
  HLER SO31 .... 65 E4
  SHAM SO14 .... 3 G3
Charden Rd *ELGH* SO50 .... 22 A5
Charlecote Dr *CHFD* SO53 .... 9 E5
Charles Knott Gdns *WSHM* SO15 .... 40 D5
Charles St *SHAM* SO14 .... 3 F4
Charleston Rd *FAWY* SO45 .... 67 H5
Charles Watts Wy *HEND* SO30 .... 43 G5
Charliejoy Gdns *SHAM* SO14 .... 53 H1
Charlotte Pl *SHAM* SO14 .... 53 E1
Charlton Rd *WSHM* SO15 .... 40 B5
Charmus Rd *TOTT* SO40 .... 36 D2
Charmwen Crs *HEND* SO30 .... 43 E2
Charnwood Cl *CHFD* SO53 .... 9 G1
  TOTT SO40 .... 37 F3
Charnwood Crs *CHFD* SO53 .... 9 G1
Charnwood Gdns *CHFD* SO53 .... 9 G1
Charterhouse Wy *HEND* SO30 .... 43 G5
Chartwell Cl *ELGH* SO50 .... 10 D5
Chatsworth Rd *ELGH* SO50 .... 10 D5
  ITCH SO19 .... 54 C2
Chaucer Rd *ITCH* SO19 .... 55 F1
Chaveney Cl *FAWY* SO45 .... 66 D4
Chawton Cl *WEND* SO18 .... 43 F4

Cheam Wy *TOTT* SO40 .... 37 F3
Cheddar Cl *ITCH* SO19 .... 54 A4
Cheltenham Gdns *HEND* SO30 .... 44 C1
Chelveston Crs *ROWN* SO16 .... 27 F5
Cheping Gdns *HEND* SO30 .... 57 G1
Chepstow Cl *CHFD* SO53 .... 9 F5
  TOTT SO40 .... 37 E4
Cherbourg Rd *ELGH* SO50 .... 20 B5
Cheriton Av *WEND* SO18 .... 43 E5
Cheriton Rd *ELGH* SO50 .... 30 B1
Cherry Dro *ELGH* SO50 .... 32 C3
Cherryton Gdns *FAWY* SO45 .... 72 B5
Cherry Wk *WSHM* SO15 .... 40 A4
Cherrywood *HEND* SO30 .... 56 B1
Cherrywood Gdns *TOTT* SO40 .... 37 E5
Cherville St *ROMY* SO51 .... 5 G3
Cherwell Crs *ROWN* SO16 .... 39 E4
Cherwell Gdns *CHFD* SO53 .... 19 H1
Chessel Av *ITCH* SO19 .... 42 A5
Chessel Crs *ITCH* SO19 .... 42 A5
Chester Rd *WEND* SO18 .... 42 C3
Chestnut Av *CHFD* SO53 .... 19 C3
  ELGH SO50 .... 19 C5
  RWIN SO21 .... 11 H2
  TOTT SO40 .... 49 E4
Chestnut Cl *CHFD* SO53 .... 19 C4
  ROMY SO51 .... 6 D5
Chestnut Ri *ELGH* SO50 .... 19 H5
Chestnut Rd *ROWN* SO16 .... 39 G2
The Chestnuts *HLER* SO31 .... 71 C3
Chettle Rd *ITCH* SO19 .... 55 C2
Chetwynd Dr *ROWN* SO16 .... 28 D5
Chetwynd Rd *ROWN* SO16 .... 28 D5
Cheviot Dr *FAWY* SO45 .... 66 B2
Cheviot Gn *HLER* SO31 .... 70 D5
Cheviot Rd *ROWN* SO16 .... 39 E4
Chichester Cl *HEND* SO30 .... 44 C3
  HLER SO31 .... 71 E2
Chichester Rd *WEND* SO18 .... 42 C3
Chickenhall La *ELGH* SO50 .... 21 E4
Chidden Holt *CHFD* SO53 .... 19 E1
Chilcomb Rd *WEND* SO18 .... 43 E4
Chilham Cl *ELGH* SO50 .... 10 C4
  TOTT SO40 .... 49 E1
Chillerton *HLER* SO31 .... 63 E4
Chillington Gdns *CHFD* SO53 .... 9 F2
Chiltern Cl *TOTT* SO40 .... 49 F2
Chiltern Gn *ROWN* SO16 .... 39 E4
Chilworth Cl *ROWN* SO16 .... 18 B5
Chilworth Dro *ROWN* SO16 .... 18 B5
Chilworth Rd *ROWN* SO16 .... 18 C5
Chine Av *ITCH* SO19 .... 54 A1
Chine Cl *HLER* SO31 .... 71 G1
Chinham Rd *TOTT* SO40 .... 47 F1
Chisholm Cl *ROWN* SO16 .... 27 F4
Church Cl *ELGH* SO50 .... 21 E2
  HLER SO31 .... 71 H2
  NBAD SO52 .... 17 G2
Churchfields *FAWY* SO45 .... 73 H5
Church Hl *HEND* SO30 .... 43 G2
Church La *BPWT* SO32 .... 33 F3
  ELGH SO50 .... 11 G3
  FAWY SO45 .... 73 G5
  HEND SO30 .... 56 B2
  HEND SO30 .... 57 G2
  HLER SO31 .... 64 B2
  LYND SO43 .... 58 D5
  PTSW SO17 .... 41 F2
  ROMY SO51 .... 5 G4
  ROWN SO16 .... 25 H4
  RWIN SO21 .... 11 H3
Church Rd *ELGH* SO50 .... 21 F1
  HLER SO31 .... 70 D5
  HLER SO31 .... 71 H2
  ITCH SO19 .... 61 H1
  ROMY SO51 .... 5 G4
Church St *ROMY* SO51 .... 5 G4
  WSHM SO15 .... 39 H4
Church View Cl *ITCH* SO19 .... 54 C1
Churchward Gdns *HEND* SO30 .... 44 C2
Cirrus Gdns *HLER* SO31 .... 69 G3
Civic Centre Rd *SHAM* SO14 .... 2 D1
Clandon Dr *ELGH* SO50 .... 10 B5
Clanfield Cl *CHFD* SO53 .... 9 H5
Clanfield Dr *CHFD* SO53 .... 9 H5
Clanfield Rd *WEND* SO18 .... 43 E5
Clanfield Wy *CHFD* SO53 .... 9 H5
Claremont Cl *ELGH* SO50 .... 10 C5
Claremont Crs *WSHM* SO15 .... 39 G5
Claremont Rd *WSHM* SO15 .... 39 G5
Clarence Rd *LYND* SO43 .... 58 D5
Clarendon Cl *ROMY* SO51 .... 6 B2
Clarendon Crs
  FHAM/STUB PO14 .... 71 H4
Clarendon Rd *CHFD* SO53 .... 9 G4
Claude Ashby Cl *WEND* SO18 .... 30 A4
Claudeen Cl *WEND* SO18 .... 30 A4

Claudius Cl *CHFD* SO53 .... 10 B4 🔳
Claudius Gdns *CHFD* SO53 .... 10 B5
Clausentum Cl *CHFD* SO53 .... 10 A4
Clausentum Rd *SHAM* SO14 .... 41 E5
Claypits La *FAWY* SO45 .... 66 A1
Cleasby Cl *ROWN* SO16 .... 39 E5
Cleethorpes Rd *ITCH* SO19 .... 54 D3
The Cleeves *TOTT* SO40 .... 49 E1
Cleveland Ct *WEND* SO18 .... 42 C3 🔳
Cleveland Dr *FAWY* SO45 .... 66 B3
Cleveland Rd *WEND* SO18........... 42 B2
Clevelands Cl *CHFD* SO53 .... 9 F1 🔳
Cliffe Av *HLER* SO31 .... 69 G2
Clifford Dibben Ms
  SHAM SO14 .... 41 E4 🔳
Clifford Pl *ELGH* SO50 .... 22 C4
Clifford St *SHAM* SO14................ 3 G1
Cliff Rd *WSHM* SO15 .... 52 B2
Clifton Gdns *WEND* SO18 .... 43 E3
Clifton Rd *WSHM* SO15 .... 39 G4
Clipper Cl *HLER* SO31 .... 71 E4
The Cloisters *ROMY* SO51 .... 5 G3 🔳
  ROWN SO16 .... 29 E5
The Close *FAWY* SO45 .... 72 D5
  HEND SO30........................... 56 B1
  WEND SO18 .... 43 E1
Clovelly Rd *SHAM* SO14............. 53 E1
Clover Cl *HLER* SO31 .... 71 E3
Clover Wy *HEND* SO30 .... 56 A1 🔳
  ROMY SO51 .... 6 C3
Clydesdale Dr *TOTT* SO40 .... 36 D4 🔳
Clydesdale Rd *HLER* SO31........... 65 H3
Clydesdale Wy *TOTT* SO40 .... 36 D4
Coach Hill Cl *CHFD* SO53 .... 9 F4
Coachmans Copse *WEND* SO18.... 42 C2
Coach Rd *HLER* SO31 .... 69 G3
Coal Park La *HLER* SO31............. 64 D1
Coalville Rd *ITCH* SO19 .... 54 D3
Coates Rd *ITCH* SO19 .... 55 F3
Coat Gdns *FAWY* SO45 .... 67 E2 🔳
Cobbett Cl *WEND* SO18 .... 42 A5
Cobbett Wy *HEND* SO30 .... 45 E5
Cobden Av *WEND* SO18.............. 41 H4
Cobden Crs *WEND* SO18 .... 42 B4
Cobden Gdns *WEND* SO18 .... 42 A3
Coblands Av *TOTT* SO40 .... 37 F5
Coburg St *SHAM* SO14............... 53 C1
Cocklydown La *TOTT* SO40......... 49 G2
Colburn Cl *ROWN* SO16 .... 38 D2
Colchester Av *ELGH* SO50 .... 21 G2
Cold East Cl *HLER* SO31 .... 65 E5
Coldeast Wy *HLER* SO31 .... 65 E5
Coldharbour La *ROWN* SO16 ...... 26 A1
Colebrook Av *WSHM* SO15 .... 40 A3
Coleman St *SHAM* SO14 .... 3 G2
Coleridge Cl *HLER* SO31............. 70 D4
Coleson Rd *WEND* SO18 .... 42 A4
Coleville Av *FAWY* SO45 .... 73 H5
College Cl *HLER* SO31 .... 69 H3 🔳
College Rd *ITCH* SO19 .... 54 A5
College St *SHAM* SO14 .... 3 H4
Collett Cl *HEND* SO30 .... 44 B2
Collier Cl *PTSW* SO17 .... 41 G4 🔳
Collingbourne Dr *CHFD* SO53....... 9 F5
Collingworth Ri *HLER* SO31 .... 65 H4
Collins Cl *NBAD* SO52 .... 8 D5 🔳
Colne Av *ROWN* SO16 .... 38 D1
Colt Cl *ROWN* SO16 .... 27 F4 🔳
Coltsfoot Cl *HEND* SO30............. 44 B5
Coltsfoot Dr *HLER* SO31 .... 71 E3
Coltsfoot Wk *ROMY* SO51 .... 6 C2 🔳
Colts Rd *ROWN* SO16 .... 27 E2
Colwell Cl *ROWN* SO16.............. 38 D4
Comfrey Cl *HEND* SO30 .... 6 C2
Comines Wy *HEND* SO30 .... 55 G1
Commercial Rd *TOTT* SO40......... 38 A5
  WSHM SO15 .... 52 D2
Commercial St *WEND* SO18 .... 42 D5
Common Cl *CHFD* SO53 .... 9 G3
Common Gdns *CHFD* SO53 .... 9 G3
Common Rd *CHFD* SO53 .... 9 G3
Compton Cl *ELGH* SO50 .... 10 B5
Compton Rd *TOTT* SO40 .... 38 A4
Compton Wk *SHAM* SO14 .... 53 E2 🔳
Condor Cl *ITCH* SO19 .... 53 H4 🔳
Conference Dr *HLER* SO31 .... 71 H2 🔳
Congleton Cl *LYND* SO43 .... 46 A4
Conifer Cl *FAWY* SO45 .... 66 D2 🔳
Conifer Rd *ROWN* SO16 .... 27 G5
Coniston Gdns *HEND* SO30 .... 56 B2
Coniston Rd *ELGH* SO50 .... 20 B4
  ROWN SO16 .... 38 C4
Connemara Crs *HLER* SO31 .... 65 H3
Consort Rd *ELGH* SO50 .... 20 D1
Constable Cl *ITCH* SO19 .... 55 E5
Constantine Av *CHFD* SO53 .... 10 A5
Constantine Cl *CHFD* SO53 .... 10 B5 🔳
Conway Cl *CHFD* SO53................ 19 F3

Cooks La *TOTT* SO40.................. 37 E2
Cook St *SHAM* SO14 .... 3 F3
Coombedale *HLER* SO31 .... 71 H3 🔳
Cooper Rd *TOTT* SO40 .... 49 E4
Cooper's Cl *WEND* SO18 .... 43 E3
Cooper's La *ITCH* SO19 .... 53 H4 🔳
Copeland Rd *ROWN* SO16 .... 38 D3
Copinger Cl *TOTT* SO40 .... 49 E1 🔳
Copperfield Rd *ROWN* SO16........ 29 E4
Copperfields *TOTT* SO40 .... 36 D5
Coppice Rd *TOTT* SO40 .... 37 E2
Copse Cl *NBAD* SO52 .... 17 F2
  TOTT SO40 .... 49 H1
Copse La *HLER* SO31 .... 69 H3
  ROWN SO16 .... 18 D5
Copse Rd *WEND* SO18 .... 42 B2
The Copse *CHFD* SO53 .... 20 A1
Copse Vw *ITCH* SO19 .... 55 G2
Copsewood Rd *FAWY* SO45 .... 66 D2
  TOTT SO40 .... 49 E4
  WEND SO18 .... 42 A2
Copthorne La *FAWY* SO45 .... 73 H5
Copythorne Crs *TOTT* SO40 .... 35 G2
Coracle Cl *HLER* SO31 .... 71 F4
Corbiere Cl *ROWN* SO16 .... 39 E1
Corbould Rd *FAWY* SO45 .... 66 D5 🔳
Cordelia Cl *FAWY* SO45 .... 66 B2
Coriander Dr *TOTT* SO40 .... 36 D5
Corinna Gdns *FAWY* SO45 .... 66 B2
Corinthian Rd *CHFD* SO53 .... 10 A4
Cork La *TOTT* SO40 .... 51 F4
Cormorant Dr *FAWY* SO45 .... 67 F3
Cornel Rd *ITCH* SO19 .... 54 B2
Cornfield Cl *NBAD* SO52 .... 8 D5
Cornflower Cl *HLER* SO31 .... 71 E3
Cornforth Rd *TOTT* SO40 .... 37 E3
Corn Market *ROMY* SO51 .... 5 G4 🔳
Cornwall Crs *WEND* SO18 .... 42 B2
Cornwall Rd *CHFD* SO53 .... 19 G3
  WEND SO18 .... 42 B2
Coronation Pde *HLER* SO31 .... 69 G2 🔳
Corsair Dr *FAWY* SO45 .... 66 B1
Cortina Wy *HEND* SO30 .... 56 C2
Corvette Av *HLER* SO31............. 71 F4
Cosford Cl *ELGH* SO50 .... 22 A4 🔳
Cossack Gn *SHAM* SO14............... 3 G4
Cosworth Dr *FAWY* SO45 .... 66 B2
Cotsalls *ELGH* SO50 .... 22 C5
Cotswold Cl *FAWY* SO45 .... 66 B2 🔳
Cotswold Rd *ROWN* SO16 .... 39 F4
Cotton Cl *ELGH* SO50 .... 21 G3
Coulsdon Rd *HEND* SO30 .... 56 C1
Coultas Rd *CHFD* SO53 .... 10 A1
Court Cl *TOTT* SO40 .... 37 E2
Court House Cl *FAWY* SO45 .... 67 E1 🔳
Courtland Gdns *ROWN* SO16 ...... 29 F4
Court Rd *WSHM* SO15 .... 40 A4
Court Royal Ms *WSHM* SO15 ...... 40 D4 🔳
Coventry Rd *WSHM* SO15 .... 52 D1
The Covert *ROMY* SO51 .... 6 B3
Cowdray Cl *ELGH* SO50 .... 21 H4 🔳
  ROWN SO16 .... 27 H5
Cowley Cl *ROWN* SO16............... 39 E2
Cowper Rd *ITCH* SO19 .... 55 F1
Cowslip Cl *HLER* SO31 .... 71 E4
Coxford Cl *ROWN* SO16 .... 39 G2
Coxford Dro *ROWN* SO16 .... 39 G2
Coxford Rd *ROWN* SO16 .... 39 F2
Cox's Dr *ITCH* SO19................... 54 D5
Cozens Cl *ITCH* SO19 .... 62 A1 🔳
Crabapple Cl *TOTT* SO40 .... 37 E5 🔳
Crabbs Wy *TOTT* SO40 .... 36 D5
Crableck La *HLER* SO31.............. 64 C5
Crabtree *ROWN* SO16 .... 39 F3 🔳
Crabwood Cl *ROWN* SO16.......... 39 F3
Crabwood Dr *ROWN* SO16.......... 43 G3
Crabwood Rd *ROWN* SO16 .... 39 E2
Cracknore Hard *TOTT* SO40 .... 52 A5
Cracknore Hard La *TOTT* SO40 .. 52 A5 🔳
Crampmoor La *ROMY* SO51 .... 6 D2
Cranbourne Gdns *CHFD* SO53 ..... 9 F3
Cranbourne Cl *WSHM* SO15 .... 40 B3 🔳
Cranbury Av *SHAM* SO14 .... 53 F1
Cranbury Gdns *HLER* SO31 .... 63 H1
Cranbury Pl *SHAM* SO14 .... 53 F1
Cranbury Rd *ELGH* SO50 .... 20 C4
  ITCH SO19 .... 54 B4
Cranford Gdns *CHFD* SO53 .... 9 F3
Cranford Wy *PTSW* SO17 .... 41 E2
Cranleigh Rd *HEND* SO30 .... 56 C4
Cranmer Dr *ROWN* SO16 .... 26 C4
Cranmore *HLER* SO31 .... 63 E3
Craven Rd *CHFD* SO53 .... 9 H5
Craven St *SHAM* SO14 .... 3 F1 🔳
Crawford Cl *ROWN* SO16 .... 26 A4
Creedy Gdns *WEND* SO18 .... 42 C1 🔳

Creighton Rd *WSHM* SO15 .... 51 F1
Crescent Rd *HLER* SO31 .... 71 F2
  NBAD SO52 .... 17 F1
The Crescent *ELGH* SO50............ 20 C2
  HLER SO31 .... 62 D4
  ITCH SO19 .... 54 C5
  ROMY SO51 .... 6 B3
  TOTT SO40 .... 48 A4
Cressey Rd *ROMY* SO51 .... 5 H4
Crest Wy *ITCH* SO19 .... 55 E3
Crete La *FAWY* SO45.................. 66 D4
Crete Rd *FAWY* SO45 .... 66 D5
Crigdon Cl *ROWN* SO16 .... 39 E4
Crispin Cl *ELGH* SO50 .... 32 C3
  HLER SO31 .... 71 H1
Crofton Cl *PTSW* SO17 .... 41 E3 🔳
Crofton Wy *HLER* SO31 .... 70 C4
The Croft *CHFD* SO53 .... 19 G3 🔳
  TOTT SO40 .... 37 E2
Cromarty Rd *ROWN* SO16 .... 27 E4
Cromer Rd *ROWN* SO16 .... 38 D3
Cromwell Rd *WSHM* SO15 .... 40 D5
Crookham Rd *ITCH* SO19 .... 62 B2 🔳
Crosshouse Rd *SHAM* SO14 .... 3 J5
Cross Rd *ITCH* SO19 .... 42 A5
Crosswell Cl *ITCH* SO19 .... 55 E2
Crown St *WSHM* SO15 .... 39 H4
Crows Nest La *BPWT* SO32......... 45 F3
Crowsport *HLER* SO31 .... 70 A2
Crowther Cl *ITCH* SO19 .... 55 E3
Croydon Cl *ROWN* SO16 .... 27 G5
Crummock Rd *CHFD* SO53 .... 9 E4
Crusader Cl *HEND* SO30 .... 56 D2
Crusaders Wy *NBAD* SO52 .... 8 D5
Cuckmere La *ROWN* SO16.......... 38 D4
Cuckoo Bushes La *CHFD* SO53 ..... 9 F3
Cudworth Md *HEND* SO30 .... 44 D3
Culford Av *TOTT* SO40 .... 49 H1
Culford Wy *TOTT* SO40 .... 49 H1
Culver Cl *HLER* SO31 .... 63 E3 🔳
Culver Cl *ROWN* SO16................ 38 D2
Culvery Gdns *WEND* SO18 .... 42 C2
Cumberland Av *CHFD* SO53 .... 20 A1
Cumberland Pl *WSHM* SO15 .... 52 D2
Cumberland St *SHAM* SO14 .... 3 G2 🔳
Cumberland Wy *FAWY* SO45 ...... 66 B2
Cumber Rd *HLER* SO31 .... 71 E2
Cumbrian Wy *ROWN* SO16 .... 39 E4
Cunard Av *WSHM* SO15 .... 40 A4
Cunard Rd *SHAM* SO14 .... 3 F7
Cunningham Crs *ITCH* SO19 .... 54 D3 🔳
Cunningham Dr *HLER* SO31 .... 71 G1
Cupernham Cl *ROMY* SO51 .... 6 A3
Cupernham La *ROMY* SO51 .... 6 A3
Curlew Cl *ROWN* SO16 .... 27 H4
Curlew Dr *FAWY* SO45 .... 67 F3
Custards Rd *LYND* SO43............. 58 D4
Cutbush La *WEND* SO18 .... 42 C1
  WEND SO18 .... 42 D4
Cutter Av *HLER* SO31 .... 71 E4
Cygnus Gdns *FAWY* SO45 .... 66 A2
Cypress Av *ITCH* SO19 .... 54 B2
Cypress Gdns *HEND* SO30 .... 45 G5
  TOTT SO40 .... 37 E5 🔳

D

Daffodil Rd *ROWN* SO16 .... 29 G5
Dahlia Rd *ROWN* SO16 .... 29 G5 🔳
Daintree Cl *ITCH* SO19 .... 55 F4
Dairy La *ROWN* SO16 .... 26 A5
Daisy La *HLER* SO31 .... 71 H2
Daisy Rd *ROWN* SO16 .... 29 G5
Dale Rd *FAWY* SO45 .... 66 D2
  ROWN SO16 .... 40 A2
Dales Wy *TOTT* SO40 .... 36 D4
Dale Valley Cl *ROWN* SO16 .... 40 A2
Dale Valley Gdns *ROWN* SO16 .... 40 A2
Dale Valley Rd *ROWN* SO16 .... 40 A1
Dalmally Gdns *WEND* SO18 .... 42 B4 🔳
Damen Cl *HEND* SO30 .... 56 B2
Danebury Gdns *CHFD* SO53 .... 19 E2 🔳
Danebury Wy *ROWN* SO16 .... 38 D1
Darlington Gdns *WSHM* SO15 ..... 40 B4
Dartington Rd *ELGH* SO50 .... 21 F1
Dart Rd *WEND* SO18.................. 42 D1
Darwin Rd *ELGH* SO50 .... 20 D2
  WSHM SO15 .... 40 B5
Dashwood Av *WSHM* SO15 .... 40 B4
Dawnay Cl *ROWN* SO16 .... 29 H4
Dawson Rd *ITCH* SO19 .... 55 E5 🔳
Dayrell Cl *TOTT* SO40 .... 36 D3
Deacon Cl *ITCH* SO19 .... 54 C2
Deacon Crs *ITCH* SO19 .... 54 C1
Deacon Rd *HLER* SO31 .... 71 H2

  ITCH SO19 .... 54 C2
Dean Ct *HEND* SO30 .... 44 B5
The Deanery *CHFD* SO53 .... 9 F3
Deanfield Cl *HLER* SO31 .... 69 H3
Dean Rd *ELGH* SO50 .... 22 B5
  WEND SO18 .... 42 C4
Dearing Cl *LYND* SO43 .... 58 D5
Dee Cl *CHFD* SO53..................... 19 E1
Deeping Cl *ITCH* SO19 .... 62 B1 🔳
Deerhurst Cl *TOTT* SO40 .... 49 F1
Deerleap Wy *FAWY* SO45 .... 67 E2
Defender Rd *ITCH* SO19 .... 53 H4
De Grouchy La *PTSW* SO17 .... 41 E3
Delft Cl *HLER* SO31 .... 71 F2
Delius Av *ITCH* SO19 .... 55 F4
Dell Cl *ELGH* SO50 .... 22 C5
Dell Rd *WEND* SO18 .... 42 B2
Dempsey Cl *ITCH* SO19 .... 54 D3
Denbigh Cl *ELGH* SO50............... 20 B1
  TOTT SO40 .... 49 F2
Denbigh Gdns *ROWN* SO16 .... 28 D5
Dene Cl *HLER* SO31 .... 71 E1
  ROWN SO16 .... 28 D2
Dene Rd *TOTT* SO40 .... 49 E5
Dene Wy *TOTT* SO40 .... 49 E4
Denham Gdns *HLER* SO31 .... 62 D5
Denmead Rd *WEND* SO18 .... 43 E4
Denny Cl *FAWY* SO45 .... 73 H5 🔳
Denzil Av *HLER* SO31................. 63 E4
Depedene La *FAWY* SO45 .... 72 B4
Derby Rd *ELGH* SO50 .... 20 B4
  SHAM SO14 .... 53 F2
Deridene Ct *TOTT* SO40 .... 49 F1
Derwent Cl *WEND* SO18 .... 42 D3
Derwent Dr *TOTT* SO40 .... 36 D4
Derwent Rd *ROWN* SO16 .... 39 E3
Desborough Rd *ELGH* SO50 .... 20 C4
Devine Gdns *ELGH* SO50 .... 21 G4 🔳
Devon Dr *CHFD* SO53................. 19 G3
Devonshire Gdns *FAWY* SO45 .... 67 E5 🔳
  HLER SO31 .... 55 H5 🔳
  HLER SO31 .... 56 A5 🔳
Devonshire Rd *WSHM* SO15 .... 52 D1
Dew La *ELGH* SO50 .... 20 B3
Dibble Dr *NBAD* SO52 .... 17 F3
Dibden Lodge Cl *FAWY* SO45 ..... 60 D5
Dibles Rd *HLER* SO31 .... 70 D4
Dickens Dell *TOTT* SO40 .... 36 D5
Didcot Rd *WSHM* SO15 .... 40 A3 🔳
Diligence Cl *HLER* SO31 .... 64 A1
Dimond Cl *WEND* SO18 .... 42 A3
Dimond Hl *WEND* SO18 .... 42 A3
Dimond Rd *WEND* SO18 .... 42 A2
Dingle Wy *HLER* SO31 .... 71 G1
Dodwell La *HLER* SO31 .... 56 B4
Dolphin Cl *ELGH* SO50 .... 21 H4
Dolton Rd *ROWN* SO16 .... 39 F1
Doncaster Rd *ELGH* SO50 .... 30 C1
Donnington Dr *CHFD* SO53 .... 19 E3
Donnington Gv *PTSW* SO17 .... 41 F2
Doric Cl *CHFD* SO53 .... 10 B4
Dorland Gdns *TOTT* SO40 .... 49 F1
Dormy Cl *HLER* SO31 .... 70 D2
The Dorrits *TOTT* SO40 .... 36 D5
Dorset Rd *CHFD* SO53 .... 19 G3 🔳
Dorset St *PTSW* SO17 .... 53 E1
Douglas Crs *ITCH* SO19 .... 55 E1
Douglas Wy *FAWY* SO45............ 66 C1
Dove Dl *ELGH* SO50 .... 19 H4
Dove Gdns *HLER* SO31 .... 65 H5 🔳
Dover St *SHAM* SO14 .... 41 F4
Dowds Cl *HEND* SO30 .... 44 B4
Downland Cl *HLER* SO31 .... 45 F5
  HLER SO31 .... 71 G1
Downland Pl *HEND* SO30 .... 56 B3
Downscroft Gdns *HEND* SO30 .... 44 B4 🔳
  HEND SO30 .... 44 B5 🔳
Downside Av *ITCH* SO19 .... 54 C1
Down's Park Av *TOTT* SO40 .... 50 A1
Down's Park Crs *TOTT* SO40 ...... 50 A1
Down's Park Rd *TOTT* SO40 .... 50 A1
Downton Rd *WEND* SO18 .... 42 B2
Downwood Cl *FAWY* SO45 .... 66 A3 🔳
Doyle Ct *ITCH* SO19 .... 62 B1
Dragoon Cl *ITCH* SO19 .... 55 E3
Drake Cl *HLER* SO31 .... 65 H5
  TOTT SO40 .... 51 F5
Drake Rd *ELGH* SO50 .... 21 G2
Drakes Cl *FAWY* SO45 .... 66 D3 🔳
Drayton Cl *ITCH* SO19 .... 62 B1
Drayton Pl *TOTT* SO40 .... 37 F5 🔳
Driftwood Gdns *TOTT* SO40 ...... 49 E1 🔳
Drinkwater Cl *ELGH* SO50 .... 20 B3
The Drive *HEND* SO30 .... 42 D1
  TOTT SO40 .... 49 H2
Drove Rd *ITCH* SO19 .... 54 D3
The Drove *ELGH* SO50 .... 32 D3
  HEND SO30 .... 43 H1

TOTT SO40 .... 36 D3
WEND SO18 .... 42 C5
Drummond Rd FAWY SO45 ...... 67 E1 🔟
HEND SO30...................... 44 C3
Drummond Wy CHFD SO53 ...... 9 F3 🔟
Dryden Rd ITCH SO19 .... 55 G2
Duddon Cl WEND SO18 .... 42 D3
Duke Rd HEND SO30 .... 56 D2
Dukes Rd SHAM SO14 .... 41 F4
Duke St SHAM SO14 .... 3 G4
Dukeswood Dr FAWY SO45 ...... 67 E1
Dumbleton Cl ITCH SO19........ 55 H3
Dumpers Dro ELGH SO50 .... 32 D3
Dunbar Cl ROWN SO16 .... 27 F4
Duncan Cl ITCH SO19............ 62 A2
Duncan Rd HLER SO31 .... 65 H5
Dundee Rd PTSW SO17 .... 41 G3
Dundonald Cl ITCH SO19 .... 61 H1 🔟
Dundry Wy HEND SO30.......... 44 C5
Dunkirk Cl ROWN SO16 .... 28 B5
Dunkirk Rd ROWN SO16 .... 28 B5
Dunnings La NBAD SO52........ 17 E1
Dunster Cl ROWN SO16 .... 28 A4
Dunvegan Dr ROWN SO16 ...... 28 A4
Durban Rd ROMY SO51.......... 6 A2
Durley Brook Rd BPWT SO32.... 33 F3
Durley Crs TOTT SO40 .... 49 F2
Durley Hall La BPWT SO32 ...... 23 H5
Durley Rd ELGH SO50 .... 33 E2
Durliston Rd ROWN SO16 ...... 38 C3
Durnford Rd SHAM SO14 .... 53 F1
Dutton La ELGH SO50 .... 20 D3
Duttons Rd ROMY SO51.......... 5 G3
Dyer Rd WSHM SO15 .... 40 A5
Dymott Cl WSHM SO15 .... 52 B2 🔟
Dyram Cl ELGH SO50 .... 20 B1
Dyserth Cl ITCH SO19............ 62 D1

E

Eadens La TOTT SO40 .... 35 H5
Eagle Cl CHFD SO53 .... 19 F2
Earls Cl ELGH SO50 .... 22 A4
Earls Rd SHAM SO14 .... 41 F4
Eastbourne Av WSHM SO15 .... 40 B4
Eastbrook Cl HLER SO31 .... 65 G5
Eastchurch Cl ROWN SO16 .... 27 F5
Eastcot Cl FAWY SO45 .... 72 B5
East Dr ELGH SO50 .... 21 E1
Eastern Rd HEND SO30 .... 43 F3
Eastgate St SHAM SO14 .... 2 C5
Eastleigh Rd ELGH SO50 .... 22 C5
Eastmeare Ct TOTT SO40........ 49 E1
East Park Ter WSHM SO15 ...... 53 E2
East Rd FAWY SO45 .... 67 H5
East St SHAM SO14.............. 2 E5
Eastville Rd ELGH SO50 .... 22 C5 🔟
E Av FAWY SO45 .... 73 E3
Edelvale Rd WEND SO18........ 42 D3
Eden Rd WEND SO18 .... 42 D2
Eden Wk CHFD SO53 .... 19 E1
Edgehill Rd WEND SO18 .... 42 D3
Edith Haisman Cl WSHM SO15 .. 52 B2 🔟
Edmunds Cl HEND SO30 .... 56 D2
Edward Av ELGH SO50 .... 21 F2
Edward Rd FAWY SO45 .... 67 E1
WSHM SO15 .... 39 H5
Edwina Cl ITCH SO19............ 54 B1
NBAD SO52.................... 17 G2
Effingham Gdns ITCH SO19 .... 55 E3
Eight Acres ROMY SO51 .... 6 B4 🔟
Elan Cl WEND SO18 .... 42 D3
Elcombes Cl LYND SO43 .... 58 D5
Elder Cl HLER SO31 .... 71 F3 🔟
Elder Gn RWIN SO21............ 12 A3
Eldridge Gdns ROMY SO51 ...... 5 H3
Electron Wy CHFD SO53 .... 9 G5
Elgar Rd ITCH SO19 .... 55 E4
Elgin Cl FAWY SO45 .... 67 F4
Elgin Rd WSHM SO15 .... 52 B2
Eling Hl TOTT SO40 .... 50 B2
Eling La TOTT SO40.............. 50 A1
Elizabeth Cl HEND SO30 .... 43 F3
Elizabeth Gdns FAWY SO45 .... 67 E4
Elland Cl ELGH SO50............ 22 C5
Elldene Ct TOTT SO40 .... 49 G2 🔟
Ellen Gdns CHFD SO53 .... 19 E1
Elliot Cl TOTT SO40 .... 49 F1
Elliot Ri HEND SO30 .... 44 C2
Ellis Rd ITCH SO19.............. 55 G2
Ellwood Av ITCH SO19.......... 55 G2
Ellwood Cl ITCH SO19 .... 55 G1
Elm Crs FAWY SO45.............. 72 A1
Elm Gdns HEND SO30............ 43 F2

Elm Gv ELGH SO50 .... 20 B4
Elmsleigh Gdns ROWN SO16...... 29 E5
Elmslie Gdns HLER SO31 ...... 63 H1
Elm St SHAM SO14 .... 3 H3
Elm Ter SHAM SO14 .... 3 H4
Elm Tree Cl TOTT SO40........ 48 D5
Elmtree Gdns ROMY SO51 ...... 6 C5
Elstree Rd ITCH SO19 .... 54 A3 🔟
Embley Cl TOTT SO40.......... 37 F2
Embsay Rd HLER SO31 .... 64 D2
Emerald Cl ITCH SO19 .... 54 D4
Emer Cl NBAD SO52 .... 17 G1 🔟
Emmett Rd ROWN SO16 ...... 27 F4
Emmons Rd HLER SO31 ...... 69 H4
Empress Rd LYND SO43 ...... 58 D5 🔟
SHAM SO14.................. 41 F5
SHAM SO14.................. 61 F1
Emsworth Rd WSHM SO15 .... 39 H4
Endeavour Cl WSHM SO15 .... 39 H5 🔟
Endeavour Wy FAWY SO45...... 60 D5
Enderwood Cl TOTT SO40 ...... 36 D4 🔟
Endle St SHAM SO14 .... 3 H4
Enfield Gv ITCH SO19.......... 54 A5
Englefield Rd WEND SO18 .... 41 H5
English Rd WSHM SO15 ...... 39 H5
Ennel Copse NBAD SO52 ...... 17 G2
Ennerdale Gdns WEND SO18 .. 42 D3 🔟
Ennerdale Rd ROWN SO16 .... 39 E2
Ensign Wy HLER SO31 .... 69 C3
Enterprise Cl HLER SO31 ...... 71 E4 🔟
Enterprise Rd ROWN SO16 .... 18 A5
Enterprise Wy SHAM SO14 .... 3 G6
Epping Cl WEND SO18 .... 42 D3
Epsom Cl ELGH SO50 .... 32 D2
Erica Cl HLER SO31 .... 71 F2
Escombe Rd ELGH SO50 ...... 21 F3
Estridge Cl HLER SO31 .... 64 A1 🔟
Ethelburt Av ROWN SO16 ...... 29 C4
Ethelred Gdns TOTT SO40 .... 49 E1
European Wy SHAM SO14 .... 3 F4
Evans St SHAM SO14 .... 3 F3
Evelyn Crs WSHM SO15 ...... 40 B4
Evenlode Rd ROWN SO16 .... 39 E3
Evesham Cl ROWN SO16 ...... 29 F4 🔟
Ewart Cr FAWY SO45 .... 61 E5
Ewell Wy TOTT SO40 .... 37 F3
Exbury Cl ELGH SO50 .... 21 H4
Exeter Cl ELGH SO50 .... 20 B1
HLER SO31 .... 71 F2
WEND SO18 .... 42 C3
Exeter Rd WEND SO18 .... 42 C4
Exford Av WEND SO18 .... 43 E4
Exford Dr WEND SO18 .... 43 E5
Exleigh Cl ITCH SO19 .... 54 D1
Exmouth Gdns ELGH SO50 .... 32 C2 🔟
Eyebright Cl ELGH SO50 ...... 32 C3 🔟
Eyeworth Wk FAWY SO45 ...... 66 A1 🔟
Eynham Av ITCH SO19 .... 55 E1
Eynham Cl ITCH SO19 .... 54 D1
Eyre Cl TOTT SO40 .... 49 F1

F

Factory Rd ELGH SO50 .... 20 C4
Fairbairn Wk NBAD SO52 ...... 8 D3
Faircross Cl FAWY SO45........ 72 C5
Fairfax Ct ITCH SO19 .... 55 G2 🔟
Fairfax Ms ITCH SO19 .... 55 G1
Fair Fld ROMY SO51............ 6 C1
Fairfield Cl FAWY SO45 .... 67 E1 🔟
Fair Gn ITCH SO19.............. 54 D2
Fairisle Rd ROWN SO16 .... 27 E5
Fairlawn Cl ROWN SO16........ 27 F2
Fairlie Cl HEND SO30 .... 44 C1 🔟
Fairmead Wy TOTT SO40 ...... 49 G2
Fairoak Rd ELGH SO50........ 21 F4
Fairview Cl FAWY SO45 .... 67 E2
ROMY SO51.................. 6 B2
Fairview Dr FAWY SO45 .... 66 D3
ROMY SO51.................. 6 B2
Fairview Pde FAWY SO45 ...... 67 E3 🔟
Fairway Gdns ROWN SO16 .... 27 E4
Fairway Rd FAWY SO45 .... 66 D1
Falaise Cl ROWN SO16 .... 28 A5
Falconer Ct FAWY SO45 .... 72 B2 🔟
Falcon Flds FAWY SO45 .... 73 H5
Falcon Sq ELGH SO50 .... 19 H5
Falcon Wy BPWT SO32 .... 45 G3
Falkland Rd CHFD SO53 ...... 19 G3
WSHM SO15 .... 39 G5
Falstaff Wy TOTT SO40 .... 49 G2 🔟
Fanshawe St SHAM SO14...... 53 E1 🔟
Faringdon Rd WEND SO18 .... 43 H3
Farley Cl ELGH SO50 .... 22 D5
Farmery Cl ELGH SO50 .... 29 H5
Farringford Rd ITCH SO19 .... 55 F1

Fastnet Cl ROWN SO16 .... 27 E4 🔟
F Av FAWY SO45 .... 73 H5
Fawley By-pass FAWY SO45 .... 73 H5
Fawley Rd FAWY SO45 .... 67 F5
FAWY SO45.................. 73 E3
WSHM SO15.................. 51 G1
Fell Cl HLER SO31 .... 71 G1
Feltham Cl ROMY SO51 .... 6 C3
Ferndale HEND SO30 .... 56 D2 🔟
Ferndene Wy WEND SO18 ...... 42 B4
Fernhills Rd FAWY SO45........ 66 B2
Fernlea Gdns ROWN SO16 .... 40 C1 🔟
Fernlea Wy FAWY SO45........ 66 B2
Fern Rd FAWY SO45 .... 66 D2
ITCH SO19 .... 54 B5 🔟
Fernyhurst Av ROWN SO16 .... 27 F3
Ferry Rd FAWY SO45 .... 66 B2
Field Cl HLER SO31 .... 71 H3
ROMY SO51.................. 6 D2
ROWN SO16 .... 29 G4 🔟
Fielden Cl NBAD SO52 .... 17 F2
Fieldfare Ct TOTT SO40 .... 37 E4
Field Vw NBAD SO52 .... 8 D5
Filton Cl TOTT SO40 .... 48 D5
Finzi Cl ITCH SO19............ 55 E4
Fir Croft Dr CHFD SO53........ 19 H1
Firecrest Cl ROWN SO16 ...... 27 H4
Firgrove Cl NBAD SO52 .... 17 F2
Firgrove Rd NBAD SO52 ...... 17 F2
WSHM SO15.................. 40 A5
Fir Rd TOTT SO40 .... 48 D5
Firs Dr HEND SO30 .... 56 A1
First Av WSHM SO15 .... 38 D5
The Firs ROWN SO16.......... 38 B4
First St FAWY SO45............ 68 A5
Fir Tree Cl ELGH SO50 .... 32 C2
Fir Tree La ELGH SO50 .... 32 B2
Fir Tree Rd TOTT SO40 .... 35 E5
Firtree Wy ITCH SO19 .... 54 D2 🔟
Firwood Cl CHFD SO53 .... 9 C3
Fisher's Rd TOTT SO40 ...... 50 A1
Fishlake Mdw ROMY SO51 .... 5 H2
Fitzhugh Pl WSHM SO15 ...... 40 D5
Fitzhugh St SHAM SO14 ...... 2 C1 🔟
Fitzroy Cl ROWN SO16 .... 28 D2
Five Elms Dr ROMY SO51 ...... 6 B5
Flamborough Cl ROWN SO16.. 38 D2
Flanders Rd HEND SO30 ...... 44 B4
Fleet End Bottom HLER SO31 .. 71 F5
Fleet Rd HLER SO31 .... 71 F5
Fleming Av NBAD SO52 ...... 17 G2
Fleming Pl ROMY SO51 .... 5 H4 🔟
RWIN SO21 .... 11 H2
Fleming Rd ROWN SO16 ...... 29 H5
Fletcher Cl FAWY SO45 .... 66 B2
Fletchwood La FAWY SO45 .... 48 D1
Fletchwood Rd TOTT SO40 .... 48 D1
Fleuret Cl FAWY SO45 .... 67 E5
Flexford Cl CHFD SO53........ 9 E3
Flexford Rd NBAD SO52 ...... 8 A5
Flint Cl ITCH SO19 .... 55 G3
Floating Bridge Rd SHAM SO14.. 3 J5
Florence Rd ITCH SO19 ...... 54 A5 🔟
The Florins ITCH SO19 .... 71 G4
Flowerdown Cl TOTT SO40 .... 37 E4
Flowers Cl HLER SO31 .... 69 G2
Foldsgate Cl LYND SO43 ...... 58 D4 🔟
Fontwell Cl TOTT SO40 .... 37 E3
Fontwell Gdns ELGH SO50 .... 32 D2 🔟
Foord Rd HEND SO30 .... 56 B3 🔟
Football Gn LYND SO43 .... 46 A4
Footner Cl ROMY SO51 .... 6 C1
Forbes Cl ROWN SO16 .... 27 F3
Ford Av CHFD SO53............ 19 H2
Foreshore North FAWY SO45 .. 73 H2
Foreshore South FAWY SO45 .. 73 H2
Forest Cl CHFD SO53 .... 9 H3
NBAD SO52.................. 17 E1
Forest Edge FAWY SO45 ...... 73 C5
Forest Front FAWY SO45 ...... 66 B5
Forest Gdns LYND SO43 ...... 58 D5
Forest Hills Dr WEND SO18 .... 42 A1
Forest Hill Wy FAWY SO45 .... 66 B5
Forest La FAWY SO45 .... 72 B2 🔟
Forest Meadow FAWY SO45 .. 67 E5
Forest Rd CHFD SO53 .... 9 H3
Forest Vw SHAM SO14 .... 2 D4
Forest Wy TOTT SO40 .... 36 C2
Forge Cl HLER SO31 .... 64 A1
Forster Rd SHAM SO14 ...... 41 E5
Forsythia Cl HEND SO30 ...... 44 B4 🔟
Fort Rd ITCH SO19 .... 55 F4
Foundry La WSHM SO15 ...... 39 H4
Four Acre HEND SO30.......... 57 G1
Fowey Cl CHFD SO53 .... 9 F4
Fowlers Rd HEND SO30........ 44 B4
Fowler's Wk NBAD SO52 ...... 18 B4

Foxbury Cl FAWY SO45 .... 67 E3
Fox Cl ELGH SO50 .... 21 H4
Foxcott Cl ITCH SO19 .... 62 B3 🔟
Foxcroft Dr FAWY SO45 .... 72 B5
The Foxgloves HEND SO30 .... 56 D2 🔟
Foxhills TOTT SO40............ 49 E3
Foxhills Cl TOTT SO40 .... 49 E4
Foxtail Dr FAWY SO45 .... 66 A4
Foy Gdns HLER SO31.......... 70 C4
Foyle Rd CHFD SO53 .... 9 F5
Frampton Cl RWIN SO21 ...... 11 H2
Frampton Wy TOTT SO40 ...... 49 H1
Franklyn Av ITCH SO19 .... 54 C3
Fraser Cl ROWN SO16 .... 27 F3
Fratton Wy ELGH SO50 .... 22 C5
Frayslea FAWY SO45 .... 67 E3 🔟
Freda Routh Gdns ELGH SO50 .. 22 D4 🔟
Frederick St SHAM SO14 ...... 53 F1
Freedom Ct FAWY SO45........ 67 E2 🔟
Freegrounds Av HEND SO30 .. 56 C1 🔟
Freegrounds Cl HEND SO30 .. 56 C1
Freegrounds Rd HEND SO30 .. 56 C1
Freemantle Cl ITCH SO19 .... 54 B2 🔟
Freemantle Common Rd
ITCH SO19.................... 54 B2
French St SHAM SO14 .... 2 D5 🔟
Frensham Cl HEND SO30 ...... 56 C1 🔟
Freshfield Rd WSHM SO15 .... 39 H5
Freshfield Sq WSHM SO15 .... 39 H5
Friarscroft HLER SO31.......... 62 D3
Friars Cft TOTT SO40 .... 36 D2
Friars Rd ELGH SO50 .... 20 B5
Friars Wy WEND SO18 .... 29 H5
Fritham Cl TOTT SO40.......... 37 E5
Fritham Rd WEND SO18 ...... 43 E4
Frobisher Gdns ITCH SO19 .... 55 E3
Froghall CHFD SO53 .... 66 D4
Frogmore La ROWN SO16...... 38 D1
Frome Cl TOTT SO40 .... 51 C5
Frome Rd WEND SO18.......... 42 C1
Frost La FAWY SO45 .... 67 G3
Fry Cl HLER SO31 .... 70 A1
Fryern Cl CHFD SO53 .... 10 A5
Fullerton Cl ITCH SO19 ...... 62 B3
Fulmar Cl ROWN SO16 .... 27 H4
Fulmar Dr FAWY SO45 .... 67 F3
Furzedale Gdns FAWY SO45.... 67 F4
Furzedale Pk FAWY SO45 ...... 67 F4
Furzedown Ms FAWY SO45 .... 67 F4 🔟
Furzedown Rd PTSW SO17 .... 41 E2
Furze Rd ITCH SO19 .... 54 C2
Fushsia Gdns ROWN SO16 .... 40 B2 🔟
Fyfeold Cl ROWN SO16 ...... 27 F3

G

Gables Ct ROWN SO16 .... 28 D4 🔟
Gage Cl TOTT SO40 .... 51 C5
Gainsford Rd ITCH SO19 ...... 54 A2
Galleon Cl HLER SO31 .... 71 H4 🔟
Galsworthy Rd TOTT SO40 .... 37 F5
Gamble Cl ITCH SO19 .... 54 B3
Ganger Farm La ROMY SO51 .. 6 C1
Ganger Rd ROMY SO51 .... 6 C1 🔟
Gannet Cl FAWY SO45 .... 67 F3
ROWN SO16 .... 27 H4
Garden Cl LYND SO43.......... 58 C5
Gardeners La ROMY SO51...... 4 B5
Garden Ms HLER SO31 .... 70 C4
Gardiner Cl TOTT SO40 .... 51 C5
Garfield Rd HLER SO31 .... 62 C4
ITCH SO19.................... 42 A5
Garnock Rd ITCH SO19 ...... 53 H5
Garratt Cl HEND SO30 .... 44 C2
Garrett Cl ITCH SO19 .... 62 C1
Garrick Gdns ITCH SO19 ...... 54 C5
Garton Rd ITCH SO19.......... 53 H4
Gatcombe HLER SO31 .... 63 E3
Gatcombe Gdns WEND SO18 .. 42 C2 🔟
Gatwick Cl ROWN SO16 ...... 27 C5
Gavan St ITCH SO19 .... 55 F2
G Av FAWY SO45 .... 73 F2
Gemini Cl ROWN SO16 .... 27 F5
Gento Cl HEND SO30 .... 57 E1
George Curl Wy ELGH SO50 .... 30 B3 🔟
George St ELGH SO50 .... 20 C3
Gerard Crs ITCH SO19 .... 55 F1
Gibbs Rd SHAM SO14 .... 2 D1
Gilbury Cl WEND SO18 .... 30 A5 🔟
Giles Cl HEND SO30 .... 44 D3 🔟
Gilpin Cl ITCH SO19............ 55 F2
The Glades HLER SO31 .... 71 G1
The Glade CHFD SO53 .... 10 B2
Gladstone Rd ITCH SO19 ...... 54 D2
Glasslaw Rd WEND SO18...... 42 C4
Glebe Ct ELGH SO50 .... 22 D4

HEND SO30 .... **45** G4 ⬛
PTSW SO17 .... **41** E2 ⬛
Glencarron Wy *ROWN* SO16 ..... **40** C1
Glencoyne Gdns *ROWN* SO16 .... **39** F2
Glenda Cl *HLER* SO31 .... **70** D5 ⬛
Glendale *HLER* SO31 .... **71** H3 ⬛
Glendowan Rd *CHFD* SO53 .... **9** E4
Glen Eyre Dr *ROWN* SO16 .... **29** E4
Glen Eyre Rd *ROWN* SO16 .... **28** D4
Glen Eyre Wy *ROWN* SO16 .... **29** E5
Glenfield Av *WEND* SO18 .... **42** B5
Glenfield Crs *WEND* SO18 .... **42** B5
Glenfield Wy *WEND* SO18 .... **42** B5
Glenlea Cl *HEND* SO30 .... **43** F3
Glenlea Dr *HEND* SO30 .... **43** F3 ⬛
Glenn Rd *HEND* SO30 .... **43** F2
HLER SO31 .... **65** E4
Glen Rd *HLER* SO31 .... **65** E3
ITCH SO19 .... **61** H1
Glenside *FAWY* SO45 .... **66** D2
Glenside Av *ITCH* SO19 .... **55** F3
Glenwood Av *ROWN* SO16 .... **29** E4
Glenwood Ct *ELGH* SO50 .... **23** E4
Gloucester Sq *SHAM* SO14 .... **2** E5
Goldcrest Gdns *ROWN* SO16 ...... **27** G4
Goldcrest La *TOTT* SO40 .... **37** E4
Golden Ct *HEND* SO30 .... **43** H2
Golden Gv *SHAM* SO14 .... **3** C1
Golden Hind Pk *FAWY* SO45 ...... **66** D3
Goldsmith Cl *TOTT* SO40 .... **37** F5 ⬛
Goldsmith Rd *ELGH* SO50 .... **20** B5
Golf Course Rd *ROWN* SO16 ...... **28** C3
Goodacre Dr *NBAD* SO52 .... **18** D1
Goodison Cl *ELGH* SO50 .... **22** B5 ⬛
Goodlands V *HEND* SO30 .... **44** A5 ⬛
Goodwin Cl *ROWN* SO16 .... **38** D2 ⬛
Goodwood Gdns *TOTT* SO40 ..... **37** E4
Goodwood Rd *ELGH* SO50 .... **20** A2
Gordon Av *SHAM* SO14 .... **41** E4
Gordon Rd *CHFD* SO53 .... **9** H2
Gordon Ter *ITCH* SO19 .... **54** C5 ⬛
Gorse Cl *HLER* SO31 .... **71** F3
Gorselands Rd *WEND* SO18 ...... **42** D3
Gort Crs *ITCH* SO19 .... **54** D3 ⬛
Gover Rd *ROWN* SO16 .... **38** C3
Grace Dieu Gdns *HLER* SO31 .... **63** H1 ⬛
Graddidge Wy *TOTT* SO40 .... **37** F5
Grafton Gdns *ROWN* SO16 .... **28** A4
Graham Rd *SHAM* SO14 .... **53** F1
Graham St *SHAM* SO14 .... **53** G1
Grainger Gdns *ITCH* SO19 .... **55** E4 ⬛
Granada Rd *HEND* SO30 .... **56** A4
Granby Gv *PTSW* SO17 .... **41** F1
Grange Cl *WEND* SO18 .... **30** A5 ⬛
Grange Dr *HEND* SO30 .... **44** D4
Grange Ms *ROMY* SO51 .... **6** C2
Grange Rd *HEND* SO30 .... **44** D5
HLER SO31 .... **62** C4
ROWN SO16 .... **39** H3
Grangewood Gdns *ELGH* SO50 .. **22** B4 ⬛
Grantham Av *HLER* SO31 .... **69** G3
Grantham Rd *ELGH* SO50 .... **20** B4
ITCH SO19 .... **54** B1
Granville St *SHAM* SO14 .... **3** H3
Grasdean Cl *WEND* SO18 .... **42** C3 ⬛
Grasmere *ELGH* SO50 .... **20** B4 ⬛
Grasmere Cl *WEND* SO18 .... **42** D3 ⬛
Gray Cl *HLER* SO31 .... **71** F3
Grayling Md *ROMY* SO51 .... **5** H2
Grays Av *FAWY* SO45 .... **67** F2
Grays Cl *ELGH* SO50 .... **11** H3
ROMY SO51 .... **6** A4
Great Br *ROMY* SO51 .... **5** G1
Greatbridge Rd *ROMY* SO51 ..... **5** G3
Great Elms Cl *FAWY* SO45 .... **72** B5
Great Well Dr *ROMY* SO51 .... **5** H3
Greatwood Cl *FAWY* SO45 .... **67** E3 ⬛
Greenaway La *HLER* SO31 .... **70** D3
Greenbank Crs *ROWN* SO16 ...... **28** D4
Green Cl *FAWY* SO45 .... **67** E1 ⬛
TOTT SO40 .... **48** B3
Greendale Cl *CHFD* SO53 .... **10** A5 ⬛
Greenfields Av *TOTT* SO40 .... **37** G3
Greenfinch Cl *ELGH* SO50 .... **19** H5 ⬛
Greenhill La *ROWN* SO16 .... **27** E1
Green La *HLER* SO31 .... **63** G1
HLER SO31 .... **64** D2
HLER SO31 .... **65** G1
HLER SO31 .... **70** A3
HLER SO31 .... **71** F4
ROMY SO51 .... **7** G3
ROWN SO16 .... **18** D5
ROWN SO16 .... **39** E2
TOTT SO40 .... **24** D5
Greenlea Crs *ROWN* SO16 .... **29** H4
Green Park Rd *ROWN* SO16 ...... **39** E5
Green's Cl *ELGH* SO50 .... **22** A5
The Green *HLER* SO31 .... **64** D4

ROMY SO51 .... **6** C1 ⬛
Greenways *CHFD* SO53 .... **9** H5
ROWN SO16 .... **29** H4
Greenwood Cl *ROWN* SO16 ...... **29** H4
Greenwood Cl *ROMY* SO51 .... **6** A3 ⬛
Greenwood La *PTSW* SO32 .... **33** G1
Gregory Gdns *TOTT* SO40 .... **37** E3 ⬛
Gregory La *BPWT* SO32 .... **33** H4
Grenadier Cl *HLER* SO31 .... **71** H3
Grendon Cl *ROWN* SO16 .... **29** F4 ⬛
Grenville Gdns *FAWY* SO45 ...... **67** E4
Gresley Gdns *HEND* SO30 .... **44** C2 ⬛
Greville Rd *WSHM* SO15 .... **40** B5
Greyhound Cl *HEND* SO30 .... **44** B1 ⬛
Greywell Av *ROWN* SO16 .... **27** H5
Griffen Cl *ELGH* SO50 .... **21** G4 ⬛
Griffin Ct *PTSW* SO17 .... **41** G4
Griffon Cl *HLER* SO31 .... **64** A1
Grosvenor Ct *PTSW* SO17 .... **41** G2
Grosvenor Gdns *HEND* SO30 .... **43** F3
PTSW SO17 .... **41** G2 ⬛
Grosvenor Rd *CHFD* SO53 .... **10** A2
PTSW SO17 .... **41** G2
Grosvenor Sq *WSHM* SO15 ...... **52** D1
Grove Gdns *ITCH* SO19 .... **62** D1
Grovely Wy *ROMY* SO51 .... **7** E2
Grove Pl *ITCH* SO19 .... **54** D5
Grove Rd *WSHM* SO15 .... **40** A5
The Grove *HLER* SO31 .... **63** F3
HLER SO31 .... **64** A1
ITCH SO19 .... **62** D1
Guernsey Cl *ROWN* SO16 .... **39** E1
Guest Rd *ELGH* SO50 .... **21** F3
Guildford Dr *CHFD* SO53 .... **19** F3
Guildford St *SHAM* SO14 .... **53** F2 ⬛
Guillemot Cl *FAWY* SO45 .... **67** F2
The Gulls *TOTT* SO40 .... **51** F5
Gullycroft Md *HEND* SO30 .... **44** B5
Gurney Rd *WSHM* SO15 .... **40** A4

H

Hack Dr *RWIN* SO21 .... **11** H3
Hackworth Gdns *HEND* SO30 .... **44** C2
Haddon Dr *ELGH* SO50 .... **20** C1
Hadleigh Gdns *ELGH* SO50 .... **20** C1
Hadley Fld *FAWY* SO45 .... **72** B3 ⬛
Hadrians Cl *CHFD* SO53 .... **10** A4
Hadrian Wy *ROWN* SO16 .... **28** C2
Haflinger Dr *HLER* SO31 .... **65** H2
Haig Rd *ELGH* SO50 .... **21** F2
Haileybury Gdns *HEND* SO30 ... **44** C3 ⬛
Halden Cl *ROMY* SO51 .... **6** B2
Hales Dr *HEND* SO30 .... **56** A2
Hallet Cl *WEND* SO18 .... **42** C2 ⬛
Hall Lands La *ELGH* SO50 .... **22** D4
Halstead Rd *WEND* SO18 .... **42** B2
Halterworth Cl *ROMY* SO51 ..... **6** B4 ⬛
Halterworth La *ROMY* SO51 ..... **6** C3
Haltons Cl *TOTT* SO40 .... **37** F3
Hambert Wy *TOTT* SO40 .... **49** G2 ⬛
Hamble Cl *HLER* SO31 .... **70** C4
Hamble Ct *CHFD* SO53 .... **19** H1 ⬛
Hamble House Gdns
HLER SO31 .... **70** A3 ⬛
Hamble La *HLER* SO31 .... **55** H5
Hamblewood *HEND* SO30 .... **57** G1
Hameldon Cl *ROWN* SO16 .... **39** F5 ⬛
Hamilton Ms *FAWY* SO45 .... **67** F4 ⬛
Hamilton Rd *ELGH* SO50 .... **21** F3
FAWY SO45 .... **67** F5
Hammonds Cl *TOTT* SO40 .... **37** G4
Hammond's Gn *TOTT* SO40 ..... **37** F4
Hammonds La *TOTT* SO40 .... **37** G4
Hammonds Wy *TOTT* SO40 ...... **37** G4
Hamtun Crs *TOTT* SO40 .... **37** G3 ⬛
Hamtun Gdns *TOTT* SO40 .... **37** G3
Hamtun Rd *ITCH* SO19 .... **55** E5
Hamtun St *SHAM* SO14 .... **2** D4
Handel Rd *WSHM* SO15 .... **52** D1
Handel Ter *WSHM* SO15 .... **52** D1 ⬛
Handford Pl *WSHM* SO15 .... **52** D1 ⬛
Hanley Rd *WSHM* SO15 .... **40** B4
Hannay Ri *ITCH* SO19 .... **55** F3
Hann Rd *ROWN* SO16 .... **27** E5
Hanns Wy *ELGH* SO50 .... **20** C4
Hanover Buildings *SHAM* SO14 . **2** D3
Harbourne Gdns *WEND* SO18 ... **42** D2
Harbour Pde *SHAM* SO14 .... **2** C2
WSHM SO15 .... **52** B1
Harcourt Rd *WEND* SO18 .... **41** H4
Harding La *ELGH* SO50 .... **22** B3
Hardley La *FAWY* SO45 .... **72** B1
Hardwicke Cl *ROWN* SO16 .... **39** F2
Hardwicke Wy *HLER* SO31 ...... **69** G2 ⬛
Hardwick Rd *CHFD* SO53 .... **9** H5 ⬛

Hardy Cl *HLER* SO31 .... **71** H1
WSHM SO15 .... **51** H1
Hardy Dr *FAWY* SO45 .... **67** F4
Hardy Rd *ELGH* SO50 .... **20** B5
Harefield Ct *ROMY* SO51 .... **6** B3 ⬛
Harefield Rd *PTSW* SO17 .... **41** G1
Harewood Cl *ELGH* SO50 .... **20** C1
Harland Crs *WSHM* SO15 .... **40** B3
Harlaxton Cl *ELGH* SO50 .... **20** B1
Harlech Dr *CHFD* SO53 .... **19** E2
Harley Rd *ROWN* SO16 .... **39** F3
Harold Cl *TOTT* SO40 .... **49** F1
Harold Rd *WSHM* SO15 .... **40** A5
The Harrage *ROMY* SO51 .... **5** H4
Harrier Cl *ROWN* SO16 .... **27** H3
Harrier Wy *FAWY* SO45 .... **72** B2
Harris Av *HEND* SO30 .... **44** C4 ⬛
Hart Hl *FAWY* SO45 .... **67** G4
Hartington Rd *SHAM* SO14 ...... **53** F2
Hartley Av *PTSW* SO17 .... **41** F1
Hartley Cl *ELGH* SO50 .... **22** A5
FAWY SO45 .... **67** E4 ⬛
Hartley Ct *ROWN* SO16 .... **29** E5
Hartley Rd *ELGH* SO50 .... **22** A4
Hartley Wk *FAWY* SO45 .... **66** D4 ⬛
Harvest Rd *NBAD* SO52 .... **8** D5
Harvey Crs *HLER* SO31 .... **71** F3
Harvey Gdns *FAWY* SO45 .... **67** F2
Harvey Rd *ELGH* SO50 .... **21** G3
Harwood Cl *TOTT* SO40 .... **37** F4
Haselbury Rd *TOTT* SO40 .... **37** H4
Haselfoot Gdns *WEND* SO18 ... **43** G5 ⬛
Haskells Cl *LYND* SO43 .... **58** C5 ⬛
Hatchley La *RWIN* SO21 .... **13** H5
Hatch Md *HEND* SO30 .... **43** E2
Hathaway Cl *ELGH* SO50 .... **20** D2
Hatherell Cl *HEND* SO30 .... **43** F3
Hatley Rd *WEND* SO18 .... **42** D4
Havelock Rd *HLER* SO31 .... **70** C4
SHAM SO14 .... **2** C1
WSHM SO15 .... **52** D2
Havendale *HEND* SO30 .... **56** D2 ⬛
Havenstone Wy *WEND* SO18 ... **29** H5 ⬛
The Haven *ELGH* SO50 .... **20** D1
H Av *FAWY* SO45 .... **73** F2
Hawfinch Cl *ROWN* SO16 .... **27** H3
Hawkeswood Rd *WEND* SO18 .. **41** G5
Hawkhill *FAWY* SO45 .... **66** A1
Hawkhurst Cl *ITCH* SO19 .... **62** C1
Hawkley Gn *ITCH* SO19 .... **62** B2
Hawswater Cl *ROWN* SO16 ...... **39** F3 ⬛
Hawthorn Cl *ELGH* SO50 .... **22** C4 ⬛
HEND SO30 .... **56** D1 ⬛
RWIN SO21 .... **12** A3
Hawthorne Rd *TOTT* SO40 ...... **37** F4
Hawthorn La *HLER* SO31 .... **65** E5
Hawthorn Rd *FAWY* SO45 .... **66** D2 ⬛
PTSW SO17 .... **41** F2
The Hawthorns *ELGH* SO50 ..... **20** A5 ⬛
Hayburn Rd *ROWN* SO16 .... **38** D2
Haydock Cl *TOTT* SO40 .... **37** E4
Hayes Md *FAWY* SO45 .... **72** B3
Hayle Rd *WEND* SO18 .... **42** D2
Hayley Cl *FAWY* SO45 .... **66** D5
Haynes Wy *FAWY* SO45 .... **66** C4 ⬛
Hayter Gdns *ROMY* SO51 .... **6** A3
Hayward Cl *TOTT* SO40 .... **37** F5
Hayward Ct *FAWY* SO45 .... **72** C4 ⬛
Hazel Cl *CHFD* SO53 .... **9** G1
RWIN SO21 .... **12** A2
Hazeldown Cl *ROWN* SO16 ..... **27** E4
Hazeleigh Av *WSHM* SO15 ...... **54** A5
Hazel Farm Rd *TOTT* SO40 ..... **37** E5
Hazel Gv *HLER* SO31 .... **71** H3
TOTT SO40 .... **48** B4
Hazel Rd *ITCH* SO19 .... **53** H4
Hazelwood Rd *WEND* SO18 ..... **42** C3 ⬛
Headland Dr *HLER* SO31 .... **71** C1
Heath Cl *ELGH* SO50 .... **22** D5
Heathcote Rd *CHFD* SO53 .... **9** H4
Heathen St *BPWT* SO32 .... **33** H5
Heatherbrae Rd *NBAD* SO52 .... **17** F2 ⬛
Heather Cha *ELGH* SO50 .... **22** A4 ⬛
Heather Ct *WEND* SO18 .... **43** E5
Heatherdeane Rd *PTSW* SO17 .. **41** E2
Heatherdene Rd *CHFD* SO53 .... **10** A2
Heatherlands Rd *ROWN* SO16 .. **28** D1
Heatherstone Av *FAWY* SO45 ... **66** D5
Heatherview *NBAD* SO52 .... **17** F1 ⬛
Heathfield *FAWY* SO45 .... **66** D3 ⬛
Heathfield Cl *ITCH* SO19 .... **55** E4 ⬛
Heathfield Rd *CHFD* SO53 .... **9** G3
ITCH SO19 .... **54** D4
Heath Gdns *HLER* SO31 .... **71** G2 ⬛
Heath House Cl *HEND* SO30 .... **56** B3
Heath House Gdns *HEND* SO30 . **56** B3

Heathhouse La *HEND* SO30 ..... **56** B3
Heathlands Cl *CHFD* SO53 .... **9** G3
Heathlands Rd *CHFD* SO53 ...... **9** G3
Heath Rd *HLER* SO31 .... **71** F2
ITCH SO19 .... **54** C2
NBAD SO52 .... **17** G3
Heath Rd North *HLER* SO31 .... **71** F2
Heath Rd South *HLER* SO31 .... **71** F2
Hedera Rd *HLER* SO31 .... **71** F2
Hedgerow Cl *ROWN* SO16 .... **27** E3
Hedgerow Dr *WEND* SO18 ...... **43** E4 ⬛
Hedley Gdns *HEND* SO30 .... **44** B1 ⬛
The Heights *HEND* SO30 .... **56** A1
Helford Gdns *WEND* SO18 .... **42** D2 ⬛
Helvellyn Rd *ROWN* SO16 .... **39** F4
Hemdean Gdns *HEND* SO30 .... **43** F3
Hemlock Wy *NBAD* SO52 .... **18** D1
Hemming Cl *TOTT* SO40 .... **49** G1
Henry Cl *FAWY* SO45 .... **72** B2 ⬛
Henry Rd *ELGH* SO50 .... **21** F2 ⬛
WSHM SO15 .... **39** H5
Henry St *WSHM* SO15 .... **52** D1 ⬛
Henstead Rd *WSHM* SO15 .... **52** D1
Hensting La *RWIN* SO21 .... **12** C4
Henty Rd *ROWN* SO16 .... **39** G4
Hepworth Cl *ITCH* SO19 .... **55** E5
Herbert Walker Av *WSHM* SO15 . **2** C4
Hereward Cl *ROMY* SO51 .... **6** B4 ⬛
Heron Sq *ELGH* SO50 .... **20** A5
Herrick Cl *ITCH* SO19 .... **55** F3
Hestia Cl *ROMY* SO51 .... **6** C3
Hewetts Ri *HLER* SO31 .... **70** C5
Hewitt's Rd *WSHM* SO15 .... **52** B2
Heyes Dr *ITCH* SO19 .... **55** E4
Heysham Rd *WSHM* SO15 .... **39** H4
Heywood Gn *ITCH* SO19 .... **55** G2
Hickory Gdns *HEND* SO30 .... **43** F1
Highbridge Rd *ELGH* SO50 ...... **11** F4
Highbury Cl *ELGH* SO50 .... **22** C5
Highclere Rd *ROWN* SO16 .... **40** B1
Highclere Wy *CHFD* SO53 .... **19** E3
Highcliff Av *SHAM* SO14 .... **41** E4 ⬛
Highcliffe Dr *ELGH* SO50 .... **10** C4
Highcrown St *PTSW* SO17 .... **41** E2
Highfield Av *PTSW* SO17 .... **40** D1
Highfield Cl *CHFD* SO53 .... **9** H5
PTSW SO17 .... **41** E2 ⬛
Highfield Crs *PTSW* SO17 .... **41** F2
Highfield La *PTSW* SO17 .... **41** E2
Highfield Rd *CHFD* SO53 .... **10** A5
PTSW SO17 .... **40** D3
Highfirs Gdns *ROMY* SO51 ...... **6** C4
High Firs Rd *ITCH* SO19 .... **54** D2
ROMY SO51 .... **6** C3
Highgrove Cl *TOTT* SO40 .... **49** F2 ⬛
Highlands Cl *FAWY* SO45 .... **67** E3
NBAD SO52 .... **17** E1 ⬛
Highlands Wy *FAWY* SO45 ...... **66** D3
High Meadow *ITCH* SO19 .... **55** E1
Highnam Gdns *HLER* SO31 ...... **71** F1
High Oaks Cl *HLER* SO31 .... **71** G2
High Rd *ELGH* SO50 .... **29** H4
ROWN SO16 .... **41** H1
High St *ELGH* SO50 .... **20** C5
FAWY SO45 .... **61** E5
HEND SO30 .... **43** G3 ⬛
HEND SO30 .... **45** G5
HLER SO31 .... **64** B3
LYND SO43 .... **58** D5
SHAM SO14 .... **2** E5
TOTT SO40 .... **38** A5
High Trees *ELGH* SO50 .... **23** E4
High View Wy *WEND* SO18 ...... **42** B4
Highwood La *ROMY* SO51 .... **6** D3
Hill Cl *ELGH* SO50 .... **22** C1
Hillcrest Av *CHFD* SO53 .... **9** H5
Hillcrest Cl *NBAD* SO52 .... **17** F1
Hillcrest Dr *CHFD* SO53 .... **9** H5 ⬛
Hilldene Wy *WEND* SO18 .... **43** G3 ⬛
Hilldown Rd *PTSW* SO17 .... **41** E1
Hill Farm Rd *WSHM* SO15 .... **52** C1
Hillgrove Rd *WEND* SO18 .... **42** B1 ⬛
Hill La *ROWN* SO16 .... **40** B1
RWIN SO21 .... **11** H2
WSHM SO15 .... **40** C3
Hill Pl *HLER* SO31 .... **64** B2
Hillside Av *ROMY* SO51 .... **6** A4
WEND SO18 .... **42** A3
Hillside Cl *CHFD* SO53 .... **9** H5
Hill St *ROMY* SO51 .... **25** E3
Hilltop Dr *ITCH* SO19 .... **55** E1
Hillview Rd *FAWY* SO45 .... **66** D2
The Hillway *CHFD* SO53 .... **9** H5
Hillyfields *ROWN* SO16 .... **26** C5
Hiltingbury Cl *CHFD* SO53 ...... **9** H2
Hiltingbury Rd *CHFD* SO53 ..... **9** F2
Hinkler Rd *ITCH* SO19 .... **55** G2
Hinton Crs *ITCH* SO19 .... **55** G2

Hirst Rd *FAWY* SO45 ... **67** F2
Hobart Dr *FAWY* SO45 ... **67** F2
Hobb La *HEND* SO30 ... **56** D1
Hobson Wy *FAWY* SO45 ... **72** D5 2
Hocombe Dr *CHFD* SO53 ... **9** F1
Hocombe Park Cl *CHFD* SO53 ... **9** F1
Hocombe Rd *CHFD* SO53 ... **9** F1
Hocombe Wood Rd *CHFD* SO53 ... **9** E1
Hodder Cl *CHFD* SO53 ... **19** F1 1
Hoe La *ROMY* SO51 ... **16** C4
Hogarth Cl *ROMY* SO51 ... **6** B2
Hogwood La *HEND* SO30 ... **31** G3
Holbury Dro *FAWY* SO45 ... **72** B4
Holcroft Rd *ITCH* SO19 ... **55** G2
Holkham Cl *ROWN* SO16 ... **39** E1 1
Holland Pk *HLER* SO31 ... **71** F2
Holland Pl *ROWN* SO16 ... **39** H3
Holland Rd *ITCH* SO19 ... **53** H5
TOTT SO40 ... **37** E5
Hollingbourne Cl *WEND* SO18 ... **41** H4
Hollman Dr *ROMY* SO51 ... **5** F3
Hollybank Crs *FAWY* SO45 ... **66** D1
Hollybank Rd *FAWY* SO45 ... **66** D2
Hollybrook Av *ROWN* SO16 ... **40** A1
Hollybrook Cl *ROWN* SO16 ... **39** H3
Hollybrook Gdns *HLER* SO31 ... **65** G5
Hollybrook Rd *ROWN* SO16 ... **40** A2
Holly Cl *FAWY* SO45 ... **72** A1
HLER SO31 ... **71** E2
Holly Dell *ROWN* SO16 ... **28** C4
Holly Gdns *HEND* SO30 ... **43** F1
Holly Hatch Rd *TOTT* SO40 ... **49** G1
Holly Hl *ROWN* SO16 ... **28** C4
Holly Hill Cl *ROWN* SO16 ... **28** C4
Holly Hill La *HLER* SO31 ... **64** D5
Holly Oak Rd *ROWN* SO16 ... **39** G1
Holly Rd *TOTT* SO40 ... **48** D5
Hollywood Cl *NBAD* SO52 ... **17** F2
Holmesland Dr *HEND* SO30 ... **45** F5
Holmesland La *HEND* SO30 ... **45** F5
Holmsley Cl *WEND* SO18 ... **43** E5 1
Holt Ct *ITCH* SO19 ... **62** A2
Holt Rd *WSHM* SO15 ... **40** D5
Holyborne Rd *ROMY* SO51 ... **6** B4
Holyrood Av *PTSW* SO17 ... **41** F2
Holyrood Ho *SHAM* SO14 ... **53** E2 3
Home Farm Cl *FAWY* SO45 ... **67** F3
Homefield *ROMY* SO51 ... **6** A2 2
Home Field Dr *ROWN* SO16 ... **26** C4
Home Rule Rd *HLER* SO31 ... **71** G1
Honeysuckle Cl *HLER* SO31 ... **65** G5
Honeysuckle Rd *ROWN* SO16 ... **29** F5
Honeysuckle Wy *NBAD* SO52 ... **9** E5
Honeywood Cl *TOTT* SO40 ... **37** F3
Hood Cl *HLER* SO31 ... **71** H1
Hood Rd *WEND* SO18 ... **42** C4 2
Hook Cl *CHFD* SO53 ... **9** E1
Hook Crs *CHFD* SO53 ... **9** E1
Hook Water Rd *CHFD* SO53 ... **9** E1
Hookwood La *ROMY* SO51 ... **8** D1
Hope Rd *HEND* SO30 ... **43** G2
Hornbeam Cl *HEND* SO30 ... **56** D1 3
Hornbeam Gdns *HEND* SO30 ... **43** F2 1
Hornbeam Rd *NBAD* SO52 ... **18** C1
Hornby Cl *HLER* SO31 ... **70** D5
Hornchurch Rd *ROWN* SO16 ... **27** F4
Horns Dro *ROWN* SO16 ... **27** E3
Horsebridge Wy *ROWN* SO16 ... **27** E4
Horsecroft *ROMY* SO51 ... **5** H3 1
Horsefair Ct *ROMY* SO51 ... **5** G4
Horseshoe Ldg *HLER* SO31 ... **71** E4
Horton Wy *ELGH* SO50 ... **21** H5
Hotspur Cl *FAWY* SO45 ... **60** D5
Hound Cl *HLER* SO31 ... **63** F5
Hound Rd *HLER* SO31 ... **63** F4
Hound Road Gdns *HLER* SO31 ... **63** F5
Hound Wy *HLER* SO31 ... **63** F4
Houndwell Pl *SHAM* SO14 ... **3** F3
Hounsdown Av *TOTT* SO40 ... **49** H2
Hounsdown Cl *TOTT* SO40 ... **49** H2
House Cl *RWIN* SO21 ... **12** A2
Hoveton Gv *CHFD* SO53 ... **9** F3
Howard Cl *CHFD* SO53 ... **19** H2
ELGH SO50 ... **22** C4
WEND SO18 ... **30** A5 4
Howard Rd *WSHM* SO15 ... **52** B1
Howard's Gv *WSHM* SO15 ... **40** A4
Hudson Ct *TOTT* SO40 ... **49** F1 2
Hulles Wy *NBAD* SO52 ... **17** F2
Hulse Rd *WSHM* SO15 ... **40** D4
Hulton Cl *ITCH* SO19 ... **61** H1
Humber Gdns *HLER* SO31 ... **64** A1 2
The Hundred *ROMY* SO51 ... **5** G4
Hungerford *HLER* SO31 ... **63** H3
Hunt Av *HLER* SO31 ... **63** E4
Hunter Cl *FAWY* SO45 ... **72** B2 3
Hunters Crs *ROMY* SO51 ... **6** C1
TOTT SO40 ... **48** D1
Hunters Hl *TOTT* SO40 ... **49** F4
Hunters Wy *ELGH* SO50 ... **22** A4
Huntingdon Cl *TOTT* SO40 ... **37** G3
Huntly Wy *WEND* SO18 ... **42** B5
Hunton Cl *ROWN* SO16 ... **40** B1
Hunts Pond Rd *HLER* SO31 ... **71** H1
Hurlingham Gdns *ROWN* SO16 ... **29** E4 1
Hurricane Dr *ROWN* SO16 ... **27** E3
Hursley Rd *CHFD* SO53 ... **9** F1
Hurst Cl *CHFD* SO53 ... **19** E2
TOTT SO40 ... **37** H4
Hurst Green Cl *ITCH* SO19 ... **62** C1
Hurst La *RWIN* SO21 ... **13** G5
Hutwood Rd *ROWN* SO16 ... **29** E1
Huxley Cl *HLER* SO31 ... **71** H3
Huxley Ct *FAWY* SO45 ... **66** A3
Hyde Cl *TOTT* SO40 ... **36** D5
WSHM SO15 ... **40** A3
Hymans Wy *TOTT* SO40 ... **37** G5
Hythe By-pass *FAWY* SO45 ... **66** D5

I

Ibbotson Wy *TOTT* SO40 ... **49** F2
Ilex Crs *HLER* SO31 ... **71** F2
Imber Cl *ITCH* SO19 ... **55** E3 2
Imber Wy *ITCH* SO19 ... **55** E3
Imperial Av *WSHM* SO15 ... **39** H5
Imperial Rd *SHAM* SO14 ... **41** F5
Ingersley Ri *HEND* SO30 ... **43** F3
Ingle Gln *FAWY* SO45 ... **67** E4 6
Ingle Gn *TOTT* SO40 ... **36** D3
Ingleside *HLER* SO31 ... **63** E3
Ingleton Rd *ROWN* SO16 ... **38** D3
Inkerman Rd *ITCH* SO19 ... **53** H4
International Wy *ITCH* SO19 ... **62** A2
Ionic Cl *CHFD* SO53 ... **10** B4
Ipley Wy *FAWY* SO45 ... **67** E3
Iris Rd *ROWN* SO16 ... **29** F5
Ironbridge Crs *HLER* SO31 ... **65** G4
Irving Rd *ROWN* SO16 ... **39** F3
Irwell Cl *CHFD* SO53 ... **19** E1
Isis Cl *ROWN* SO16 ... **39** E4
Itchen Av *ELGH* SO50 ... **21** H4
Itchenside Cl *WEND* SO18 ... **30** B5
Itchen Wy *ELGH* SO50 ... **10** D5
ITCH SO19 ... **53** H4
Itchin Cl *TOTT* SO40 ... **49** F1
Ivanhoe Rd *WSHM* SO15 ... **40** B3
Ivor Cl *FAWY* SO45 ... **72** C4
Ivy Cl *TOTT* SO40 ... **37** G2
Ivy Dene *ITCH* SO19 ... **55** F3
Ivy La *HEND* SO30 ... **42** D2
Ivy Rd *PTSW* SO17 ... **41** G4

J

Jackdaw Ri *ELGH* SO50 ... **19** H5 3
Jackie Wigg Gdns *TOTT* SO40 ... **37** H5
Jackmans Cl *ITCH* SO19 ... **53** H4 3
Jacobs Cl *ROMY* SO51 ... **6** A4 1
Jacob's Gutter La *TOTT* SO40 ... **49** H2
Jacobs Wk *TOTT* SO40 ... **49** G3
James Grieve Av *HLER* SO31 ... **71** G3
James St *SHAM* SO14 ... **3** G2
Janaway Gdns *PTSW* SO17 ... **41** G4
Janson Rd *WSHM* SO15 ... **40** A5
Jarvis Flds *HLER* SO31 ... **64** B2
Jasmine Rd *HEND* SO30 ... **44** B4
Java Rd *SHAM* SO14 ... **61** F1
J Av *FAWY* SO45 ... **73** F2
Jeffries Cl *ROWN* SO16 ... **27** E4
Jenkins Cl *HEND* SO30 ... **45** G5
Jenner Wy *ROMY* SO51 ... **6** C3
Jennings Rd *TOTT* SO40 ... **38** A4
Jerome Ct *ITCH* SO19 ... **55** F1
Jerrett's La *ROWN* SO16 ... **38** D1
Jersey Cl *ROWN* SO16 ... **39** E1
Jesmond Gv *HLER* SO31 ... **71** G4
Jessamine Rd *ROWN* SO16 ... **39** H2
Jessop Cl *FAWY* SO45 ... **60** D5
Jetty Rd *FAWY* SO45 ... **73** H3
Jex Blake Cl *ROWN* SO16 ... **27** H5
Jockey La *ELGH* SO50 ... **21** G1
Johnson St *SHAM* SO14 ... **3** F2 1
John's Rd *ITCH* SO19 ... **53** H4
John St *SHAM* SO14 ... **3** F5
Jones La *FAWY* SO45 ... **66** D1
Jubilee Cl *ELGH* SO50 ... **20** B5 1
Jubilee Gdns *WEND* SO18 ... **42** C5
Jubilee Rd *ROMY* SO51 ... **5** G3
Julian Cl *ROWN* SO16 ... **28** D3
Julian Rd *ITCH* SO19 ... **54** D4
Julius Cl *CHFD* SO53 ... **10** A5
Junction Rd *TOTT* SO40 ... **38** A5
Juniper Cl *NBAD* SO52 ... **17** F1
Juniper Rd *WEND* SO18 ... **42** B5
Jupiter Cl *ROWN* SO16 ... **27** E5
Jurds Lake Wy *ITCH* SO19 ... **61** H1
Jurd Wy *HLER* SO31 ... **63** H1
Justinian Cl *CHFD* SO53 ... **10** B4
Jutland Cl *FHAM* PO15 ... **65** H3

K

Kanes Hl *ITCH* SO19 ... **55** H1
Kathleen Rd *ITCH* SO19 ... **54** D4
Katrine Crs *CHFD* SO53 ... **9** E4
Kayak Cl *HLER* SO31 ... **71** E4
Kayleigh Cl *TOTT* SO40 ... **49** F1
Keats Rd *WEND* SO18 ... **55** E1
Keble Cl *CHFD* SO53 ... **19** G2 1
Keble Rd *CHFD* SO53 ... **19** G2
Keepers Cl *CHFD* SO53 ... **9** F5
Kelburn Cl *CHFD* SO53 ... **9** F4
Kellett Rd *WSHM* SO15 ... **40** B4
Kelmscott Gdns *CHFD* SO53 ... **9** E2
Kelsey Cl *FHAM/STUB* PO14 ... **71** H4
Kelvin Cl *FAWY* SO45 ... **67** E2
Kelvin Gv *HLER* SO31 ... **63** E4
Kelvin Rd *ELGH* SO50 ... **20** B4
Kendal Av *ROWN* SO16 ... **38** D3
Kendal Cl *CHFD* SO53 ... **10** A4
Kenilworth Dr *ELGH* SO50 ... **10** C5
Kenilworth Gdns *HEND* SO30 ... **43** G3
Kenilworth Rd *WSHM* SO15 ... **52** D1 3
Kenmore Cl *TOTT* SO40 ... **49** F2
Kennedy Rd *ROWN* SO16 ... **39** F1
Kennet Cl *WEND* SO18 ... **42** D1
Kennett Rd *ROMY* SO51 ... **6** C3
Kennington La *TOTT* SO40 ... **35** F5
Kensington Cl *ELGH* SO50 ... **21** F1 2
Kensington Flds *FAWY* SO45 ... **66** B3
Kenson Gdns *ITCH* SO19 ... **54** C3
Kentish Rd *WSHM* SO15 ... **40** A5
Kent Rd *CHFD* SO53 ... **19** G3
PTSW SO17 ... **41** G3
Kent St *SHAM* SO14 ... **53** G2
Kenwyn Cl *WEND* SO18 ... **42** D2
Kern Cl *ROWN* SO16 ... **39** F1
Kerry Cl *CHFD* SO53 ... **9** G5
Kesteven Wy *WEND* SO18 ... **42** C4
Kestrel Cl *BPWT* SO32 ... **45** G3
ROWN SO16 ... **27** H4
Kestrel Rd *ELGH* SO50 ... **20** A4
Keswick Rd *ITCH* SO19 ... **53** H4
Kevlyn Crs *HLER* SO31 ... **63** H1 2
Kewlake La *ROMY* SO51 ... **34** B2
Kew La *HLER* SO31 ... **64** A3
Keynsham Rd *ITCH* SO19 ... **54** D1
Khartoum Rd *PTSW* SO17 ... **41** E2
Kielder Cl *CHFD* SO53 ... **9** E4
Kilford Ct *HEND* SO30 ... **57** G1
Killarney Cl *ITCH* SO19 ... **55** G4 3
Kiln Cl *FAWY* SO45 ... **66** C2
Kiln La *RWIN* SO21 ... **10** D1
Kilnyard Cl *TOTT* SO40 ... **37** F3
Kimberley Cl *ELGH* SO50 ... **22** D4
Kineton Rd *WSHM* SO15 ... **40** C3
King Cup Av *HLER* SO31 ... **71** F3
King Edward Av *ROWN* SO16 ... **39** G4
Kingfisher Cl *HLER* SO31 ... **70** A1 1
Kingfisher Copse *HLER* SO31 ... **71** H2
Kingfisher Wy *ROMY* SO51 ... **5** H3 2
King George's Av *WSHM* SO15 ... **51** F1
Kings Av *HLER* SO31 ... **69** G2
Kingsbury Rd *SHAM* SO14 ... **41** F5 3
Kingsclere Av *ITCH* SO19 ... **62** B1
Kingsclere Cl *ITCH* SO19 ... **62** B1 3
King's Cl *CHFD* SO53 ... **9** H4
LYND SO43 ... **58** D5
Kings Copse Av *HEND* SO30 ... **44** D5
Kings Copse Rd *HEND* SO30 ... **56** C2
Kingsdown Wy *WEND* SO18 ... **42** B2
Kings Fld *HLER* SO31 ... **64** A1
Kings Field Gdns *HLER* SO31 ... **64** A1
Kingsfold Av *WEND* SO18 ... **42** B1
Kingsley Gdns *TOTT* SO40 ... **36** D5
Kingsley Rd *WSHM* SO15 ... **39** H5
Kings Park Rd *WSHM* SO15 ... **53** E1
King's Rd *CHFD* SO53 ... **9** G5
Kingston *HLER* SO31 ... **63** E3 4
Kingston Rd *WSHM* SO15 ... **52** B1
King St *SHAM* SO14 ... **3** F4
Kingsway *CHFD* SO53 ... **9** H5
Kingsway Gdns *CHFD* SO53 ... **10** A3
Kinross Rd *TOTT* SO40 ... **37** H5
Kinsbourne Cl *ITCH* SO19 ... **55** H1 1
Kinsbourne Ri *ITCH* SO19 ... **55** H2
Kinsbourne Wy *ITCH* SO19 ... **55** G1 2
Kinver Cl *ROMY* SO51 ... **6** B2
Kipling Ct *ITCH* SO19 ... **62** B1 4
Kipling Rd *ELGH* SO50 ... **20** B3
Kirk Gdns *TOTT* SO40 ... **49** H2
Kitchener Rd *PTSW* SO17 ... **41** G1
Knatchbull Cl *ROMY* SO51 ... **5** H4 2
Knellers La *TOTT* SO40 ... **49** F3
Knighton Rd *ITCH* SO19 ... **54** B4
Knights Cl *HLER* SO31 ... **71** E4 3
Knightstone Gra *FAWY* SO45 ... **67** E3 3
Knightwood Av *LYND* SO43 ... **58** D5
Knightwood Cl *LYND* SO43 ... **58** D5
TOTT SO40 ... **48** D5
Knightwood Rd *FAWY* SO45 ... **67** F3
NBAD SO52 ... **8** D3
Knottgrass Rd *HLER* SO31 ... **71** E3
Knowle Hl *ELGH* SO50 ... **10** D4
Knowle La *ELGH* SO50 ... **32** D2
Knyght Cl *ROMY* SO51 ... **6** A5
Kootenay Av *WEND* SO18 ... **43** G5
Kytes La *BPWT* SO32 ... **33** H4

L

Laburnum Cl *NBAD* SO52 ... **17** G1
Laburnum Crs *FAWY* SO45 ... **67** F5 1
Laburnum Gv *ELGH* SO50 ... **20** C3 1
Laburnum Rd *HEND* SO30 ... **56** D1
ROWN SO16 ... **29** G5
Lackford Av *TOTT* SO40 ... **49** G1
Lacon Cl *WEND* SO18 ... **42** A4
Ladycross Rd *FAWY* SO45 ... **67** E3
Ladywood *ELGH* SO50 ... **10** B5
Lake Farm Cl *HEND* SO30 ... **44** C4 4
Lakelands Dr *WSHM* SO15 ... **52** A1 1
Lake Rd *CHFD* SO53 ... **10** A3
ITCH SO19 ... **53** H5
Lakeside *ELGH* SO50 ... **30** B1
Lakeside Av *ROWN* SO16 ... **27** E4
Lakewood Cl *CHFD* SO53 ... **9** H3
Lakewood Rd *CHFD* SO53 ... **9** H3
TOTT SO40 ... **49** E4
Lamberhurst Cl *ITCH* SO19 ... **62** C2
Lambourne Cl *FAWY* SO45 ... **66** D4 3
Lambourne Dr *HLER* SO31 ... **71** G2
Lambourne Rd *WEND* SO18 ... **42** D2
Lambourn Sq *CHFD* SO53 ... **9** E5
Lammas Rd *FAWY* SO45 ... **67** E3
Lancaster Cl *HLER* SO31 ... **64** A1 3
Lancaster Rd *ROWN* SO16 ... **39** F1
Lance's Hl *ITCH* SO19 ... **42** B5
Landguard Rd *WSHM* SO15 ... **52** B1
Landseer Rd *ITCH* SO19 ... **55** E4
Lands End Rd *HLER* SO31 ... **64** B3
Lanehays Rd *FAWY* SO45 ... **66** D2
Lanesbridge Cl *TOTT* SO40 ... **48** B2
The Lane *FAWY* SO45 ... **73** H5 4
Langbar Cl *ITCH* SO19 ... **54** A1
Langdale Cl *ROWN* SO16 ... **39** F4 2
Langdown Lawn *FAWY* SO45 ... **67** E3
Langdown Lawn Cl
FAWY SO45 ... **67** E3 4
Langdown Rd *FAWY* SO45 ... **67** E2
Langham Cl *NBAD* SO52 ... **17** F2
Langhorn Rd *ROWN* SO16 ... **29** G5
Langley Rd *WSHM* SO15 ... **51** G1
Langrish Rd *ROWN* SO16 ... **27** H5
Lansdowne Cl *ROMY* SO51 ... **5** G3 2
Lansdowne Hl *SHAM* SO14 ... **2** D4 2
Lansdowne Rd *WSHM* SO15 ... **39** G5
Lapwing Dr *TOTT* SO40 ... **37** E4
Larch Av *FAWY* SO45 ... **72** C3
Larch Cl *HEND* SO30 ... **43** F1
Larchdale Cl *HLER* SO31 ... **70** D5 3
Larch Rd *ROWN* SO16 ... **39** G1
Larch Wy *HLER* SO31 ... **63** H2
Larchwood Rd *TOTT* SO40 ... **49** E1
Larkspur Cha *ITCH* SO19 ... **55** G2
Larkspur Cl *HLER* SO31 ... **71** F3 4
Larkspur Dr *NBAD* SO52 ... **8** D5
Larkspur Gdns *FAWY* SO45 ... **72** B4
HEND SO30 ... **56** C1 3
Laser Cl *HLER* SO31 ... **71** E4
Latchmore Dr *FAWY* SO45 ... **66** A1
Latelie Cl *HLER* SO31 ... **63** E5 1
Latham Cl *ELGH* SO50 ... **22** B4
Latham Ct *WSHM* SO15 ... **39** H5
Latham Rd *ELGH* SO50 ... **22** B4
ROMY SO51 ... **6** A3 2
Latimer St *ROMY* SO51 ... **5** G4
SHAM SO14 ... **3** F5
Launcelyn Cl *NBAD* SO52 ... **17** F3
Launceston Dr *ELGH* SO50 ... **20** B1 1
Laundry Rd *ROWN* SO16 ... **39** H2
Laurel Cl *FAWY* SO45 ... **66** C2
HLER SO31 ... **71** H1 1

Laurel Gdns *HLER* SO31 .... **71** H1
Laurel Rd *HLER* SO31 .... **71** H1
Lauriston Dr *CHFD* SO53 .... **9** F2 🗋
Lavender Cl *ITCH* SO19 .... **54** B2 🗋
Laverstoke Cl *ROWN* SO16 ...... **27** E3 🗋
Lavington Gdns *NBAD* SO52 ...... **17** F3
Lawford Wy *TOTT* SO40 .... **37** G4
Lawn Dr *HLER* SO31 .... **71** G3
Lawn Rd *ELGH* SO50 .... **20** D2
  PTSW SO17 .... **41** F4
Lawnside Rd *WSHM* SO15........ **39** G4
Lawrence Gv *ITCH* SO19 .... **54** B5
Lawson Cl *HLER* SO31 .... **64** D2 🗋
Laxton Cl *HLER* SO31 .... **71** H2
  ITCH SO19 .... **54** C5
Leander Cl *ELGH* SO50 .... **20** C1 🗋
Leaside Wy *ROWN* SO16 .... **29** G4
Leatherhead Gdns *HEND* SO30 .. **44** D2 🗋
Lebanon Rd *WSHM* SO15 .... **38** D5
Leckford Cl *WEND* SO18 .... **43** F4 🗋
Lee Church La *ROMY* SO51 ...... **25** H1
Lee Dro *ROMY* SO51 .... **16** A5
Lee La *ROMY* SO51 .... **16** A2
Leicester Rd *WSHM* SO15 .... **40** B2
Leigh Rd *CHFD* SO53 .... **19** C2
  ELGH SO50 .... **20** D3 🗋
  PTSW SO17 .... **41** E3
Leighton Av *WSHM* SO15 .... **39** H4
Leighton Rd *ITCH* SO19 .... **54** A4
Lemon Rd *WSHM* SO15 .... **39** H5
Lennox Cl *CHFD* SO53 .... **10** A3
  ROWN SO16 .... **27** F4
Leven Cl *CHFD* SO53 .... **9** E3
Lewes Cl *ELGH* SO50 .... **10** C5
Lewin Cl *RWIN* SO21 .... **12** A3
Lewis Cl *FAWY* SO45 .... **66** A3
Lewis Silkin Wy *ROWN* SO16 ... **27** C5
Lewry Cl *HEND* SO30 .... **44** C5
Lexby Rd *TOTT* SO40 .... **50** A1
Leybourne Av *WEND* SO18 ...... **42** B4
Leyton Rd *SHAM* SO14 .... **53** G1
Library Rd *TOTT* SO40 .... **38** A5
Lichen Wy *TOTT* SO40 .... **51** F5
Liddel Wy *CHFD* SO53 .... **19** E1
Lilac Rd *ROWN* SO16 .... **29** F5
Lime Av *ITCH* SO19 .... **54** C2
Lime Cl *FAWY* SO45 .... **66** C3
  ITCH SO19 .... **54** C2
  RWIN SO21 .... **12** A3
Lime Gdns *HEND* SO30 .... **43** F1
Lime Kiln La *FAWY* SO45 .... **72** B4
Lime St *SHAM* SO14 .... **3** F4
Lime Wk *FAWY* SO45 .... **66** C3
Linacre Rd *ITCH* SO19 .... **55** F3
Lincoln Cl *WSHM* SO15 .... **40** B2 🗋
Lincolns Ri *ELGH* SO50 .... **10** D3
Linda Rd *FAWY* SO45 .... **73** H5 🗋
Linden Gdns *HEND* SO30 .... **56** D2
Linden Gv *CHFD* SO53 .... **9** G3
Linden Rd *ROMY* SO51 .... **5** H4
  ROWN SO16 .... **27** C5
Linden Wk *NBAD* SO52 .... **17** F1
Lindsay Rd *ITCH* SO19 .... **55** G1
Lindway *HLER* SO31 .... **65** G4
Linford Crs *ROWN* SO16 .... **40** B1
Ling Dl *ROWN* SO16 .... **28** D2
Lingfield Gdns *WEND* SO18 .... **42** B2 🗋
Lingwood Cl *ROWN* SO16 .... **28** D2
Lingwood Wk *ROWN* SO16 ...... **28** D2 🗋
Link Rd *ROWN* SO16 .... **39** F1
Links View Wy *ROWN* SO16 ..... **28** D3
Linnet Sq *ELGH* SO50 .... **19** H5
The Linnets *TOTT* SO40 .... **37** E4 🗋
Lionheart Wy *HLER* SO31 .... **63** H1
Lipizzaner Flds *HLER* SO31 ..... **65** H2
Lisbon Rd *WSHM* SO15 .... **52** B1
Litchfield Crs *WEND* SO18 ...... **42** B3
Litchfield Rd *WEND* SO18 .... **42** B3
Little Abshot Rd
  FHAM/STUB PO14 .... **71** H5
Littlefield Crs *NBAD* SO52 ...... **8** C5
Little Lance's Hl *ITCH* SO19 .... **42** A4
Littlemeads *ROMY* SO51 .... **5** F4
Little Oak Rd *ROWN* SO16 .... **28** D5
Little Park Cl *HEND* SO30 .... **56** B1 🗋
Little Quob La *HEND* SO30 ...... **43** G2
Littlewood Gdns *HEND* SO30 ... **43** F3
  HLER SO31 .... **71** E2 🗋
Liverpool St *SHAM* SO14 .... **41** E5
Livingstone Rd *SHAM* SO14 .... **41** E4
Loane Rd *ITCH* SO19 .... **54** B4
Lobelia Rd *ROWN* SO16 .... **29** G5
Lockerley Crs *ROWN* SO16 ...... **39** F2
Locke Rd *HEND* SO30 .... **44** C5
Locksheath Park Rd *HLER* SO31 .. **71** H4
Locksley Rd *ELGH* SO50 .... **20** A5
Locks Rd *HLER* SO31 .... **71** G1
Lockswood Rd *HLER* SO31 ...... **71** G5

Lodge Dr *FAWY* SO45 .... **66** D4
Lodge Rd *HLER* SO31 .... **71** H2
  SHAM SO14 .... **41** E5
Lofting Cl *ELGH* SO50 .... **21** G4 🗋
Logan Cl *ROWN* SO16 .... **27** F4
Lomax Cl *HEND* SO30 .... **44** C3 🗋
London Rd *WSHM* SO15 .... **52** D1
Long Beech Dr *TOTT* SO40 ..... **49** F1
Longbridge La *TOTT* SO40 ...... **37** F2
Longclose Rd *HEND* SO30 ...... **44** D5
Long Copse *FAWY* SO45 .... **73** E5
Long Dr *HEND* SO30 .... **43** G2
Long La *FAWY* SO45 .... **72** C3
  HLER SO31 .... **64** A1
Long Lane Cl *FAWY* SO45....... **72** D5
Longleat Gdns *ROWN* SO16 .... **27** H4
Longmead Av *ELGH* SO50 ...... **21** F2
Longmeadow Gdns *FAWY* SO45 .. **67** E1
Longmead Rd *WEND* SO18 ..... **42** B2 🗋
Longmore Av *ITCH* SO19 .... **53** H5
Longmore Crs *ITCH* SO19 ...... **53** H5 🗋
Longridge Rd *HEND* SO30 ...... **56** C1
Longstock Cl *ITCH* SO19 .... **62** C2 🗋
Longstock Crs *TOTT* SO40 ..... **37** F5
Loperwood *TOTT* SO40 .... **36** B2
Loperwood La *TOTT* SO40 ...... **24** C5
Lord Mountbatten Cl
  WEND SO18 .... **30** A5 🗋
Lord's Hill Centre East
  ROWN SO16 .... **27** F4
Lord's Hill Centre West
  ROWN SO16 .... **27** F5
Lord's Hill Wy *ROWN* SO16 ..... **27** F4
Lordswood *ELGH* SO50 .... **11** G4
Lordswood Cl *ROWN* SO16 ..... **40** B1 🗋
Lordswood Gdns *ROWN* SO16 .. **28** B5
Lordswood Rd *ROWN* SO16 .... **28** A5
Loreille Cl *ROWN* SO16 .... **27** E2
Loughwood Cl *ELGH* SO50 ..... **10** C5
Lovage Gdns *TOTT* SO40 .... **37** E5
Love La *ROMY* SO51 .... **5** G4
Lower Alfred St *SHAM* SO14.... **53** F1
Lower Banister St *WSHM* SO15 .. **52** D1
Lower Baybridge La *RWIN* SO21 .. **13** H2
Lower Brownhill Rd
  ROWN SO16 .... **38** C2
Lower Canal Wk *SHAM* SO14 ... **2** E5
Lower Duncan Rd *HLER* SO31 .. **65** H5
Lower Moors Rd *RWIN* SO21 ... **11** H2
Lower Mortimer Rd *ITCH* SO19 .. **53** H4
Lower Mullin's La *FAWY* SO45 .. **66** C1
Lower New Rd *HEND* SO30...... **43** F3
Lower Northam Rd *HEND* ... **44** C5
Lower St Helens Rd *HEND* SO30 .. **56** C2
Lower Swanwick Rd
  HLER SO31 .... **64** D2 🗋
Lower Vicarage Rd *ITCH* SO19 .. **53** H4
Lower William St *SHAM* SO14 .. **53** G2
Lower York St *SHAM* SO14 ..... **53** H1
Lowford Hl *HLER* SO31 .... **63** H1
Lowry Gdns *ITCH* SO19 .... **55** E5
Lucas Cl *ROWN* SO16 .... **27** F4 🗋
Luccombe Pl *WSHM* SO15....... **40** B3
Luccombe Rd *WSHM* SO15 ..... **40** B2
Lucerne Gdns *HEND* SO30 ...... **56** A1
Ludlow Rd *ITCH* SO19 .... **54** A3
Lukin Dr *ROWN* SO16 .... **26** C4
Lulworth Cl *CHFD* SO53 .... **19** F3
  ROWN SO16 .... **39** E2
Lulworth Gn *ROWN* SO16 .... **39** E2
Lumsden Av *WSHM* SO15 .... **40** A5
Lundy Cl *ROWN* SO16 .... **27** E4
Lunedale Rd *FAWY* SO45 .... **66** C5
Lupin Rd *ROWN* SO16 .... **29** G4
Luton Rd *ITCH* SO19 .... **54** D3
Luxton Cl *HEND* SO30 .... **45** F4
Luzborough La *ROMY* SO51 .... **16** B2
Lyburn Cl *ROWN* SO16 .... **28** A5 🗋
Lydgate *TOTT* SO40 .... **37** F5 🗋
Lydgate Cl *ITCH* SO19 .... **55** F3
Lydgate Gn *ITCH* SO19 .... **55** F3 🗋
Lydgate Rd *ITCH* SO19 .... **55** F3 🗋
Lydiard Cl *ELGH* SO50 .... **20** C1
Lydlynch Rd *TOTT* SO40 .... **37** G5
Lyme Cl *ELGH* SO50 .... **20** B1 🗋
Lymer La *ROWN* SO16 .... **26** C3
Lyndale Rd *HLER* SO31 .... **71** H1
Lynden Ga *ITCH* SO19 .... **54** A2 🗋
Lyndhurst Rd *TOTT* SO40 .... **34** C5
  TOTT SO40 .... **49** E5
Lyndock Cl *ITCH* SO19 .... **54** A5 🗋
Lyndock Pl *ITCH* SO19 .... **54** A5
Lynton Cl *TOTT* SO40 .... **49** G5
Lynton Rd *HEND* SO30 .... **44** C5
Lynx Cl *ELGH* SO50 .... **20** C4
Lyon St *SHAM* SO14 .... **53** E1
Lytham Rd *WEND* SO18 .... **42** C4

Lytton Rd *FAWY* SO45 .... **67** F3

M

Macarthur Crs *WEND* SO18 ..... **42** C4 🗋
Macnaghten Rd *WEND* SO18 ... **41** H5
Maddison St *SHAM* SO14 .... **2** D4 🗋
Maddoxford Wy *BPWT* SO32 ... **45** F3
Magazine La *TOTT* SO40 .... **51** G4
Magnolia Cl *FAWY* SO45 .... **66** A1 🗋
Magnolia Gv *ELGH* SO50 .... **23** E4
Magnolia Rd *ITCH* SO19 .... **54** B2
Magpie Dr *TOTT* SO40 .... **37** E5
Magpie Gdns *ITCH* SO19 .... **54** D3
Magpie La *ELGH* SO50 .... **20** A4
Main Rd *FAWY* SO45 .... **60** B5
  FAWY SO45 .... **72** C2
  RWIN SO21 .... **10** D1
  RWIN SO21 .... **11** H1
  TOTT SO40 .... **49** C3
Mainstone *ROMY* SO51 .... **5** F5
Mainstream Ct *ELGH* SO50 ..... **21** F3 🗋
Majestic Rd *ROWN* SO16 .... **26** B5
Malcolm Cl *CHFD* SO53 .... **10** A2
  HLER SO31 .... **71** H2
Malcolm Rd *CHFD* SO53.......... **10** A2
Maldon Cl *ELGH* SO50 .... **21** F3
Maldon Rd *ITCH* SO19 .... **54** A3
Malibres Rd *CHFD* SO53.......... **10** B3
Malin Cl *ROWN* SO16 .... **27** E5
Mallard Cl *ROMY* SO51 .... **5** H3
Mallard Gdns *HEND* SO30 ...... **44** C2
Mallards Rd *HLER* SO31 .... **63** H3
Mallett Cl *HEND* SO30 .... **45** E2
Mallow Rd *HEND* SO30 .... **56** A1
Malmesbury Cl *ELGH* SO50 .... **22** C4 🗋
Malmesbury Pl *WSHM* SO15.... **40** B5
Malmesbury Rd *ROMY* SO51 ... **5** G3
  WSHM SO15 .... **40** B5
Malory Cl *ITCH* SO19 .... **55** F1
Malthouse Cl *ROMY* SO51 ...... **5** G3 🗋
Malvern Dr *FAWY* SO45 .... **66** B2
Malvern Gdns *HEND* SO30 ...... **44** D2
Malvern Rd *ROWN* SO16 .... **40** A2
Malwood Av *ROWN* SO16 .... **40** B1
Malwood Gdns *TOTT* SO40 ..... **37** E4
Malwood Rd *FAWY* SO45 .... **66** C1
Malwood Rd West *FAWY* SO45 .. **66** C1
Mandela Wy *WSHM* SO15 .... **52** C2
Manley Rd *HLER* SO31 .... **63** H1
Manns Cl *WEND* SO18 .... **43** E2
Manor Cl *HLER* SO31 .... **63** H1 🗋
  TOTT SO40 .... **49** G1
Manor Crs *HLER* SO31 .... **63** H1
Manor Farm Gv *ELGH* SO50 .... **21** G4 🗋
Manor Farm Rd *HEND* SO30 ... **41** H3
Manor House Av *WSHM* SO15 .. **51** E1
Manor Rd *ELGH* SO50 .... **21** G4
  FAWY SO45 .... **72** C4
  ROWN SO16 .... **18** B5
Manor Rd North *ITCH* SO19 .... **54** A3
Manor Rd South *ITCH* SO19 .... **54** A4
Mans Br *WEND* SO18 .... **30** B5
Mansbridge Rd *ELGH* SO50 .... **20** C5
  WEND SO18 .... **30** B5
Mansel Ct *ROWN* SO16 .... **39** E2
Mansell Cl *FAWY* SO45 .... **66** C5
Mansel Rd East *ROWN* SO16... **39** E3
Mansel Rd West *ROWN* SO16 .. **38** D2
Mansion Rd *WSHM* SO15 .... **52** A1
Maple Cl *ROMY* SO51 .... **6** C5
Maple Gdns *TOTT* SO40 .... **49** E1 🗋
Maple Rd *FAWY* SO45 .... **67** F5 🗋
  WEND SO18 .... **42** A5
Maple Sq *ELGH* SO50 .... **20** A5 🗋
The Maples *CHFD* SO53 .... **9** G3
Mapleton Rd *HEND* SO30 .... **56** D1 🗋
Maplewood Cl *TOTT* SO40....... **49** E1
Maplin Rd *ROWN* SO16 .... **38** D2
Marathon Pl *ELGH* SO50 .... **22** B4
Marchwood By-pass *TOTT* SO40 .. **49** H2
  WSHM SO15 .... **51** H1
Marcus Cl *ELGH* SO50 .... **22** B4
Mardale Rd *ROWN* SO16 .... **38** D4
Mardon Cl *ELGH* SO50 .... **30** A4
Margam Av *ITCH* SO19 .... **54** B2
Marianne Cl *WSHM* SO15 .... **51** F1 🗋
Marie Rd *ITCH* SO19 .... **55** E4
Marine Pde *SHAM* SO14 .... **3** H3
Mariner's Cl *HLER* SO31 .... **70** A1
Mariners Ms *FAWY* SO45 .... **67** E1 🗋
Mariners Wy *HLER* SO31 .... **70** C4
Maritime Av *TOTT* SO40 .... **51** G4
Maritime Wk *SHAM* SO14 .... **3** G7
Maritime Wy *SHAM* SO14 .... **3** F6

Mark Cl *WSHM* SO15 .... **39** G5
Marken Cl *HLER* SO31 .... **71** E2 🗋
Market Pl *SHAM* SO14 .... **2** E5
Market St *ELGH* SO50 .... **20** D5
Marlborough Ct *FAWY* SO45 .... **66** C3 🗋
Marlborough Gdns
  HEND SO30 .... **44** C1 🗋
Marlborough Rd *CHFD* SO53 ... **10** A2
  WSHM SO15 .... **39** H4
Marlhill Cl *WEND* SO18 .... **42** B2
Marls Rd *HEND* SO30 .... **56** D1 🗋
Marne Rd *WEND* SO18 .... **42** C5
Marsh Gdns *HEND* SO30 .... **44** C1 🗋
Marsh La *FAWY* SO45 .... **73** H4
  SHAM SO14 .... **3** F4
The Marsh *FAWY* SO45........... **61** E5
Marston Rd *ITCH* SO19 .... **55** F2
The Martins *ELGH* SO50 .... **22** D5 🗋
Martley Gdns *HEND* SO30 ...... **44** D2
Marvin Wy *HEND* SO30 .... **44** D5 🗋
  WEND SO18 .... **55** E1
Marybridge Cl *TOTT* SO40 ...... **49** G1
Maryfield *SHAM* SO14 .... **3** G3
Maryland Cl *WEND* SO18 .... **42** B1
Masefield Cl *ELGH* SO50 .... **20** B3 🗋
Masefield Gn *ITCH* SO19 .... **55** F1 🗋
Matheson Rd *ROWN* SO16 ...... **27** F3
Matley Gdns *TOTT* SO40 .... **36** D5
Maunsell Wy *HEND* SO30 .... **44** C1
Mauretania Rd *ROWN* SO16 ... **26** B5
Maxwell Rd *ITCH* SO19 .... **54** C4
Maybray King Wy *ITCH* SO19 ... **42** C5
Maybush Rd *ROWN* SO16 .... **39** E2
May Cl *FAWY* SO45 .... **72** D5
May Copse *FAWY* SO45 .... **72** D5
May Crs *FAWY* SO45 .... **72** D5
Mayfair Ct *HEND* SO30 .... **45** G5
Mayfair Gdns *WSHM* SO15 ..... **40** D5
Mayfield Av *TOTT* SO40 .... **37** G4
Mayfield Rd *PTSW* SO17 .... **41** F1
Mayflower Cl *CHFD* SO53 .... **19** F2
Mayflower Rd *WSHM* SO15 ..... **40** A4 🗋
Mayflower Rbt *WSHM* SO15 .... **2** C5
The Mayflowers *ROWN* SO16 ... **29** E5
Maynard Rd *TOTT* SO40 .... **37** H5
May Rd *WSHM* SO15 .... **40** A5 🗋
Maytree Cl *HLER* SO31 .... **71** G2
Maytree Rd *CHFD* SO53 .... **9** G1
Meacher Cl *TOTT* SO40 .... **37** G4 🗋
Meadbrook Gdns *CHFD* SO53 .. **9** G5
Mead Cl *ROMY* SO51 .... **6** B4
Mead Crs *WEND* SO18 .... **41** H1
Meadcroft Cl *HLER* SO31 .... **70** D5
Meadow Av *HLER* SO31 .... **71** G1
Meadow Cl *HEND* SO30 .... **43** G2
  NBAD SO52 .... **17** G3
  TOTT SO40 .... **49** H2
Meadowhead Rd *ROWN* SO16 .. **40** D1 🗋
Meadow La *HLER* SO31 .... **70** A3
Meadowmead Av *WSHM* SO15 .. **39** H4
Meadowside Cl *WEND* SO18 ... **30** A5 🗋
Meadowsweet Wy *ELGH* SO50 .. **32** C3
The Meadow *ROMY* SO51 .... **5** H2 🗋
Meadow Wy *FAWY* SO45 .... **73** H5 🗋
Mead Rd *CHFD* SO53 .... **9** G5
The Meads *CHFD* SO53 .... **19** E1
  ROMY SO51 .... **5** F4
The Mead *FAWY* SO45 .... **66** C2
Mears Rd *ELGH* SO50 .... **22** D4
Medina Cl *CHFD* SO53 .... **20** A1 🗋
Medina Rd *WSHM* SO15.......... **39** H3
Medlar Cl *HEND* SO30 .... **56** D1 🗋
Medwall Gn *ITCH* SO19 .... **55** F2
Medway Dr *CHFD* SO53 .... **9** E3
Megan Rd *HEND* SO30 .... **43** F2
Meggeson Av *WEND* SO18 ..... **42** C2
Melbourne Rd *HEND* SO30 ..... **56** C1
Melbourne St *SHAM* SO14....... **3** H3
Melchet Rd *WEND* SO18 .... **43** E4
Melick Cl *TOTT* SO40 .... **51** F5
Melrose Ct *TOTT* SO40 .... **37** E3
Melrose Rd *WSHM* SO15 .... **40** B3
Melville Cl *ROWN* SO16 .... **28** A4
Mendip Gdns *FAWY* SO45 .... **66** B3 🗋
Mendip Rd *ROWN* SO16.......... **39** F4
Menzies Cl *ROWN* SO16 .... **27** F4
Meon Cl *ROMY* SO51 .... **6** C4
Meon Ct *WEND* SO18 .... **43** F4
Meon Crs *CHFD* SO53 .... **9** H5
Meon Rd *ROMY* SO51 .... **6** C4
Mercer Wy *ROMY* SO51 .... **5** H3 🗋
  ROMY SO51 .... **6** A3 🗋
Mercury Cl *ROWN* SO16.......... **27** F5
Mercury Gdns *HLER* SO31 ...... **70** A1
Merdon Av *CHFD* SO53 .... **9** H3
Merdon Cl *CHFD* SO53 .... **9** H3
Meredith Gdns *TOTT* SO40 ..... **49** F1
Merlin Gdns *HEND* SO30 .... **44** B5

Mermaid Wy *SHAM* SO14 .... 3 G6 🔲
Merrick Wy *CHFD* SO53 .... 8 D3
Merridale Rd *ITCH* SO19 .... 54 A3
Merrieleas Cl *CHFD* SO53 .... 9 G4
Merrieleas Dr *CHFD* SO53 .... 9 G4
Merrivale Cl *FAWY* SO45 .... 66 C2
Merry Gdns *NBAD* SO52 .... 17 G1
Merryoak Gn *ITCH* SO19 .... 54 B2 🔲
Merryoak Rd *ITCH* SO19 .... 54 B3
Mersea Gdns *ITCH* SO19 .... 54 C3
Mersham Gdns *WEND* SO18 ...... 42 C5 🔲
Merton Rd *PTSW* SO17 .... 41 F2
Methuen St *SHAM* SO14 .... 41 E5
Metuchen Wy *HEND* SO30 .... 56 C3
The Mews *ROWN* SO16 .... 27 F3
Meynell Cl *ITCH* SO19 .... 20 B3
Michaels Wy *ELGH* SO50 .... 22 D4
    FAWY SO45 .... 66 D1
Michelmersh Cl *ROWN* SO16 ... 27 E4 🔲
Michigan Wy *TOTT* SO40 .... 36 D4
Midanbury Crs *WEND* SO18 .... 42 B3
Midanbury La *WEND* SO18 .... 42 A4
Middlebridge St *ROMY* SO51 .... 5 G5
Middle Rd *HLER* SO31 .... 65 H5
    ITCH SO19 .... 54 C4
    NBAD SO52 .... 17 G1
Middle St *SHAM* SO14 .... 41 E5 🔲
Middleton Cl *WEND* SO18 .... 42 C2
Midlands Est *HEND* SO30 .... 43 E2
Midway *FAWY* SO45 .... 66 D2 🔲
Milbury Crs *ITCH* SO19 .... 54 C1
Milford Gdns *CHFD* SO53 .... 10 A5
Milkwood Ct *TOTT* SO40 .... 37 E5 🔲
Millais Rd *ITCH* SO19 .... 54 A4
Millbank St *SHAM* SO14 .... 53 G1
Millbridge Gdns *ITCH* SO19 .... 54 D3 🔲
Millbrook Cl *CHFD* SO53 .... 19 F1
Millbrook Point Rd *WSHM* SO15 . 51 G1
Millbrook Rd East *WSHM* SO15 .. 52 A2
Millbrook Rd West *WSHM* SO15... 39 E5
Mill Cl *ROWN* SO16 .... 26 D4
Mill Hl *HEND* SO30 .... 45 G5
Mill La *LYND* SO43 .... 46 C5
    ROMY SO51 .... 5 F4
    ROWN SO16 .... 25 G5
The Mill Pond *FAWY* SO45 .... 72 B2
Mill Rd *TOTT* SO40 .... 38 A5
    WSHM SO15 .... 39 G5
Millstream Ri *ROMY* SO51 .... 5 F4
Millvina Cl *TOTT* SO40 .... 48 B3
Mill Wy *TOTT* SO40 .... 49 G2
Milne Cl *FAWY* SO45 .... 66 A3
Milner Ct *WSHM* SO15 .... 40 A4
Milton Gv *HLER* SO31 .... 71 H4
Milton Rd *ELGH* SO50 .... 20 D1 🔲
    WSHM SO15 .... 52 C1
Milverton Rd *TOTT* SO40 .... 50 A1
Mimosa Dr *ELGH* SO50 .... 23 C4
Minstead Av *WEND* SO18 .... 43 E4
Mintern Cl *ELGH* SO50 .... 21 F1 🔲
Mirror Cl *HLER* SO31 .... 71 H3
Missenden Acres *HEND* SO30 .... 44 C4 🔲
Misslebrook La *NBAD* SO52 .... 18 B2
Mitchell Dr *ELGH* SO50 .... 22 C3
Mitchell Rd *ELGH* SO50 .... 20 D4
Mitchells Cl *ROMY* SO51 .... 5 H4
Mitchell Wy *ELGH* SO50 .... 30 C2
Mitre Copse *ELGH* SO50 .... 21 H4
Moat Cl *FAWY* SO45 .... 72 B5
Moat Hl *WEND* SO18 .... 42 B1
Monarch Cl *HLER* SO31 .... 71 G3
Monarch Wy *HEND* SO30 .... 43 G2 🔲
Monastery Rd *WEND* SO18 .... 42 A5
Mon Crs *WEND* SO18 .... 42 A5
Monks Brook Cl *ELGH* SO50 ...... 20 A5
Monks Pl *TOTT* SO40 .... 49 F1
Monks Rd *HLER* SO31 .... 62 D4
Monks Wk *FAWY* SO45 .... 66 C5
Monks Wy *ELGH* SO50 .... 20 B5
    WEND SO18 .... 30 A5
Monks Wood Cl *ELGH* SO50 ...... 29 F3
Monkton La *TOTT* SO40 .... 49 E1
Monmouth Cl *CHFD* SO53 .... 9 F5
Monnow Gdns *WEND* SO18 .... 42 D3
Montague Av *ITCH* SO19 .... 55 F4
Montague Cl *ITCH* SO19 .... 55 F4 🔲
Monterey Dr *HLER* SO31 .... 71 G3
Montfort Cl *ROMY* SO51 .... 6 C4
Montfort Hts *ROMY* SO51 .... 6 C4 🔲
Montfort Rd *ROMY* SO51 .... 6 C5
Montgomery Rd *TOTT* SO40 ...... 37 F4
Montgomery Rd *WEND* SO18..... 42 C4
Montgomery Wy *CHFD* SO53 ...... 9 F5
Montrose Cl *HEND* SO30 .... 57 E1 🔲
Moonscross Av *TOTT* SO40 .... 49 H3
Moore Crs *HLER* SO31 .... 62 D4
Moorgreen Rd *HEND* SO30 .... 43 G3

Moorhill Gdns *WEND* SO18 .... 43 G5
Moorhill Rd *HEND* SO30 .... 43 F4
Moorland Cl *FAWY* SO45 .... 66 B2 🔲
    HLER SO31 .... 71 C1
Moorlands Crs *WEND* SO18 .... 42 C4
Moors Cl *RWIN* SO21 .... 11 H2
Mordaunt Rd *SHAM* SO14 .... 41 E5
Morgan Rd *HEND* SO30 .... 56 C2 🔲
Morland Rd *WSHM* SO15 .... 40 A3
Morley Cl *ITCH* SO19 .... 54 B1
Morpeth Av *TOTT* SO40 .... 37 H4
Morris Cl *FAWY* SO45 .... 66 B4
Morris Rd *WSHM* SO15 .... 52 C2
Mortimer Cl *HLER* SO31 .... 62 D4
    TOTT SO40 .... 37 F3
Mortimer Rd *HEND* SO30 .... 57 C1
    ITCH SO19 .... 54 D3
Mortimers Dr *ELGH* SO50 ...... 22 D4 🔲
Mortimers La *ELGH* SO50 .... 22 D4
Mortimer Wy *NBAD* SO52 .... 17 F3
Mosaic Cl *ITCH* SO19 .... 55 H3 🔲
Moss Dr *TOTT* SO40 .... 51 F5
Mossleigh Av *ROWN* SO16 .... 27 F4
Mottisfont Cl *WSHM* SO15 ...... 51 G1 🔲
Mottisfont Rd *ELGH* SO50 .... 20 C2
Mountain Ash Cl *WEND* SO18 ... 43 E5 🔲
Mountbatten Av *ROMY* SO51 ..... 5 H4
Mountbatten Rd *ELGH* SO50 .. 20 C1 🔲
    TOTT SO40 .... 37 F4
Mountbatten Wy *WSHM* SO15... 52 B2
Mount Dr *CHFD* SO53 .... 20 A2
Mountfield *FAWY* SO45 .... 66 C5
Mount House Cl *FAWY* SO45 .... 61 E5 🔲
Mount Pleasant Rd *SHAM* SO14 . 41 F5
The Mount *ROWN* SO16 .... 28 D5 🔲
    ROWN SO16 .... 39 G3
Mount Vw *ELGH* SO50 .... 20 D2
Mousehole La *FAWY* SO45 .... 67 E2
    WEND SO18 .... 42 B4
Mowbray Rd *ITCH* SO19 .... 54 D3
Mulberry Wk *WSHM* SO15 .... 40 A4
Mullen Cl *ITCH* SO19 .... 54 A3
Mullin's La *FAWY* SO45 .... 66 D3
Munro Crs *WSHM* SO15 .... 39 F5
Murray Cl *TOTT* SO40 .... 55 C1
Mussett Cl *TOTT* SO40 .... 37 G5
Mustang Av *FHAM* PO15 .... 65 H3
Myrtle Av *TOTT* SO40 .... 49 F1
Myrtle Rd *ROWN* SO16 .... 27 H5
Myvern Cl *FAWY* SO45 .... 72 C5

N

Napier Rd *ITCH* SO19 .... 55 G2
Narrow La *ROMY* SO51 .... 5 G4 🔲
Nash Cl *FAWY* SO45 .... 66 B3
Nash Rd *FAWY* SO45 .... 66 B4
Navigator's Wy *HEND* SO30 ...... 44 C4
Neath Wy *CHFD* SO53 .... 19 E1
Neilson Cl *CHFD* SO53 .... 9 G4
Nelson Cl *FAWY* SO45 .... 72 C5
    ROMY SO51 .... 5 H3 🔲
Nelson Rd *ELGH* SO50 .... 21 F2
    WSHM SO15 .... 52 A1
Nelsons Gdns *HEND* SO30 .... 44 C1
Neptune Wy *SHAM* SO14 .... 3 C6
Nerquis Cl *ROMY* SO51 .... 6 B3 🔲
Nether Hill La *BPWT* SO32 .... 45 H2
Netley Cl *CHFD* SO53 .... 19 F3 🔲
Netley Firs Rd *ITCH* SO19 .... 55 H3
Netley Hill Est *ITCH* SO19 .... 55 H3
Netley Lodge Cl *HLER* SO31 ...... 63 E5
Nettlestone *HLER* SO31 .... 63 E3 🔲
Neva Rd *WEND* SO18 .... 42 B4
Neville Dr *ROMY* SO51 .... 5 H3 🔲
Newbridge *HLER* SO31 .... 63 E4 🔲
Newbridge Rd *TOTT* SO40 .... 34 D1
Newbury Cl *ELGH* SO50 .... 22 B4 🔲
Newbury Pl *WSHM* SO15 .... 71 F3
Newbury Rd *WSHM* SO15 .... 40 A3 🔲
New Cliffe Gdns *HEND* SO30 .. 56 B2 🔲
Newcombe Rd *WSHM* SO15 ...... 52 C1
New Inn La *TOTT* SO40 .... 47 F1
New Inn Rd *TOTT* SO40 .... 47 F1
Newlands Av *WSHM* SO15 .... 40 A5
Newlands Cl *NBAD* SO52 .... 18 C1
Newlyn Wk *ROMY* SO51 .... 6 A2
Newman St *ROWN* SO16 .... 39 H4 🔲
Newmarket Cl *ELGH* SO50 ..... 32 D2 🔲
Newport Cl *CHFD* SO53 .... 19 E2 🔲
New Rd *ELGH* SO50 .... 22 B4
    FAWY SO45 .... 67 F5
    HLER SO31 .... 62 D4
    HLER SO31 .... 65 F2
    HLER SO31 .... 70 D5
    ROMY SO51 .... 6 B3

O

Oakbank Rd *ELGH* SO50 .... 21 E3
    ITCH SO19 .... 53 H4

RWIN SO21 .... 11 H2
    SHAM SO14 .... 2 E1
    TOTT SO40 .... 49 E5
Newton La *ROMY* SO51 .... 5 G4
Newton Rd *WEND* SO18 .... 42 A3
Newtown Rd *ELGH* SO50 .... 20 C2
    HLER SO31 .... 70 C5
    ITCH SO19 .... 54 C5
Nichol Rd *CHFD* SO53 .... 9 H2
Nicholson Wk *ROWN* SO16 .... 26 D3
Nichols Rd *SHAM* SO14 .... 53 F2 🔲
Nickleby Gdns *TOTT* SO40 ..... 36 D5 🔲
Nickson Cl *CHFD* SO53 .... 9 F3
Nightingale Av *ELGH* SO50 .... 19 H4
Nightingale Cl *ROMY* SO51 ..... 6 B4 🔲
Nightingale Dr *TOTT* SO40 .... 37 E4
Nightingale Gv *WSHM* SO15 ..... 40 A5
Nightingale Rd *HLER* SO31 .... 63 F2
Nightingale Wk *HLER* SO31 ...... 69 E1
Nile Rd *PTSW* SO17 .... 41 E2
Ninian Cl *ELGH* SO50 .... 22 C5
Noads Cl *FAWY* SO45 .... 66 D3 🔲
Noads Wy *FAWY* SO45 .... 66 C4
Noble Rd *HEND* SO30 .... 56 D1
Nob's Crook *RWIN* SO21 .... 12 A4
Nogarth Cl *ROMY* SO51 .... 6 B2 🔲
Nomad Cl *WEND* SO18 .... 42 D3 🔲
The Nook *HEND* SO30 .... 56 D1
Norbury Cl *CHFD* SO53 .... 9 F4
Norbury Gdns *HLER* SO31 .... 69 G3
Norcliffe Rd *PTSW* SO17 .... 41 E4
Nordik Gdns *HEND* SO30 .... 56 C2
Norfolk Rd *WSHM* SO15 .... 40 B4
Norham Av *ROWN* SO16 .... 40 A2
Norham Cl *ROWN* SO16 .... 40 A2
Normandy Cl *ROWN* SO16 .... 26 D3
Normandy Wy *TOTT* SO40 .... 51 F4
Norman Gdns *HEND* SO30 ..... 56 A2 🔲
Norris Cl *ROMY* SO51 .... 6 C1 🔲
Norris Hl *WEND* SO18 .... 42 A3
Northam Br *WSHM* SO15 .... 53 G1
Northam Rd *SHAM* SO14 .... 3 G1
Northbourne Cl *FAWY* SO45 .... 67 E4 🔲
Northbrook Rd *SHAM* SO14 ...... 53 F2
North Cl *HLER* SO31 .... 6 C2
Northcote Rd *PTSW* SO17 .... 41 E2
Northdene Rd *CHFD* SO53 .... 19 G1
North East Cl *ITCH* SO19 .... 54 D2
North East Rd *ITCH* SO19 .... 54 C3
North End Cl *CHFD* SO53 .... 19 G2
Northern Anchorage *ITCH* SO19 .... 58 C5
Northover Av *LYND* SO43 .... 58 C5
Northerwood Cl *NBAD* SO52 ... 17 F2 🔲
Northfield Rd *WEND* SO18 .... 42 B1
North Front *SHAM* SO14 .... 3 F1
Northlands Cl *TOTT* SO40 .... 37 H4
Northlands Gdns *WSHM* SO15 ... 40 C5
Northlands Rd *ELGH* SO50 ..... 20 C3 🔲
    ROMY SO51 .... 6 C5
    TOTT SO40 .... 40 C5
    WSHM SO15 .... 40 C5
North Millers Dl *CHFD* SO53 .... 9 F4
Northmore Cl *HLER* SO31 ...... 65 H5 🔲
Northmore Rd *HLER* SO31 .... 65 H5
Northolt Gdns *ROWN* SO16 .... 27 G5
North Rd *FAWY* SO45 .... 66 B3
    PTSW SO17 .... 41 E3
North Trestle Rd *FAWY* SO45 .... 73 H2
Northumberland Rd *SHAM* SO14 . 53 F1 🔲
Northwood Cl *ROWN* SO16 ..... 29 E3 🔲
Norton Cl *ITCH* SO19 .... 54 A4
Norton Welch Cl *NBAD* SO52 ... 17 H2
Norwich Cl *HLER* SO31 .... 71 E1
Norwich Rd *WEND* SO18 .... 42 B2
Noyce Dr *ELGH* SO50 .... 22 D5
Nursery Gdns *CHFD* SO53 .... 19 G3
    ITCH SO19 .... 54 D1
    ROMY SO51 .... 6 A4 🔲
Nursery Gv *HEND* SO30 .... 56 D2
Nursery Rd *WEND* SO18 .... 41 H3
Nursling St *ROWN* SO16 .... 26 C4
Nutbeem Rd *ELGH* SO50 .... 20 C4
Nutburn Rd *NBAD* SO52 .... 17 H1
Nutfield Ct *WSHM* SO15 .... 39 E1
Nutfield Rd *ROWN* SO16 .... 26 D5
Nutsey Av *TOTT* SO40 .... 37 F2
Nutsey La *TOTT* SO40 .... 37 G2
Nutshalling Av *ROWN* SO16 ...... 27 E4
Nutshalling Cl *TOTT* SO40 .... 37 E3
Nutwood Wy *TOTT* SO40 .... 37 G2

Oak Cl *FAWY* SO45 .... 66 C4
    WSHM SO15 .... 38 C5
Oak Coppice Cl *ELGH* SO50 ...... 22 A4
Oakdene *TOTT* SO40 .... 36 D5
Oak Dr *ELGH* SO50 .... 22 C4
Oakenbrow *FAWY* SO45 .... 66 B3
Oakfield Rd *TOTT* SO40 .... 35 F5
    TOTT SO40 .... 37 H5
Oakfields *ELGH* SO50 .... 10 C4
Oak Green Wy *WEND* SO18....... 42 C4
Oakgrove Rd *ELGH* SO50 .... 21 G4
Oakhill *HLER* SO31 .... 64 B1
Oakhill Cl *CHFD* SO53 .... 20 A1
    HLER SO31 .... 64 B1
Oakhurst Cl *HLER* SO31 .... 63 E4 🔲
Oakhurst Rd *PTSW* SO17 ...... 41 E1 🔲
Oakhurst Wy *HLER* SO31 .... 63 E4
Oaklands Av *TOTT* SO40 .... 37 H5
The Oaklands *CHFD* SO53 ...... 19 G3 🔲
Oaklands Wy *FAWY* SO45 .... 66 A3
    ROWN SO16 .... 28 D5
Oakleigh Crs *TOTT* SO40 .... 49 G1
Oakleigh Gdns *ROMY* SO51 ..... 6 A4 🔲
Oakley Cl *FAWY* SO45 .... 72 C4
Oakley Rd *ROWN* SO16 .... 39 F4
Oakmount Av *CHFD* SO53 .... 19 H2
    PTSW SO17 .... 41 E3
    TOTT SO40 .... 37 H4
Oakmount Rd *CHFD* SO53 .... 10 A4
    CHFD SO53 .... 19 H2
Oakridge Rd *WSHM* SO15 .... 38 D4
Oak Rd *FAWY* SO45 .... 66 C4
    HLER SO31 .... 63 G2
    ITCH SO19 .... 53 H5
The Oaks *HLER* SO31 .... 63 H2
    ITCH SO19 .... 54 B2
Oak Tree Cl *RWIN* SO21 .... 11 H3
Oak Tree Gdns *HEND* SO30 ... 56 B1 🔲
Oak Tree Rd *WEND* SO18 .... 41 H3
Oak Tree Wy *ELGH* SO50 .... 20 C1
Oak V *HEND* SO30 .... 42 D1
Oakwood Cl *HLER* SO31 .... 70 D5
    ROMY SO51 .... 5 H3
Oakwood Ct *HEND* SO30 ...... 43 G2 🔲
Oakwood Dr *ROWN* SO16 .... 27 H4
Oakwood Rd *CHFD* SO53 .... 9 H3
Oakwood Wy *HLER* SO31 ...... 70 A2 🔲
Oatfield Gdns *TOTT* SO40 .... 37 H4
Oatlands *ROMY* SO51 .... 5 H3 🔲
Oatlands Cl *BPWT* SO32 .... 45 F3
Oatlands Rd *BPWT* SO32 .... 45 F3
Obelisk Rd *ITCH* SO19 .... 53 H5
Ocean Rd *SHAM* SO14 .... 61 E1
Ocean Wy *SHAM* SO14 .... 3 G7
Ocknell Gv *FAWY* SO45 .... 66 A2
O'Connell Rd *ELGH* SO50 .... 20 A4
Octavia Gdns *CHFD* SO53 .... 10 B4
Octavia Rd *WEND* SO18 .... 30 A5
Odiham Cl *ROWN* SO16 .... 27 F5
Ogle Rd *SHAM* SO14 .... 2 D2
Okement Cl *WEND* SO18 .... 42 D2
Oldbarn Cl *TOTT* SO40 .... 49 H3
Old Bridge House Rd *HLER* SO31.. 64 B2
Oldbury Ct *ROWN* SO16 .... 38 D2
Old Common *HLER* SO31 .... 71 G1
Old Common Gdns *HLER* SO31 ... 71 G2
Old Cracknore Cl *TOTT* SO40 .... 51 F5
Oldenburg *HLER* SO31 .... 65 H2
Old Farm Dr *WEND* SO18 .... 42 B2
Old Ivy La *HEND* SO30 .... 42 D2
Old Lyndhurst Rd *TOTT* SO40 ... 34 D4
Old Magazine Cl *TOTT* SO40 .... 51 F5
Old Mill Wy *ROWN* SO16 .... 39 G3
Old Priory Cl *HLER* SO31 .... 70 A3
Old Redbridge Rd *WSHM* SO15 ... 38 B4
Old Rd *ROMY* SO51 .... 6 A3
    SHAM SO14 .... 3 G6
Old Romsey Rd *TOTT* SO40 ...... 34 C4
Old Salisbury La *ROMY* SO51 ..... 4 A2
Old Salisbury Rd *ROMY* SO51 ... 24 A2
Old School Cl *FAWY* SO45 .... 72 B2
    HLER SO31 .... 63 F3 🔲
Old School Gdns *HEND* SO30 ... 43 G2
Old Shamblehurst La
    HEND SO30 .... 44 C2
The Old Well Cl *ITCH* SO19........ 55 E4
Oleander Cl *HLER* SO31 .... 65 G5
Olive Rd *ROWN* SO16 .... 27 G5
Oliver Rd *WEND* SO18 .... 41 H1
Olivers Cl *TOTT* SO40 .... 36 D5
Olympic Wy *ELGH* SO50 .... 22 A3 🔲
    ELGH SO50 .... 22 B3 🔲
Omdurman Rd *PTSW* SO17 .... 41 E2
Onibury Cl *WEND* SO18 .... 42 C3
Onibury Rd *WEND* SO18 .... 42 C3
Onslow Rd *SHAM* SO14 .... 53 E1
Orchard Av *ELGH* SO50 .... 21 H5
Orchard Cl *FAWY* SO45 .... 73 H5

NBAD S052 .... 17 F1
RWIN S021 .... 11 H2
TOTT S040 .... 49 H2
Orchard Ct *HEND* S030 .... 45 E5
Orchard Ho *SHAM* S014 .... 53 E2
Orchard La *ROMY* S051 .... 5 G4
  SHAM S014 .... 3 F4
Orchard Pl *SHAM* S014 .... 2 E6
Orchard Rd *ELGH* S050 .... 22 C4
  HLER S031 .... 71 F3
Orchards Wy *HEND* S030 .... 43 F3
  PTSW S017 .... 41 E2
The Orchard *ROWN* S016 .... 18 C5
Orchard Wy *FAWY* S045 .... 66 C3
Ordnance Rd *WSHM* S015 .... 53 E1
Ordnance Wy *TOTT* S040 .... 51 G4
Oregon Cl *ITCH* S019 .... 54 C3
Orion Cl *ROWN* S016 .... 27 F5
Orkney Cl *ROWN* S016 .... 27 E5
Ormesby Dr *CHFD* S053 .... 9 F3
Ormond Cl *ELGH* S050 .... 22 B3
Orpen Rd *ITCH* S019 .... 55 E4
Orwell Cl *ROWN* S016 .... 39 E5
Osborne Dr *CHFD* S053 .... 20 A1
Osborne Gdns *ELGH* S050 .... 22 D5
Osborne Rd *HLER* S031 .... 70 C5
  TOTT S040 .... 38 A5
Osborne Rd North *PTSW* S017 .... 41 G4
Osborne Rd South *PTSW* S017 .... 41 G4
Oslands Dr *HLER* S031 .... 64 D3
Osprey Cl *ROWN* S016 .... 27 H4
Osterley Cl *HEND* S030 .... 45 C5
Osterly Rd *ITCH* S019 .... 54 A3
Otterbourne HI *CHFD* S053 .... 10 C2
Otter Cl *ELGH* S050 .... 22 A4
Ouse Cl *CHFD* S053 .... 9 E3
Outer Cir *ROWN* S016 .... 27 C5
Overbrook *FAWY* S045 .... 66 D3
Overbrook Wy *NBAD* S052 .... 17 E1
Overcliff Ri *ROWN* S016 .... 28 C5
Oviat Cl *TOTT* S040 .... 36 D5
Owen Rd *ELGH* S050 .... 20 B4
Oxburgh Cl *ELGH* S050 .... 20 B1
Oxford Av *SHAM* S014 .... 53 E2
Oxford Rd *SHAM* S014 .... 41 E5
Oxford St *SHAM* S014 .... 3 F5
Oxlease Cl *ROMY* S051 .... 6 A2
Ozier Rd *WEND* S018 .... 42 C2

P

Pacific Cl *SHAM* S014 .... 3 H7
Packridge La *ROMY* S051 .... 17 F5
The Paddocks *FAWY* S045 .... 73 H5
The Paddock *ELGH* S050 .... 10 D5
  TOTT S040 .... 37 E2
Padwell Rd *SHAM* S014 .... 41 E5
Paget St *SHAM* S014 .... 3 H4
Paignton Rd *ROWN* S016 .... 39 F4
Painswick Cl *HLER* S031 .... 65 F4
Pallet Cl *RWIN* S021 .... 11 H3
Pallot Cl *HLER* S031 .... 63 H2
Palmers Cl *ELGH* S050 .... 22 D4
Palmerston Rd *SHAM* S014 .... 2 E1
Palmerston St *ROMY* S051 .... 5 G4
  ROMY S051 .... 5 H4
Palm Rd *ROWN* S016 .... 39 F1
Pangbourne Cl *ITCH* S019 .... 54 C3
Pansy Rd *ROWN* S016 .... 29 E5
Pantheon Rd *CHFD* S053 .... 10 B4
Panwell Rd *WEND* S018 .... 42 C5
Paradise La *TOTT* S040 .... 47 H1
Pardoe Cl *HEND* S030 .... 56 C2
Parham Dr *ELGH* S050 .... 20 B2
Park Cl *FAWY* S045 .... 67 F1
Park Hill Cl *FAWY* S045 .... 72 C5
Parklands *HLER* S031 .... 71 C1
  WEND S018 .... 42 A4
Parklands Cl *CHFD* S053 .... 9 G4
Park La *ELGH* S050 .... 10 D2
  FAWY S045 .... 72 B4
  TOTT S040 .... 50 C5
Park Rd *CHFD* S053 .... 9 G3
  WSHM S015 .... 52 A1
Parkside *TOTT* S040 .... 49 H2
Parkside Av *ROWN* S016 .... 38 D4
Park St *ROWN* S016 .... 39 H4
Park Vw *HEND* S030 .... 44 B5
  HEND S030 .... 45 C5
Parkville Rd *ROWN* S016 .... 29 H5
Park Wk *SHAM* S014 .... 2 E1
Parkway Gdns *CHFD* S053 .... 9 G4
The Parkway *ROWN* S016 .... 29 E4
Parnell Rd *ELGH* S050 .... 20 B4
Parry Rd *ITCH* S019 .... 55 F3
Parsonage La *BPWT* S032 .... 33 H3

Parsonage Rd *SHAM* S014 .... 53 F1
Partridge Rd *FAWY* S045 .... 66 D4
Partry Cl *CHFD* S053 .... 9 E3
Passage La *HLER* S031 .... 70 B4
Passfield Av *ELGH* S050 .... 20 A4
Passfield Cl *ELGH* S050 .... 20 A4
Pat Bear Cl *WSHM* S015 .... 38 C4
Patricia Cl *HEND* S030 .... 43 F2
Patricia Dr *HEND* S030 .... 44 D5
Paulet Cl *WEND* S018 .... 42 C3
Paulet Lacave Av *ROWN* S016 .... 26 D3
Pauletts La *TOTT* S040 .... 36 D1
Paulson Cl *CHFD* S053 .... 9 G3
Pauncefoot HI *ROMY* S051 .... 15 E1
Pavilion Cl *ELGH* S050 .... 32 C1
Pavilion Rd *HEND* S030 .... 44 D4
Paxton Cl *HEND* S030 .... 56 D2
Payne's Rd *WSHM* S015 .... 51 H1
Peach Rd *ROWN* S016 .... 27 G5
Peak Cl *ROWN* S016 .... 39 F4
Peartree Av *ITCH* S019 .... 54 A4
Pear Tree Cl *BPWT* S032 .... 45 F2
Peartree Cl *ITCH* S019 .... 53 H3
Peartree Rd *FAWY* S045 .... 66 C3
  ITCH S019 .... 53 H3
Pebble Ct *TOTT* S040 .... 51 F5
Pedula Wy *ELGH* S050 .... 21 G1
Peel Cl *ROMY* S051 .... 6 C2
Peel St *SHAM* S014 .... 53 G2
Peewit HI *HLER* S031 .... 56 A4
Peewit Hill Cl *HLER* S031 .... 56 A4
Pegasus Cl *HLER* S031 .... 69 H3
  ROWN S016 .... 27 F5
Pembers Cl *ELGH* S050 .... 22 D4
Pemberton Rd *LYND* S043 .... 59 E5
Pembrey Cl *ROWN* S016 .... 27 F4
Pembroke Cl *ELGH* S050 .... 20 B1
  ROMY S051 .... 5 H4
  TOTT S040 .... 38 A4
Pembroke Rd *ITCH* S019 .... 54 D3
Pendle Cl *ROWN* S016 .... 39 F4
Penelope Gdns *HLER* S031 .... 55 H5
Penhale Gdns *FHAM/STUB* P014... 71 H4
Penhale Wy *TOTT* S040 .... 49 G2
Penistone Cl *ITCH* S019 .... 62 D1
Pennard Wy *CHFD* S053 .... 19 E2
Pennine Gdns *FAWY* S045 .... 66 B3
Pennine Rd *ROWN* S016 .... 39 F5
Pennine Wy *CHFD* S053 .... 19 H2
Pennington Cl *ELGH* S050 .... 11 H3
Pennycress *HLER* S031 .... 71 E3
Penrhyn Cl *ITCH* S019 .... 20 B1
Penshurst Wy *ELGH* S050 .... 10 C5
Pentire Av *WSHM* S015 .... 40 B2
Pentire Wy *WSHM* S015 .... 40 B2
Pentland Cl *FAWY* S045 .... 66 B3
Pentridge Wy *TOTT* S040 .... 49 F2
Peppard Cl *WEND* S018 .... 42 C5
Peppercorn Wy *HEND* S030 ...... 44 B1
Pepys Av *ITCH* S019 .... 55 F2
Percy Cl *FAWY* S045 .... 60 D5
Percy Rd *ROWN* S016 .... 39 G4
Peregrine Cl *TOTT* S040 .... 49 E1
Pern Dr *HEND* S030 .... 45 G5
Perran Rd *ROWN* S016 .... 38 D3
Perryvale Rd *NBAD* S052 .... 18 D1
Perrywood Cl *FAWY* S045 .... 72 C5
Perrywood Gdns *TOTT* S040 ..... 36 D4
Pershore Cl *HLER* S031 .... 71 G2
Persian Dr *HLER* S031 .... 65 H3
Peters Cl *HLER* S031 .... 71 E2
Peters Rd *HLER* S031 .... 71 E2
Pettinger Gdns *PTSW* S017 .... 41 H4
Petty Cl *ROMY* S051 .... 6 A5
Petworth Gdns *ELGH* S050 .... 20 C1
  ROWN S016 .... 27 H4
Pevensey Cl *ROWN* S016 .... 38 D3
Peverells Rd *CHFD* S053 .... 10 A5
Peverells Wood Av *CHFD* S053 .. 10 A4
Peverells Wood Cl *CHFD* S053 .. 10 B4
Peveril Rd *ITCH* S019 .... 54 A3
Pewsey Pl *WSHM* S015 .... 40 B2
Phillimore Rd *ROWN* S016 .... 29 H5
Phillips Cl *ROWN* S016 .... 27 E3
Phoenix Cl *HLER* S031 .... 64 A1
Pickwick Cl *TOTT* S040 .... 36 D5
Pikes HI *LYND* S043 .... 58 C3
Pilands Wood Rd *HLER* S031 .... 63 H2
Pilchards Av *HLER* S031 .... 22 B3
Pilgrim Pl *WEND* S018 .... 30 A5
Pilgrims Cl *NBAD* S052 .... 18 D1
Pimpernel Cl *HLER* S031 .... 71 E3
Pine Cl *FAWY* S045 .... 66 D3
  NBAD S052 .... 17 F1
  TOTT S040 .... 49 E4
Pine Crs *CHFD* S053 .... 9 G3
Pine Dr *WEND* S018 .... 43 F5
Pine Dr East *WEND* S018 .... 43 G5

Pinefield Rd *WEND* S018 .... 42 B2
Pinegrove Rd *ITCH* S019 .... 54 B4
Pinehurst Rd *ROWN* S016 .... 28 D2
Pinelands Rd *ROWN* S016 .... 28 D1
Pine Rd *CHFD* S053 .... 9 G2
  ROMY S051 .... 6 C5
Pineview Cl *HLER* S031 .... 64 A1
Pine Wk *HLER* S031 .... 65 G5
  ROWN S016 .... 28 D2
Pine Wy *ROWN* S016 .... 28 D2
Pinewood Cl *ROMY* S051 .... 4 C5
Pinewood Crs *FAWY* S045 .... 67 F3
Pinewood Dr *FAWY* S045 .... 67 F3
Pinewood Pk *ITCH* S019 .... 55 H2
Pinto Cl *FHAM* P015 .... 65 H3
Pipers Cl *TOTT* S040 .... 49 F1
Piping Cl *RWIN* S021 .... 11 H3
Piping Rd *RWIN* S021 .... 11 H3
Pirelli St *SHAM* S014 .... 2 C2
  WSHM S015 .... 2 C2
Pirrie Cl *WSHM* S015 .... 40 B3
Pitchponds Rd *HLER* S031 .... 70 C5
Pitmore Cl *ELGH* S050 .... 10 D3
Pitmore Rd *ELGH* S050 .... 10 D3
Pitt Rd *WSHM* S015 .... 52 A1
Platform Rd *SHAM* S014 .... 2 E6
Players Crs *TOTT* S040 .... 49 G2
Plover Cl *ROWN* S016 .... 27 H4
Plover Rd *TOTT* S040 .... 37 E5
P.l.p.h. Rd *FAWY* S045 .... 71 F3
Pointout Cl *ROWN* S016 .... 40 C1
Pointout Rd *ROWN* S016 .... 40 C1
Polesden Cl *CHFD* S053 .... 9 F3
Pollards Moor Rd *TOTT* S040 .... 35 E3
The Polygon *WSHM* S015 .... 52 C2
Pond Cl *TOTT* S040 .... 51 F5
Pondhead Cl *FAWY* S045 .... 72 C5
Pond Rd *HLER* S031 .... 65 F4
Pooksgreen *TOTT* S040 .... 50 D5
Poole Rd *ITCH* S019 .... 54 A3
Popes La *TOTT* S040 .... 37 H5
Poplar Rd *ITCH* S019 .... 54 B1
Poplar Wy *HEND* S030 .... 44 D5
  NBAD S052 .... 17 F1
Poppy Cl *HLER* S031 .... 71 F3
Poppyfields *NBAD* S052 .... 9 E5
Poppy Rd *ROWN* S016 .... 29 G4
Porchester Rd *ITCH* S019 .... 54 A4
Porlock Rd *ROWN* S016 .... 38 C3
Portal Rd *ELGH* S050 .... 21 F3
  ITCH S019 .... 54 D3
  TOTT S040 .... 37 F5
Portchester Ri *ELGH* S050 .... 10 C4
Portelet Pl *HEND* S030 .... 56 C2
Porteous Crs *CHFD* S053 .... 10 B5
Portersbridge St *ROMY* S051 ...... 5 G4
Porter's La *SHAM* S014 .... 2 D4
Portland St *SHAM* S014 .... 2 D2
Portland Ter *SHAM* S014 .... 2 D2
Portsmouth Rd *BPWT* S032 ...... 23 H2
  ELGH S050 .... 12 C5
  HLER S031 .... 63 H1
  ITCH S019 .... 53 H4
  RWIN S021 .... 13 F5
Portswood Av *PTSW* S017 .... 41 F4
Portswood Pk *PTSW* S017 .... 41 F4
Portswood Rd *PTSW* S017 .... 41 F4
Portview Rd *WEND* S018 .... 42 B2
Portway Cl *WEND* S018 .... 42 D5
Pouliner Cl *ITCH* S019 .... 62 C1
Pound La *ROMY* S051 .... 7 H1
  TOTT S040 .... 35 G2
  TOTT S040 .... 49 G4
Pound Rd *HLER* S031 .... 63 G1
Pound St *WEND* S018 .... 42 C5
Pound Tree Rd *SHAM* S014 .... 2 E2
Powell Crs *TOTT* S040 .... 49 H2
Precosa Rd *HEND* S030 .... 57 E2
Preshaw Cl *ROWN* S016 .... 27 H5
Prestwood Rd *HEND* S030 .... 56 C1
Pretoria Rd *HEND* S030 .... 56 B2
Priestlands *ROMY* S051 .... 5 G3
Priestlands Cl *TOTT* S040 .... 48 C1
Priestley Cl *TOTT* S040 .... 37 F5
Priestwood Cl *WEND* S018 .... 43 F5
Primrose Cl *HEND* S030 .... 56 C2
  NBAD S052 .... 18 D2
Primrose Rd *ROWN* S016 .... 29 E5
Primrose Wy *HLER* S031 .... 71 F3
  ROMY S051 .... 6 C2
Prince of Wales Av *WSHM* S015 . 39 C5
Prince Rd *ROWN* S016 .... 27 E2
Princes Ct *SHAM* S014 .... 53 G1
Princes Crs *LYND* S043 .... 59 E5
Princes Rd *ROMY* S051 .... 5 G3
  WSHM S015 .... 52 B1
Princess Cl *HEND* S030 .... 43 G2
Princess Rd *TOTT* S040 .... 48 D5

Prince's St *SHAM* S014 .... 53 G1
Priory Av *PTSW* S017 .... 41 H3
Priory Cl *PTSW* S017 .... 41 H3
Priory Rd *ELGH* S050 .... 20 B5
  HLER S031 .... 62 D4
  PTSW S017 .... 41 G4
Proctor Cl *ITCH* S019 .... 55 F2
Proctor Dr *NBAD* S052 .... 17 F3
The Promenade *FAWY* S045 ...... 61 E5
Prospect Pl *CHFD* S053 .... 9 G5
  FAWY S045 .... 61 E5
Providence HI *HLER* S031 .... 56 A5
Prunus Cl *ROWN* S016 .... 28 A4
Pudbrooke Gdns *HEND* S030 ..... 44 B4
Puffin Cl *ROWN* S016 .... 27 H4
Purbrook Cl *ROWN* S016 .... 28 A5
Purcell Rd *ITCH* S019 .... 55 F4
Purkess Cl *CHFD* S053 .... 9 H4
Purkiss Cl *TOTT* S040 .... 47 G2
Purvis Gdns *ITCH* S019 .... 54 D5
Pycroft Cl *ITCH* S019 .... 54 B2
Pyland's La *HLER* S031 .... 56 B4
Pylewell Rd *FAWY* S045 .... 67 E1

Q

The Quadrangle *ELGH* S050 ...... 20 C2
Quantock Rd *ROWN* S016 .... 39 E4
The Quantocks *FAWY* S045 .... 66 B3
Quay Hvn *HLER* S031 .... 64 D2
Quayside Rd *WEND* S018 .... 41 H5
Quayside Wk *TOTT* S040 .... 51 F4
Quebec Gdns *HLER* S031 .... 63 H1
Queens Cl *FAWY* S045 .... 67 E2
Queen's Ho *SHAM* S014 .... 53 E2
Queens Pde *LYND* S043 .... 58 D5
Queens Ride *NBAD* S052 .... 17 E2
Queen's Rd *CHFD* S053 .... 9 H2
  HLER S031 .... 70 C5
  WSHM S015 .... 40 A2
Queen's Ter *SHAM* S014 .... 3 F5
Queenstown Rd *WSHM* S015 ..... 52 B1
Queens Vw *HLER* S031 .... 62 D4
Queen's Wy *SHAM* S014 .... 2 E5
Querida Cl *HLER* S031 .... 64 D2
Quilter Cl *ITCH* S019 .... 55 F3
Quob Farm Cl *HEND* S030 .... 43 G1
Quob La *HEND* S030 .... 43 G1

R

Racecourse Vw *LYND* S043 .... 58 D4
Rachel Cl *ELGH* S050 .... 22 B4
Radcliffe Rd *SHAM* S014 .... 53 F2
Radleigh Gdns *TOTT* S040 .... 36 D4
Radley Cl *HEND* S030 .... 44 C3
Radstock Rd *ITCH* S019 .... 54 A4
Radway Crs *WSHM* S015 .... 40 B4
Radway Rd *WSHM* S015 .... 40 B4
Raeburn Dr *HEND* S030 .... 44 C5
Raglan Cl *CHFD* S053 .... 18 D2
Raley Rd *HLER* S031 .... 71 G3
Ramalley La *CHFD* S053 .... 9 F4
Rampart Rd *WEND* S018 .... 41 H5
Randall Cl *TOTT* S040 .... 37 E2
Randall Rd *CHFD* S053 .... 9 H1
Randolph St *WSHM* S015 .... 40 A5
Ranelagh Gdns *WSHM* S015 ...... 40 A5
Ranfurly Gdns *FAWY* S045 .... 66 C3
Range Gdns *ITCH* S019 .... 54 D4
Ratcliffe Rd *FAWY* S045 .... 66 D4
  HEND S030 .... 44 C5
Raven Rd *SHAM* S014 .... 53 F1
Ravenscroft Cl *HLER* S031 .... 63 H1
Ravenscroft Wy *BPWT* S032 ..... 45 F2
Raven Sq *ELGH* S050 .... 19 H4
Raymond Cl *FAWY* S045 .... 72 D5
  HEND S030 .... 43 H1
Raymond Rd *WSHM* S015 .... 40 B4
Rayners Gdns *ROWN* S016 .... 29 H5
The Recess *ELGH* S050 .... 20 D1
Rectory Ct *HEND* S030 .... 45 F5
Redbridge Cswy *WSHM* S015 .... 38 B4
Redbridge HI *ROWN* S016 .... 39 F3
Redbridge La *ROWN* S016 .... 38 B2
Redbridge Rd *WSHM* S015 .... 38 C3
Redcote Cl *WEND* S018 .... 42 D5
Redcroft La *HLER* S031 .... 64 A1
The Redfords *TOTT* S040 .... 37 F2
Redhill *ROWN* S016 .... 28 C5
Redhill Cl *ROWN* S016 .... 28 C5
Red Hill Crs *ROWN* S016 .... 28 C5
Red Hill Wy *ROWN* S016 .... 40 C1
Redlands Dr *ITCH* S019 .... 54 B1

Red Ldg *CHFD* SO53 19 F3
Redmoor Cl *ITCH* SO19 54 A1
Red Oaks Dr *FHAM* PO15 65 H5
Redrise Cl *FAWY* SO45 72 B5
Redward Rd *ROWN* SO16 27 F4
Redwing Gdns *TOTT* SO40 37 E4 7
Redwood Cl *FAWY* SO45 66 B2
HEND SO30 43 E2
Redwood Gdns *TOTT* SO40 37 E5
Redwood Wy *ROWN* SO16 29 E3
Reed Dr *TOTT* SO40 51 F5
Reeves Wy *HLER* SO31 63 H1 5
Regent Rd *CHFD* SO53 9 H5
Regents Ga *HLER* SO31 65 E5
Regent's Gv *WSHM* SO15 39 H4 4
Regent's Park Gdns
WSHM SO15 39 H5 2
Regent's Park Rd *WSHM* SO15 39 G5
Regent St *SHAM* SO14 2 D2
Reliant Cl *CHFD* SO53 19 F2 1
Renda Rd *FAWY* SO45 72 C4
Renown Cl *CHFD* SO53 19 F1
Reservoir La *HEND* SO30 56 A1
The Retreat *ELGH* SO50 20 D2
TOTT SO40 49 H2
Reynolds Dl *TOTT* SO40 49 F2
Reynolds Rd *ELGH* SO50 22 D5
WSHM SO15 40 A4
Rhinefield Cl *ELGH* SO50 21 H4 2
Rhyme Hall Ms *FAWY* SO45 73 H5 8
Ribble Cl *CHFD* SO53 19 H1
Ribble Ct *ROWN* SO16 39 E3
Richards Cl *HLER* SO31 71 H2
Richlans Rd *HEND* SO30 56 C1
Richmond Cl *CHFD* SO53 9 F2
TOTT SO40 36 D3
Richmond Gdns *PTSW* SO17 41 F3
Richmond La *ROMY* SO51 6 A2
Richmond Rd *WSHM* SO15 52 A1
Richmond St *SHAM* SO14 3 F4
Richville Rd *ROWN* SO16 39 G4
Ridding Cl *WSHM* SO15 39 H4
Ridge La *ROMY* SO51 14 D5
Ridgemount Av *ROWN* SO16 28 D4
Ridgeway Cl *CHFD* SO53 20 A1
ELGH SO50 22 C3 1
Ridgewood Cl *FAWY* SO45 66 A2 1
The Ridings *ELGH* SO50 22 A4
Ridley Cl *FAWY* SO45 72 C4 3
Rigby Rd *SHAM* SO14 41 F4
The Ring *ROWN* SO16 28 C2
Ringwood Dr *NBAD* SO52 17 E1
Ringwood Rd *TOTT* SO40 36 C5
Ripstone Gdns *PTSW* SO17 41 F1
Ritchie Ct *ITCH* SO19 54 D3
Riverdene Pl *WEND* SO18 41 H4 2
River Gn *HLER* SO31 70 A3
Rivermead Cl *ROMY* SO51 5 F4
Riversdale Cl *ITCH* SO19 62 A2 2
Riverside *ELGH* SO50 21 F3
Riverside Cl *TOTT* SO40 47 G1
Riverside Gdns *ROMY* SO51 5 G5
Riverview *TOTT* SO40 49 H2
River View Rd *WEND* SO18 41 H2
River Wk *WEND* SO18 42 A1
Robert Cecil Av *WEND* SO18 30 A5
Roberts Rd *FAWY* SO45 66 D1
TOTT SO40 49 H2
WSHM SO15 52 B2
Robert Whitworth Dr
ROMY SO51 5 H2
Robin Gdns *TOTT* SO40 37 E4
Robinia Gn *ROWN* SO16 28 A4
Robin Sq *ELGH* SO50 19 G5
Rochester St *SHAM* SO14 3 J1
Rockall Cl *ROWN* SO16 27 E4
Rockery Cl *FAWY* SO45 66 A1
Rockleigh Dr *TOTT* SO40 49 F3
Rockleigh Rd *ROWN* SO16 40 B1
Rockram Cl *TOTT* SO40 35 F5
Rockram Gdns *FAWY* SO45 66 A2 2
Rockstone La *SHAM* SO14 53 E1
Rockstone Pl *WSHM* SO15 52 D1
Roewood Cl *FAWY* SO45 72 C5 2
Roewood Rd *FAWY* SO45 72 C5
Rogers Cl *ELGH* SO50 21 G2
Rogers Rd *ELGH* SO50 21 G2
Roker Wy *ELGH* SO50 22 B5
Rollestone Rd *FAWY* SO45 72 B5
Roman Cl *CHFD* SO53 10 A4
Roman Dr *ROWN* SO16 28 C2
Roman Gdns *FAWY* SO45 66 B4 1
Roman Rd *FAWY* SO45 66 C5
FAWY SO45 72 B2
ROWN SO16 18 C5
Roman Wy *FAWY* SO45 66 B4
Romford Rd *HLER* SO31 70 D5
Romill Cl *WEND* SO18 42 D1
Romsey Cl *ELGH* SO50 20 C3
Romsey Rd *ELGH* SO50 20 C3
LYND SO43 58 D4
ROMY SO51 24 A4
ROWN SO16 26 D4
TOTT SO40 34 D4
Rookery Av *HLER* SO31 65 H3
Rookley *HLER* SO31 63 E3
Rooksbridge *FAWY* SO45 66 A2 3
Rookwood Cl *ELGH* SO50 10 D5 2
Ropley Cl *ITCH* SO19 62 C2 2
Rosebank Cl *ROWN* SO16 27 E4
Rosebay Cl *ELGH* SO50 32 C3 4
Rosebery Crs *ELGH* SO50 10 D5
Rosebury Av *FAWY* SO45 67 E4
Rose Cl *FAWY* SO45 67 E3 5
HEND SO30 44 C4
Rosedale Av *ROMY* SO51 6 A4
Roselands *HEND* SO30 43 F4 3
Roselands Cl *ELGH* SO50 22 B3
Roselands Gdns *PTSW* SO17 41 E2
Roseleigh Dr *TOTT* SO40 49 G1
Rosemary Gdns *HEND* SO30 56 C2
Rosemoor Gv *CHFD* SO53 9 F2
Rosendale Rd *CHFD* SO53 19 H2 1
Rose Rd *SHAM* SO14 41 E4
TOTT SO40 50 A1
Rosewall Rd *ROWN* SO16 39 F1
Rosoman Rd *ITCH* SO19 54 B3
Ross Gdns *ROWN* SO16 39 G2
Rossington Av *WEND* SO18 42 B5
Rossington Wy *WEND* SO18 42 B5
Rosslyn Cl *NBAD* SO52 17 G2
Rostron Cl *WEND* SO18 42 C1 2
Rosyth Rd *WEND* SO18 42 B5
Rotary Ct *HLER* SO31 62 D4
Rothbury Cl *ITCH* SO19 54 C3 1
TOTT SO40 37 F3
Rother Cl *WEND* SO18 42 D3
Rother Dl *ITCH* SO19 55 G4
Rothsbury Dr *CHFD* SO53 9 F5
Rothschild Cl *ITCH* SO19 62 A2 3
Rothville Pl *CHFD* SO53 9 F1 2
Roundcopse *FAWY* SO45 66 A2 4
Roundhill Cl *WEND* SO18 42 C3
Roundhouse Dr *TOTT* SO40 48 D1
Routs Wy *ROWN* SO16 27 E2
Rowan Cl *HLER* SO31 63 H2
ROMY SO51 6 C5
ROWN SO16 39 F1
TOTT SO40 49 F1
Rowan Gdns *HEND* SO30 56 D1
Rowborough Rd *WEND* SO18 42 B4
Rowe Ashe Wy *HLER* SO31 71 F2 1
Rowhill Dr *FAWY* SO45 66 A2
Rowlands Cl *CHFD* SO53 19 E2
Rowley Cl *HEND* SO30 45 F4 1
Rowley Dr *HEND* SO30 45 F4
Rownhams Cl *ROWN* SO16 27 E3
Rownhams La *NBAD* SO52 17 F1
ROMY SO51 17 F5
ROWN SO16 27 F2
Rownhams Rd *NBAD* SO52 17 G3
ROWN SO16 39 F2
Rownhams Rd North
ROWN SO16 27 F4
Rownhams Wy *ROWN* SO16 27 E3
Rowse Cl *ROMY* SO51 5 H2 2
Royal Crescent Rd *SHAM* SO14 3 G5
Royston Av *ELGH* SO50 20 C1
Royston Cl *PTSW* SO17 41 F2
Ruby Rd *ITCH* SO19 54 C1
Rufford Cl *ELGH* SO50 10 C5
Rufus Cl *CHFD* SO53 10 A3
ROWN SO16 26 D3
Rufus Gdns *TOTT* SO40 37 E5
Rumbridge Gdns *TOTT* SO40 38 A5 1
Rumbridge St *TOTT* SO40 49 H1
Runnymede *HEND* SO30 43 F3 4
The Rushes *TOTT* SO40 51 F5
Rushington Av *TOTT* SO40 49 H1
Rushington La *TOTT* SO40 49 G2
Ruskin Rd *ELGH* SO50 20 C2
Rusland Cl *CHFD* SO53 9 F4
Russell Pl *PTSW* SO17 41 F3
Russell St *SHAM* SO14 3 F4
Rustan Cl *ELGH* SO50 22 D4
HEND SO30 56 B1 4
Rutland Gdns *HLER* SO31 64 A1
Rutland Wy *WEND* SO18 42 C3
Ruxley Cl *FAWY* SO45 72 C4
Ryde Ter *SHAM* SO14 3 H4
Rye Cl *NBAD* SO52 8 D5
Rye Dl *TOTT* SO40 49 E4
Rye Paddock La *FAWY* SO45 73 H4
Rylandes Ct *ROWN* SO16 39 F1

S

Saddlers Cl *ELGH* SO50 10 C5
Sadlers La *FAWY* SO45 67 E4
St Agatha's Rd *HLER* SO31 70 A1 2
St Alban's Rd *SHAM* SO14 53 F2 3
St Andrews Cl *NBAD* SO52 17 E1
St Andrews Pk *ELGH* SO50 32 C3
St Andrews Rd *SHAM* SO14 53 E2
St Anne's Gdns *ITCH* SO19 54 A5
St Anne's Rd *ITCH* SO19 54 A5
St Aubin's Av *ITCH* SO19 54 C2
St Augustine Gdns *PTSW* SO17 41 H3 1
St Austell Cl *ELGH* SO50 21 G3 1
St Barbe Cl *ROMY* SO51 6 A5 2
St Blaize Rd *ROMY* SO51 6 B3 5
St Catherine's Rd *ELGH* SO50 20 C1
WEND SO18 42 A3
St Catherines Vw *HEND* SO30 56 A1 3
St Christophers Cl *NBAD* SO52 17 F2
St Clements Cl *ROMY* SO51 5 G3 4
St Cuthberts Cl *HLER* SO31 71 H1 2
St Cuthberts La *HLER* SO31 71 H1
St David's Cl *TOTT* SO40 37 E3
St Davids Rd *HLER* SO31 71 F2
St Denys' Rd *PTSW* SO17 41 F3
PTSW SO17 41 F3
St Edmund Cl *FHAM/STUB* PO14 71 H4
St Edmund's Rd *ROWN* SO16 39 H4
St Edwards Rd *HLER* SO31 62 D3
St Elizabeth's Av *WEND* SO18 42 D5
St Evox Cl *ROWN* SO16 27 F4
St Francis Av *WEND* SO18 42 D4
St Gabriel's Rd *WEND* SO18 42 D5
St George Cl *HLER* SO31 63 H1
St Georges Rd *HLER* SO31 71 F2
St Georges St *SHAM* SO14 2 E3
St Helena Gdns *WEND* SO18 42 B1
St James Rd *HEND* SO30 43 F2
St James's Cl *WSHM* SO15 40 A3
St James's Park Rd *ROWN* SO16 40 A2
St James's Rd *WSHM* SO15 40 A3
St Johns Cl *ROWN* SO16 27 E2
St Johns Gdns *ROMY* SO51 5 H3 7
St Johns Glebe *ROWN* SO16 27 F2
St John's Rd *ELGH* SO50 20 D2
HEND SO30 56 A3
HLER SO31 71 H3
St John's St *FAWY* SO45 67 E1
St Lawrence Rd *ELGH* SO50 20 C2
SHAM SO14 3 G5
St Lukes Cl *HEND* SO30 44 C3 4
St Margaret's Cl *WEND* SO18 42 D5
St Martin's Cl *ROWN* SO16 39 E1
St Mary's Pl *SHAM* SO14 3 F2
St Mary's Rd *ELGH* SO50 21 F2
HLER SO31 63 E4
SHAM SO14 53 E2
St Mary St *SHAM* SO14 3 G3
St Michaels Rd *HLER* SO31 71 F3
TOTT SO40 37 H3
St Michael's St *SHAM* SO14 2 D4
St Monica Rd *ITCH* SO19 54 C4
St Paul's Rd *HLER* SO31 65 E4
St Philip's Wy *WEND* SO18 42 D5 2
St Simon Cl *HLER* SO31 71 H2 2
St Swithun's Cl *ROMY* SO51 6 D2 1
St Tristan Cl *HLER* SO31 71 H2
St Vigor Wy *RWIN* SO21 11 H2
St Winifred's Rd *ROWN* SO16 40 A2
Salcombe Cl *CHFD* SO53 19 F2
Salcombe Crs *TOTT* SO40 49 G1
Salcombe Rd *TOTT* SO40 49 G1
WSHM SO15 39 H5
Salem St *WSHM* SO15 40 A3
Salerno Rd *ROWN* SO16 28 A5
Salisbury Cl *ELGH* SO50 20 D2 1
Salisbury Rd *PTSW* SO17 41 E1
ROMY SO51 4 A3
TOTT SO40 24 D5
Salmon Dr *ELGH* SO50 21 H4
Salterns La *FAWY* SO45 73 H4
HLER SO31 64 A4
Saltmarsh Rd *SHAM* SO14 3 H5
Saltmead *PTSW* SO17 41 H3 2
Salwey Rd *HEND* SO30 56 D2
Sampan Cl *HLER* SO31 71 E4
Sandhurst Rd *WSHM* SO15 52 D1
Sandlewood Cl *TOTT* SO40 37 E4 8
Sandown Rd *WSHM* SO15 39 H3
Sandpiper Rd *ROWN* SO16 27 G4
Sandringham Cl *NBAD* SO52 18 D2
Sandringham Rd *WEND* SO18 42 A3
Sandycroft *HLER* SO31 70 D5
Sandy La *ELGH* SO50 22 B4
NBAD SO52 17 H1 1
Saracens Rd *CHFD* SO53 10 B4
Sarnia Ct *ROWN* SO16 39 E1
Sarum Rd *CHFD* SO53 10 A5
Satchell La *HLER* SO31 70 A2
Saturn Cl *ROWN* SO16 27 F5
Savernake Cl *ROMY* SO51 6 B2 3
Saville Cl *ELGH* SO50 21 F1
Saxholm Cl *ROWN* SO16 28 D3
Saxholm Dl *ROWN* SO16 28 D3
Saxholm Wy *ROWN* SO16 28 D3
Saxon Cl *HLER* SO31 71 E4
Saxon Gdns *HEND* SO30 56 A2
Saxon Rd *WSHM* SO15 52 B2
Saxon Wy *ROMY* SO51 6 B4
Sayers Rd *ELGH* SO50 21 F4
Scantabout Av *CHFD* SO53 10 A4
School Cl *CHFD* SO53 19 F1
School La *CHFD* SO53 19 E2
HLER SO31 70 A4
School Rd *FAWY* SO45 67 E1
FAWY SO45 73 H5
HLER SO31 64 A2
ROMY SO51 6 C2
TOTT SO40 50 A1
Schooner Wy *HLER* SO31 71 F4
Scotland Cl *ELGH* SO50 23 E4
Scott Cl *RWIN* SO21 12 A3
Scotter Rd *ELGH* SO50 21 F3
Scott Rd *ELGH* SO50 20 B4
ITCH SO19 62 B1
Scullards La *SHAM* SO14 2 D2
Seacombe Gn *ROWN* SO16 38 D3
Seafield Rd *ROWN* SO16 38 D2
Seaford Cl *HLER* SO31 63 H1 6
Seagarth La *ROWN* SO16 40 B1
Sea Rd *ITCH* SO19 53 H3
Seaton Cl *WEND* SO18 43 E3
Seaward Rd *FAWY* SO45 67 F2
ITCH SO19 54 A3
Second Av *WSHM* SO15 38 D5
Second St *FAWY* SO45 68 A5
Sedbergh Rd *ROWN* SO16 38 D3
Sedgefield Cl *TOTT* SO40 37 E4
Sedgemead *HLER* SO31 62 D5 1
Sedgewick Rd *ELGH* SO50 21 F3
ITCH SO19 55 E2
Selborne Av *WEND* SO18 43 E4
Selbourne Dr *ELGH* SO50 20 C2
Selbourne Rd *TOTT* SO40 37 F4 2
Selhurst Wy *ELGH* SO50 22 C5
Sellwood Rd *HLER* SO31 63 E4
Selsdon Av *ROMY* SO51 6 B3
Selsey Cl *ROWN* SO16 39 E2
Selwyn Gdns *ELGH* SO50 20 C1
Sengana Cl *HEND* SO30 56 D1 7
Senlac Rd *ROMY* SO51 6 B4
Seps 4 Rd *FAWY* SO45 73 H4
September Cl *HEND* SO30 43 F3
Serle Cl *TOTT* SO40 36 D5
Serle Gdns *TOTT* SO40 49 F1
Setters Cl *RWIN* SO21 11 H3
Settle Cl *ROWN* SO16 39 H4 3
Severn Rd *ROWN* SO16 39 E4
Severn Wy *HEND* SO30 43 F3 5
Seward Ri *ROMY* SO51 6 C3 1
Seymour Cl *CHFD* SO53 20 A1
TOTT SO40 37 E3
Seymour La *NBAD* SO52 17 F2
Seymour Rd *ROWN* SO16 40 A1
Shaftesbury Av *CHFD* SO53 19 G2
PTSW SO17 41 F3
Shaggs Meadow *LYND* SO43 58 D5
Shakespeare Dr *TOTT* SO40 37 F2
Shakespeare Rd *ELGH* SO50 20 C2
Shalcombe *HLER* SO31 63 E3
Shaldon Cl *ROWN* SO16 27 H5
Shales Rd *WEND* SO18 42 D5
Shamblehurst La *HEND* SO30 44 C3
Shamblehurst La North
BPWT SO32 44 D1
Shamblehurst La South
HEND SO30 44 C4
Shamrock Rd *ITCH* SO19 53 H4 4
Shamrock Wy *FAWY* SO45 61 E5
Shanklin Crs *WSHM* SO15 40 B3
Shanklin Rd *WSHM* SO15 40 B2
Shannon Wy *CHFD* SO53 9 F5
Shapton Cl *FAWY* SO45 72 B4 1
Sharon Rd *HEND* SO30 43 E2
Shaw Cl *TOTT* SO40 37 F5 5
WEND SO18 42 C2
Shawford Cl *ROWN* SO16 28 C5 1
TOTT SO40 36 D5 2
Shears Rd *ELGH* SO50 21 G3
Sheffield Cl *ELGH* SO50 21 F1
Sheldrake Gdns *ROWN* SO16 27 H4
Shellcroft *HLER* SO31 70 D5 6
Shelley La *ROMY* SO51 14 A5

Shelley Rd *ELGH* SO50 .... 20 B5
  ITCH SO19 .... 55 F1
  TOTT SO40 .... 37 F2
Shepherds Cl *TOTT* SO40 .... 47 F1
Shepherds Hey Rd
  TOTT SO40 .... 36 D3
Shepherds Purse Cl
  HLER SO31 .... 71 F3 🔟
Shepherds Rd *TOTT* SO40 .... 47 F1
Shepherds Wy *ROWN* SO16 ...... 26 C4
Sherborne Ct *ELGH* SO50 .... 10 B5
Sherborne Rd *PTSW* SO17 .... 41 F2
Sherborne Wy *HEND* SO30 .... 56 C1
Sheridan Cl *ITCH* SO19............ 55 E2
Sheridan Gdns *TOTT* SO40 .... 37 F5
Sherringham Cl *FAWY* SO45 ...... 73 H5
Sherwood Av *HEND* SO30 .... 56 C3
Sherwood Cl *ROWN* SO16 .... 40 C1 🔟
Sherwood Gdns *HLER* SO31 ...... 71 E1
Sherwood Rd *CHFD* SO53 .... 10 A2
Shetland Cl *TOTT* SO40 .... 36 D4
Shetland Ri *HLER* SO31 .... 65 H4
Shire Cl *HLER* SO31.................. 65 H3
The Shires *HEND* SO30.............. 56 A1
Shirley Av *WSHM* SO15 .... 40 A4
Shirley High St *WSHM* SO16 ...... 39 H4
Shirley Park Rd *ROWN* SO16 ...... 39 H4
Shirley Rd *WSHM* SO15 .... 40 A4
Sholing Rd *ITCH* SO19.............. 54 A3
Shooters Hill Cl *ITCH* SO19 ...... 54 D4
Shop La *HLER* SO31 .... 55 C4
Shorefield Rd *TOTT* SO40 .... 51 F5
Shore Rd *FAWY* SO45................ 67 F1
Shorewell *HLER* SO31................ 63 E3 🔟
Shorewood Cl *HLER* SO31.......... 71 G4
Short HI *ROMY* SO51 .... 6 C2
Shorts Rd *ELGH* SO50................ 22 B4
Shraveshill Cl *TOTT* SO40 .... 37 F3
Shrubland Cl *WEND* SO18 .... 42 D4
The Sidings *HLER* SO31 .... 63 F5
Silkin Gdns *TOTT* SO40.............. 49 F1
Silver Birches *HLER* SO31 .... 63 H2
Silverdale Rd *WSHM* SO15 .... 40 C5
Silvers End *FAWY* SO45 .... 67 E4 🔟
Silver St *LYND* SO43 .... 58 B5
Silvers Wd *TOTT* SO40 .... 37 E5
Simmons Cl *HEND* SO30 .... 44 C4
Simnel St *SHAM* SO14.............. 2 D4 🔟
Simon Wy *WEND* SO18 .... 43 G5
Sinclair Rd *ROWN* SO16 .... 27 C4
Singleton Wy *TOTT* SO40 .... 36 D4
Sir Christopher Cl *FAWY* SO45 .. 67 F1 🔟
Sirdar Rd *PTSW* SO17 .... 41 C1
Sir Galahad Rd *NBAD* SO52 ...... 8 D5 🔟
Sir George's Rd *WSHM* SO15 .... 52 B1
Sir Lancelot Cl *NBAD* SO52 ...... 8 D5
Siskin Cl *ROWN* SO16 .... 27 C4
Sissinghurst Cl *ITCH* SO19........ 62 C1
Six Oaks Rd *NBAD* SO52 .... 17 C1
Sixpenny Cl *HLER* SO31............ 71 G4
Sizer Wy *FAWY* SO45 .... 66 A1
Skipton Rd *CHFD* SO53 .... 19 H2
Skys Wood Rd *NBAD* SO52 ...... 8 D4
Slater Cl *TOTT* SO40 .... 36 D4
Sloane Av *FAWY* SO45 .... 72 D4 🔟
Sloane Ct *FAWY* SO45 .... 72 D4 🔟
Smithe Cl *ELGH* SO50 .... 20 C3 🔟
Smith Gv *HEND* SO30 .... 56 C2
Smith's Fld *ROMY* SO51 .... 6 A2 🔟
Smythe Rd *ITCH* SO19 .... 55 F4
Snakemoor La *BPWT* SO32 ...... 33 E4
Snapdragon Cl *HLER* SO31 ...... 71 F3 🔟
Snellgrove Cl *TOTT* SO40.......... 37 E2
Snellgrove Pl *TOTT* SO40 .... 37 E2 🔟
Solent Av *ITCH* SO19 .... 55 C1
Solent Cl *CHFD* SO53 .... 10 A5
Solent Dr *FAWY* SO45................ 66 D1
Solent Mdw *HLER* SO31 .... 70 A4
Solent Rd *FAWY* SO45 .... 66 C5
Solent Wy *SHAM* SO14.............. 2 E6
Solona Cl *CHFD* SO53 .... 10 B4 🔟
Somerford Cl *ITCH* SO19 .... 54 C1 🔟
Somerset Av *WEND* SO18.......... 43 E5
Somerset Crs *CHFD* SO53 .... 19 C3
Somerset Rd *PTSW* SO17 .... 41 C2
Somerset Ter *WSHM* SO15 .... 51 H1
Somerton Av *WEND* SO18.......... 42 D5
Sopwith Wy *HLER* SO31 .... 65 E2
Sorrel Cl *ROMY* SO51 .... 6 C2
Sorrell Cl *HLER* SO31 .... 71 F3
Southampton Rd *ELGH* SO50 .... 30 C1
  FAWY SO45 .... 66 C1
  FAWY SO45 .... 67 E2
  LYND SO43 .... 59 C4
  ROMY SO51 .... 6 A5
  TOTT SO40 .... 34 C4
  TOTT SO40 .... 34 D5
Southampton St *WSHM* SO15 .. 52 D1 🔟

South Av *FAWY* SO45 .... 73 E5
Southbourne Av *FAWY* SO45 .... 72 C4
Southcliff Rd *SHAM* SO14.......... 41 E5
South Ct *ROMY* SO51 .... 6 C2 🔟
South Ct *HLER* SO31................ 69 C3
Southdene Rd *CHFD* SO53 .... 19 C1
South East Crs *ITCH* SO19 .... 54 C3
South East Rd *ITCH* SO19 .... 54 C3
Southern Gdns *TOTT* SO40 .... 37 C5
Southern Rd *HEND* SO30 .... 43 F4
  WSHM SO15 .... 2 A2
South Front *SHAM* SO14............ 3 F2
South Millers Dl *CHFD* SO53 ...... 9 F4
South Mill Rd *WSHM* SO15 ...... 39 F5
South Rd *PTSW* SO17................ 41 C4
South St *ELGH* SO50 .... 30 C1
  FAWY SO45 .... 67 E2
South View Rd *WSHM* SO15...... 40 B4
South Wood Gdns *HLER* SO31 .. 71 C4
Sovereign Crs *FHAM/STUB* PO14.. 71 C4
Sovereign Dr *HEND* SO30 .... 56 D1
Sovereign Wy *ELGH* SO50.......... 10 B5
Sowden Cl *HEND* SO30 .... 44 B5
Spalding Rd *ITCH* SO19 .... 55 F2
Spaniard's La *ROMY* SO51........ 15 H3
Spa Rd *SHAM* SO14.................. 2 D3
Sparrow Sq *ELGH* SO50 .... 19 H4
Sparsholt Rd *ITCH* SO19 .... 54 D4
Speakers Corner Rbt *SHAM* SO14 .. 2 E4
Spear Rd *SHAM* SO14 .... 41 E4
Speedwell Cl *HLER* SO31 .... 71 F3 🔟
Speggs Wk *HEND* SO30 .... 56 C1
Spencer Rd *ELGH* SO50 .... 20 A4
  ITCH SO19 .... 55 F1
Spenser Cl *HLER* SO31 .... 70 D5 🔟
Spicer's HI *TOTT* SO40 .... 49 H2
Spicer's Wy *TOTT* SO40 .... 49 C1
Spindlewood Cl *ROWN* SO16 .... 29 E3
Spinney Dl *FAWY* SO45.............. 67 F3 🔟
Spinney Gdns *FAWY* SO45 .... 67 F3 🔟
The Spinney *ELGH* SO50 .... 22 A4
  ROWN SO16 .... 28 D3
  TOTT SO40 .... 37 E3
Spinney Wk *WEND* SO18 .... 42 B1
Spitfire Loop *ELGH* SO50 .... 30 B2
Spitfire Wy *HLER* SO31 .... 69 H5
Spring Cl *ELGH* SO50 .... 22 C4
  ITCH SO19 .... 54 B3
Spring Crs *PTSW* SO17.............. 41 F4
Springfield Av *FAWY* SO45 .... 72 D4
Springfield Dr *TOTT* SO40 .... 49 C1 🔟
Springfield Gv *FAWY* SO45........ 72 D4
Springfields Cl *ROWN* SO21 ...... 11 H2
Springford Cl *ROWN* SO16 .... 27 H5
Springford Crs *ROWN* SO16 ...... 39 H1
Springford Gdns *ROWN* SO16 .... 27 H5
Springford Rd *ROWN* SO16 ...... 39 H1
Spring Gdns *NBAD* SO52 .... 17 F1
Spring Gv *HLER* SO31 .... 64 A1
Springhill Rd *CHFD* SO53.......... 9 C5
Spring Hills *ITCH* SO19 .... 55 E3
Spring La *ELGH* SO50 .... 21 F3
  RWIN SO21 .... 11 H2
Spring Pl *ROMY* SO51 .... 5 C4 🔟
Spring Rd *FAWY* SO45 .... 67 E1
  HLER SO31 .... 65 F4
  ITCH SO19 .... 54 B1
Spruce Cl *HLER* SO31 .... 70 D5
Spruce Dr *ITCH* SO19 .... 55 C2
The Square *FAWY* SO45 .... 73 H5 🔟
Squires Wk *ITCH* SO19 .... 62 A1
Squirrel Cl *ELGH* SO50 .... 21 H4 🔟
Squirrel Dr *ITCH* SO19 .... 54 C4
Squirrels Wk *FAWY* SO45 .... 66 D3
Stafford Rd *WSHM* SO15............ 40 B5
Stagbrake Cl *FAWY* SO45 .... 72 B5 🔟
Stag Cl *ELGH* SO50 .... 21 H4
Stainer Cl *ITCH* SO19 .... 55 F4
Staith Cl *ITCH* SO19 .... 55 E2
Stalybridge Cl *HLER* SO31 .... 65 C4
Stamford Wy *ELGH* SO50 .... 22 C5 🔟
Standen Rd *ROWN* SO16 .... 26 C4
Standford St *SHAM* SO14 .... 3 H3 🔟
Stanier Wy *HEND* SO30 .... 44 C2
Stanley Rd *FAWY* SO45 .... 72 D4
  PTSW SO17 .... 41 C3
  TOTT SO40 .... 37 F3
Stannington Crs *TOTT* SO40 ...... 37 H4
Stannington Wy *TOTT* SO40 ...... 37 H4
Stanstead Rd *ELGH* SO50 .... 20 B2
Stanton Rd *WSHM* SO15 .... 39 F5
Stapleford Cl *ROMY* SO51 .... 6 B1
Stapleford La *BPWT* SO32........ 33 F4
Staplehurst Cl *ITCH* SO19 .... 62 C2
Starling Sq *ELGH* SO50 .... 19 H4 🔟
Station HI *ELGH* SO50 .... 20 D3
  HLER SO31 .... 64 B3

Station La *CHFD* SO53 .... 9 C5
Station Rd *HLER* SO31 .... 20 D5
  HLER SO31 .... 64 B2
  ITCH SO19 .... 54 C4
  ROMY SO51 .... 5 C4
  ROWN SO16 .... 26 A5
  WSHM SO15 .... 38 C4
Station Rd North *TOTT* SO40 .... 38 A5 🔟
Station Rd South *TOTT* SO40 .... 38 B5 🔟
Steele Cl *CHFD* SO53 .... 19 H2
Stenbury Wy *HLER* SO31 .... 63 E3
Stephenson Rd *TOTT* SO40 .... 37 F2
Stephenson Wy *HEND* SO30...... 44 B1
Steuart Rd *WEND* SO18 .... 41 H5
Steventon Rd *WEND* SO18 .... 43 E5
Stinchar Dr *CHFD* SO53 .... 19 E1
Stirling Cl *TOTT* SO40 .... 38 A4
Stirling Crs *HEND* SO30 .... 44 C3
  TOTT SO40 .... 38 A4
Stockholm Dr *HEND* SO30 .... 56 C2 🔟
Stockley Cl *FAWY* SO45 .... 72 C5 🔟
Stockton Cl *HEND* SO30............ 44 D5 🔟
Stoddart Av *ITCH* SO19 .... 54 B1
Stoke Common Rd *ELGH* SO50 .. 21 C1
Stoke Hts *ELGH* SO50 .... 22 B3
Stoke Park Rd *ELGH* SO50 .... 21 C2
Stoke Rd *ROWN* SO16 .... 39 C3
Stokesay Cl *FAWY* SO45............ 67 E5 🔟
Stoke Wood Cl *ELGH* SO50 ...... 22 B4 🔟
Stonechat Dr *TOTT* SO40 .... 37 F5
Stone Crop Cl *HLER* SO31 .... 71 E4
Stoneham Cemetery Rd
  WEND SO18 .... 30 B5
Stoneham Cl *ROWN* SO16 .... 29 H4 🔟
Stoneham La *ELGH* SO50 .... 30 A1
  ROWN SO16 .... 29 H4
Stoneham Wy *ELGH* SO50 .... 30 B5
Stonymoor Cl *FAWY* SO45 .... 72 C5
Stour Cl *WEND* SO18 .... 42 C1
Stourvale Gdns *CHFD* SO53 ...... 19 H1
Stowe Cl *HEND* SO30 .... 44 D3
The Straight Mile *ROMY* SO51 .. 7 E2
Strand *SHAM* SO14.................... 2 E3
Stratfield Dr *CHFD* SO53 .... 9 F2 🔟
Stratford Pl *ELGH* SO50 .... 20 D2 🔟
Stratton Rd *WSHM* SO15............ 40 A3
Strawberry HI *HLER* SO31 .... 71 F2
Street End *NBAD* SO52 .... 17 H1
Strides Wy *TOTT* SO40 .... 36 D5
Strongs Cl *ROMY* SO51 .... 6 B3 🔟
Stroudley Wy *HEND* SO30.......... 44 D2
Stroudwood La *BPWT* SO32 ...... 23 C3
  RWIN SO21 .... 23 C1
Stubbington Wy *ELGH* SO50 .... 22 D5
Stubbs Dro *HEND* SO30............ 44 D5
Stubbs Rd *ITCH* SO19 .... 55 E5 🔟
Studland Cl *ROWN* SO16 .... 38 D3
Studland Rd *ROWN* SO16 .... 38 D3
Studley Av *FAWY* SO45 .... 72 C5
Suffolk Av *WSHM* SO15............ 40 C5
Suffolk Cl *CHFD* SO53 .... 19 C4
Suffolk Dr *CHFD* SO53 .... 19 C4
  FHAM PO15 .... 65 H3
  FHAM PO15 .... 65 H3
Sullivan Rd *ITCH* SO19 .... 55 F4 🔟
Summerfield Gdns
  ROWN SO16 .... 29 H4 🔟
Summerfields
  FHAM/STUB PO14 .... 71 H4
Summerlands Rd *ELGH* SO50 .... 22 C4
Summers St *SHAM* SO14 .... 53 F1
Summit Wy *WEND* SO18 .... 42 B3
Sunningdale *FAWY* SO45 .... 66 D3
Sunningdale Cl *ELGH* SO50 ...... 21 H4 🔟
Sunningdale Gdns
  WEND SO18 .... 42 D5 🔟
Sunninghill Ri *HLER* SO31 .... 64 A1 🔟
Sunny Wy *TOTT* SO40 .... 37 H5 🔟
Sunset Av *TOTT* SO40................ 37 C4
Sunset Rd *TOTT* SO40 .... 37 C4
Sunvale Cl *ITCH* SO19 .... 54 D4
Surbiton Rd *ELGH* SO50 .... 20 D1
Surrey Cl *TOTT* SO40 .... 49 F2
Surrey Rd *CHFD* SO53 .... 19 C3
  ITCH SO19 .... 53 H5
Sussex Rd *CHFD* SO53 .... 19 H3
  SHAM SO14...................... 2 E2
Sutherland Rd *ROMY* SO51 ...... 6 B2 🔟
Sutherland Rd *ROWN* SO16 ...... 27 F4
Sutherlands Ct *CHFD* SO53 ...... 9 C5 🔟
Sutherlands Wy *CHFD* SO53 .... 9 F4
Sutton Rd *TOTT* SO40 .... 37 C4
Swale Dr *CHFD* SO53 .... 9 E4
Swallow Cl *TOTT* SO40 .... 48 D1
Swallow Sq *ELGH* SO50 .... 19 H4 🔟
Swanage Cl *ITCH* SO19 .... 54 A4
Swan Cl *HLER* SO31 .... 64 D3
Swanley Cl *ELGH* SO50.............. 20 C1

Swanmore Av *ITCH* SO19 .... 54 D4
Swanton Gdns *CHFD* SO53 .... 9 F4
Swanwick La *HLER* SO31 .... 64 D2
Swanwick Shore Rd
  HLER SO31 .... 64 D3 🔟
Swaythling Rd *HEND* SO30........ 42 D2
Sweethills Crs *HLER* SO31 .... 65 H2
Swift Cl *ELGH* SO50 .... 19 H4
Swift Gdns *ITCH* SO19 .... 61 H1
Swift Hollow *ITCH* SO19 .... 61 H1 🔟
Swift Rd *ITCH* SO19 .... 61 H1
Swincombe Ri *WEND* SO18 ...... 42 D3 🔟
Sycamore Av *CHFD* SO53 .... 9 C2
Sycamore Cl *HLER* SO31 .... 63 H2
  NBAD SO52 .... 17 F1
  ROMY SO51 .... 6 C5
Sycamore Dr *FAWY* SO45 .... 72 B3
Sycamore Rd *FAWY* SO45 .... 66 D2
  ROWN SO16 .... 39 C2
Sydmanton Cl *ROMY* SO51 ...... 6 A5 🔟
Sydney Av *HLER* SO31 .... 69 C2
Sydney Rd *ELGH* SO50 .... 21 F2
  WSHM SO15 .... 39 H3
Sylvan Av *ITCH* SO19 .... 55 E1
Sylvan Dr *NBAD* SO52 .... 17 F2
Sylvan La *HLER* SO31 .... 70 A3
The Sylvans *FAWY* SO45 .... 66 B2 🔟
Sylvia Crs *TOTT* SO40 .... 37 C3
Symes Rd *ROMY* SO51 .... 6 B4
Symonds Cl *CHFD* SO53 .... 19 H2

Tadburn Cl *CHFD* SO53 .... 19 H1
  ROMY SO51 .... 6 A4 🔟
Tadburn Rd *ROMY* SO51 .... 6 A5
Tadfield Rd *ROMY* SO51 .... 6 A4
Talbot Cl *ROWN* SO16 .... 28 D5
Talbot Ct *SHAM* SO14 .... 53 F2 🔟
Talbot Rd *FAWY* SO45 .... 66 B4
Talland Rd *FHAM/STUB* PO14...... 71 H4
Tamar Gv *FAWY* SO45................ 66 C2
Tamarisk Gdns *WEND* SO18 ...... 42 A4
Tamarisk Rd *HEND* SO30 .... 44 B5
Tamella Rd *HEND* SO30 .... 57 E1
Tamorisk Dr *TOTT* SO40 .... 49 E1
Tangmere Dr *ROWN* SO16.......... 27 F5
Tanhouse Cl *HEND* SO30 .... 56 C2
Tanhouse La *HEND* SO30 .... 56 D2
Tankerville Rd *ITCH* SO19.......... 54 B5
Tanner's Brook Wy *WSHM* SO15 .. 51 F1
Tanners Rd *NBAD* SO52 .... 17 C2
Tansy Meadow *NBAD* SO52 ...... 18 D2 🔟
The Tanyards *CHFD* SO53 .... 9 F2 🔟
Taplin Dr *HEND* SO30 .... 44 C4
Taranto Rd *ROWN* SO16 .... 28 A5
Tasman Cl *SHAM* SO14.............. 3 H7
Tatchbury La *TOTT* SO40 .... 36 B3
Tate Rd *WSHM* SO15 .... 38 C4
Tates Rd *FAWY* SO45 .... 67 F2 🔟
  FAWY SO45 .... 67 F3 🔟
Tatwin Cl *ITCH* SO19 .... 55 F2
Tatwin Crs *ITCH* SO19 .... 55 F2
Taunton Dr *WEND* SO18 .... 42 D5
Taverners Cl *ITCH* SO19 .... 55 F4
Tavistock Cl *ROMY* SO51 .... 6 B2 🔟
Tavy Cl *CHFD* SO53 .... 9 F5
Taw Dr *CHFD* SO53 .... 9 F4
Teachers Wy *FAWY* SO45 .... 72 B5 🔟
Teal Cl *TOTT* SO40 .... 37 E5 🔟
Tebourba Wy *WSHM* SO15 .... 39 F5
Tedder Rd *WEND* SO18 .... 42 C4
Tedder Wy *TOTT* SO40 .... 37 F5
Tees Cl *CHFD* SO53 .... 9 E4
Telegraph Rd *HEND* SO30 .... 43 C4
Telford Gdns *HEND* SO30 .... 44 D2 🔟
Teme Crs *ROWN* SO16 .... 39 E4
Teme Rd *ROWN* SO16 .... 39 E4 🔟
Templars Mede *CHFD* SO53 ...... 19 F3
Templars Wy *NBAD* SO52 .... 18 D2
Templecombe Rd *ELGH* SO50.... 21 H4
Temple Gdns *ITCH* SO19 .... 54 B5 🔟
Temple Rd *ITCH* SO19 .... 54 B5
Tenby Cl *WEND* SO18 .... 42 C4
Tenby Dr *CHFD* SO53 .... 19 E2
Tench Wy *ROMY* SO51 .... 6 A4
Tennyson Rd *FAWY* SO45.......... 72 B3 🔟
Tennyson Rd *ELGH* SO50 .... 20 B4
  PTSW SO17 .... 41 F4
  TOTT SO40 .... 37 F2
Tenterton Av *ITCH* SO19 .... 62 D1
Terminus Ter *SHAM* SO14 .... 3 C5
Tern Cl *FAWY* SO45 .... 67 F3
Terrier Cl *HEND* SO30 .... 44 C1
Terriote Cl *CHFD* SO53 .... 9 C4
Testbourne Av *TOTT* SO40 .... 37 F5

Testbourne Cl TOTT SO40 .... 37 F5
Testbourne Rd TOTT SO40 .... 37 F5
Testlands Av ROWN SO16 .... 26 D3
Test La ROWN SO16 .... 38 B3
Test Rd SHAM SO14 .... 61 F2
Test Wy ROMY SO51 .... 4 C1
  TOTT SO40 .... 38 A3
Testwood Av TOTT SO40 .... 37 G3
Testwood Crs TOTT SO40 .... 37 F2
Testwood La TOTT SO40 .... 37 H3
Testwood Pl TOTT SO40 .... 38 A4
Testwood Rd WSHM SO15 .... 51 H1
Tetney Cl ROWN SO16 .... 39 E1
Teviot Rd CHFD SO53 .... 19 E1
Thackeray Rd PTSW SO17 .... 41 F4
Thames Cl WEND SO18 .... 42 D2
The Itchen Br SHAM SO14 .... 3 K5
Thetford Gdns CHFD SO53 .... 9 E4
The Thicket ROMY SO51 .... 6 C5
Third Av WSHM SO15 .... 51 F1
Thirlmere ELGH SO50 .... 20 B4
Thirlmere Rd ROWN SO16 .... 39 G2
Thirlstane Firs CHFD SO53 .... 19 F2
Thistle Rd HEND SO30 .... 56 B1
  NBAD SO52 .... 18 D1
Thomas Cl TOTT SO40 .... 49 F1
Thomas Lewis Wy PTSW SO17 .. 41 F4
Thomas Rd NBAD SO52 .... 17 G2
Thompson's La RWIN SO21 .... 13 F4
Thornbury Av WSHM SO15 .... 40 C5
Thornbury Hts CHFD SO53 .... 10 B2
Thornbury Wd CHFD SO53 .... 10 B2
Thorn Cl ELGH SO50 .... 20 C1
Thorndike Cl ROWN SO16 .... 39 G2
Thorness Cl ROWN SO16 .... 38 C3
Thornhill Av ITCH SO19 .... 55 F1
Thornhill Park Rd WEND SO18.... 43 F5
Thornhill Rd ROWN SO16 .... 28 B5
Thornleigh Rd ITCH SO19 .... 54 A5
Thornton Av HLER SO31 .... 70 C4
Thornycroft Av ITCH SO19 .... 53 H5
Thorold Rd CHFD SO53 .... 10 A2
  WEND SO18 .... 42 A3
Threefield La SHAM SO14 .... 3 F4
Three Oaks ITCH SO19 .... 55 G2
Thurmell Cl HEND SO30 .... 56 C3
Thurston Cl CHFD SO53 .... 9 H4
Tichborne Rd ELGH SO50 .... 30 B1
  WEND SO18 .... 43 F4
Tickleford Dr ITCH SO19 .... 62 C1
Tickner Rd HEND SO30 .... 56 D2
Ticonderoga Gdns ITCH SO19 ... 62 A1
Tides Reach WEND SO18.... .... 41 H4
Tides Wy TOTT SO40 .... 51 F5
Tilbrook Rd WSHM SO15 .... 39 G4
Timberly Cl FAWY SO45 .... 72 C4
Timor Cl HLER SO31 .... 65 H2
Timsbury Dr ROWN SO16 .... 39 F2
Timson Cl TOTT SO40 .... 49 E1
Tindale Rd ROWN SO16 .... 39 E2
Tinker Aly ELGH SO50 .... 30 C2
Tintern Gv WSHM SO15 .... 52 C2
Tiptree Cl ELGH SO50 .... 20 C1
Tithewood Cl CHFD SO53 .... 9 F1
Tivoli Cl CHFD SO53 .... 10 B4
Tolefrey Gdns NBAD SO52 .... 8 D5
Tollbar Wy HEND SO30 .... 44 B2
Tollgate CHFD SO53 .... 19 G4
Toogoods Wy ROWN SO16 .... 26 D4
Toothill Rd ROMY SO51 .... 16 C5
Topiary Gdns HLER SO31 .... 71 H1
Torch Cl ELGH SO50 .... 22 B4
Torcross Cl ITCH SO19 .... 54 A5
Tormead FAWY SO45 .... 66 D2
Tornay Gv NBAD SO52 .... 17 F2
Torquay Gv WSHM SO15 .... 40 A4
Torque Cl ITCH SO19 .... 10 C5
Torre Cl ELGH SO50 .... 10 C5
Torridge Gdns WEND SO18 .... 42 D1
Torrington Cl ITCH SO19 .... 54 C3
Torwood Gdns ELGH SO50 .... 21 H4
Tosson Cl ROWN SO16 .... 39 E4
Totland Cl ROWN SO16 .... 39 E4
Totnes Cl ELGH SO50 .... 20 B1
Tottehale Cl NBAD SO52 .... 17 F3
Totton By-pass TOTT SO40 .... 50 A1
Tower La ROWN SO16 .... 26 B4
Tower Pl HEND SO30 .... 43 F3
Townhill Wy WEND SO18 .... 42 C3
Town Quay SHAM SO14.... .... 2 D6
Toynbee Cl ELGH SO50 .... 20 C3
Toynbee Rd ELGH SO50 .... 20 C3
Trafalgar Cl CHFD SO53 .... 19 F1
Trafalgar Rd WSHM SO15 .... 52 A1
Trafalgar Wy FAWY SO45 .... 67 F4
Trafford Wy ELGH SO50 .... 22 B5
Tranby Rd ITCH SO19 .... 54 A3
Treagore Rd TOTT SO40 .... 37 E3

Trearnan Cl ROWN SO16 .... 39 F4
Treeside Av TOTT SO40 .... 38 A5
Treeside Rd WSHM SO15 .... 40 A4
Treloyhan Cl CHFD SO53 .... 19 H2
Tremona Rd ROWN SO16 .... 39 H1
Trenley Cl FAWY SO45 .... 72 C5
Trent Cl WEND SO18 .... 42 B3
Trent Rd WEND SO18 .... 42 B3
Tresillian Gdns WEND SO18 .... 42 D2
Trevone Cl TOTT SO40 .... 49 G2
Trevose Cl CHFD SO53 .... 19 H2
Trevose Crs CHFD SO53 .... 19 H2
Trevose Wy FHAM/STUB PO14.... 71 H4
Trimaran Cl HLER SO31 .... 71 E4
Trimaran Rd HLER SO31 .... 71 E4
Trotts La TOTT SO40.... .... 50 C3
Trowbridge Cl ROWN SO16 .... 27 E3
Truro Ri ELGH SO50 .... 21 G3
Tudor Cl TOTT SO40 .... 37 E4
Tudor Gdns HEND SO30.... .... 56 A2
Tudor Wood Cl ROWN SO16 .... 28 D5
Tuffin Cl ROWN SO16 .... 26 C4
Tulip Gdns HLER SO31 .... 71 F2
Tulip Rd ROWN SO16 .... 29 G5
Tumulus Cl ITCH SO19 .... 55 H3
Tunstall Rd ITCH SO19 .... 55 G3
Turnpike Wy HEND SO30 .... 56 A1
Turnstone Gdns ROWN SO16 .... 27 H4
Tuscan Wk CHFD SO53 .... 10 A5
The Tussocks TOTT SO40.... .... 51 F5
Tutland Rd NBAD SO52 .... 17 F2
Tutor Cl HLER SO31 .... 69 H2
Tweed Cl CHFD SO53 .... 9 E4
Twiggs End Cl HLER SO31 .... 71 F1
Twyford Av WSHM SO15 .... 40 A3
Twyford Rd ELGH SO50 .... 10 D5
The Tyleshades ROMY SO51 .... 6 A5
Tyne Cl CHFD SO53 .... 19 E1
Tyne Wy HEND SO30 .... 43 G2
Tyrell Rd CHFD SO53 .... 9 G4
Tytherley Rd WEND SO18 .... 43 E4

U

Ullswater Av WEND SO18 .... 42 D3
Ullswater Rd ROWN SO16 .... 39 E3
Underwood Cl ROWN SO16 .... 28 C5
Underwood Rd ELGH SO50 .... 21 F2
  ROWN SO16 .... 28 C5
Union Rd SHAM SO14 .... 53 F1
University Crs PTSW SO17 .... 41 F1
University Pkwy ROWN SO16 .... 18 A5
University Rd PTSW SO17 .... 41 E1
Unwin Cl ITCH SO19 .... 61 H1
Uplands Wy PTSW SO17 .... 41 E2
Upper Banister St
  WSHM SO15 .... 52 D1
Upper Barn Copse ELGH SO50 ... 22 B3
Upper Brook Dr HLER SO31 .... 71 E3
Upper Brownhill Rd
  ROWN SO16 .... 39 F1
Upper Bugle St SHAM SO14 .... 2 D4
Upper Crescent Rd NBAD SO52 .. 17 F2
Upper Deacon Rd ITCH SO19 .... 54 D1
Upper Market St ELGH SO50 .... 20 D3
Upper Mead Cl ELGH SO50 .... 22 D4
Upper Moors Rd ELGH SO50.... 11 H2
  RWIN SO21 .... 11 H2
Upper Mullin's La FAWY SO45 .... 66 C2
Upper New Rd HEND SO30 .... 43 F3
Upper Northam Cl HEND SO30 ... 56 A1
Upper Northam Dr HEND SO30 ... 55 G1
Upper Northam Rd HEND SO30.... 44 A5
Upper St Helens Rd HEND SO30 .. 56 B3
Upper Shaftesbury Av
  PTSW SO17 .... 41 F2
Upper Shirley Av WSHM SO15 .... 40 A3
Upper Spinney HLER SO31 .... 70 C5
Upper Toothill Rd ROWN SO16 .... 17 E5
Upper Weston La ITCH SO19 .... 54 C5
Upton Crs ROWN SO16 .... 26 C2
Upton La ROWN SO16 .... 26 B4

V

Vale Dr WEND SO18 .... 42 B3
Valentine Av ITCH SO19 .... 55 E4
Valerian Cl HEND SO30 .... 32 C3
Valerian Rd HEND SO30 .... 56 C1
The Vale FAWY SO45 .... 66 D2
  HLER SO31 .... 71 H3
Valley Cl RWIN SO21 .... 11 H3
Valleydene FAWY SO45 .... 66 D3
Valley Ri HLER SO31 .... 71 E1

Valley Rd CHFD SO53 .... 9 G4
  TOTT SO40 .... 49 H2
Vanburgh Wy CHFD SO53 .... 9 F2
Vanguard Rd WEND SO18 .... 42 C4
Vardy Cl ITCH SO19 .... 55 F4
Varna Rd WSHM SO15 .... 52 A2
Vaudrey Cl WSHM SO15 .... 40 A3
Vaughan Cl ITCH SO19 .... 55 G2
Vaughan Rd FAWY SO45 .... 66 A1
Vear's La RWIN SO21 .... 12 A3
Vellan Ct ROWN SO16 .... 38 C3
Velmore Rd CHFD SO53 .... 19 F2
Velsheda Ct FAWY SO45 .... 66 D5
Venture Rd ROWN SO16 .... 18 B5
Verbena Wy HEND SO30 .... 56 D1
Verdon Av HLER SO31 .... 69 G2
Vermont Cl ROWN SO16 .... 28 D5
Verona Rd CHFD SO53 .... 10 A4
Verulam Rd SHAM SO14 .... 41 F5
Vespasian Rd WEND SO18 .... 41 H5
Vespasian Wy CHFD SO53 .... 10 A5
Vesta Wy CHFD SO53 .... 10 A4
Vicarage Dr HEND SO30 .... 56 B2
Vicarage La TOTT SO40 .... 35 F3
Viceroy Rd ITCH SO19 .... 54 C4
Victena Rd ELGH SO50 .... 22 C4
Victoria Cl HLER SO31 .... 71 G4
Victoria Gld HLER SO31 .... 63 H5
Victoria Rd ELGH SO50 .... 20 D1
  HLER SO31 .... 62 C4
  ITCH SO19 .... 61 H1
Victoria St WSHM SO15 .... 3 J1
Victor St WSHM SO15 .... 40 A4
Victory Cl CHFD SO53 .... 19 F1
Victory Crs WSHM SO15 .... 51 H1
Victory Rd WSHM SO15 .... 51 H1
Victory Sq WSHM SO15 .... 51 H1
Viking Cl ROWN SO16.... .... 27 E4
The Vikings ROMY SO51 .... 6 B4
Villiers Rd FAWY SO45 .... 66 D5
  WSHM SO15 .... 40 A5
Vincent Av ROWN SO16 .... 40 A4
Vincent Rd WSHM SO15 .... 40 A4
Vincent's Gv WSHM SO15 .... 40 A4
Vincent's Wk SHAM SO14 .... 2 E4
Vine Bank WEND SO18 .... 43 E4
Vine Cl HLER SO31 .... 70 D2
Vine Rd ROWN SO16 .... 39 G1
Vinery Gdns ROWN SO16 .... 39 H2
Vinery Rd ROWN SO16 .... 40 A2
Vineyard Cl ITCH SO19 .... 53 H4
The Vineyards NBAD SO52 .... 17 G2
Viney Av ROMY SO51 .... 6 B3
Violet Cl NBAD SO52.... .... 9 E5
Violet Rd ROWN SO16 .... 29 E5
Vokes Cl ITCH SO19 .... 54 D2
Vulcan Cl WSHM SO15 .... 51 F1
Vulcan Rd WSHM SO15 .... 51 F1
Vyse La SHAM SO14 .... 2 D5

W

Wadhurst Gdns ITCH SO19 .... 62 C2
Wadhurst Rd HEND SO30 .... 56 C1
Wakefield Ct WEND SO18 .... 42 C3
Wakefield Rd WEND SO18 .... 42 C3
Waldegrave Cl ITCH SO19 .... 61 H1
Waldon Gdns WEND SO18 .... 42 C3
Walkers Cl ELGH SO50 .... 22 D4
Wallace Rd ITCH SO19 .... 62 B1
Wallington Dr CHFD SO53.... .... 9 E3
Walmer Cl ELGH SO50 .... 10 C4
Walnut Av WEND SO18 .... 30 A4
Walnut Cl CHFD SO53 .... 9 G1
  ROWN SO16 .... 39 G3
Walnut Gv ROWN SO16 .... 39 F4
Wainwright Gdns HEND SO30 .... 44 C1
Walpole La HLER SO31 .... 65 E3
Walsingham Gdns WEND SO18 ... 42 A1
Waltham Crs ROWN SO16 .... 27 H5
Walton Rd ITCH SO19 .... 55 F3
Waltons Av FAWY SO45 .... 72 D4
Wansbeck Cl CHFD SO53 .... 19 F1
Warbler Cl ROWN SO16 .... 27 H3
Warblington Cl CHFD SO53 .... 19 F3
Warburton Cl ITCH SO19 .... 55 G3
Warburton Rd ITCH SO19 .... 55 F2
Warden Cl HEND SO30 .... 43 F3
Wardle Rd ELGH SO50 .... 11 F4
Warlock Cl ITCH SO19 .... 55 F4
Warren Av CHFD SO53 .... 20 A1
  ROWN SO16 .... 39 G2
Warren Cl CHFD SO53 .... 20 A1
  ROWN SO16 .... 39 G2
Warren Crs ROWN SO16 .... 39 G2

Warren Pl TOTT SO40 .... 37 E2
The Warren FAWY SO45 .... 72 B5
Warrior Cl CHFD SO53 .... 19 F2
Warrys Cl FAWY SO45 .... 67 G5
Warsash Rd HLER SO31 .... 70 D4
Warwick Cl CHFD SO53 .... 19 E2
Warwick Rd TOTT SO40 .... 37 H4
  WSHM SO15 .... 40 B2
Waterbeech Dr HEND SO30 .... 44 C4
Waterhouse La WSHM SO15 .... 39 H5
Waterhouse Wy WSHM SO15.... 39 H5
Water La FAWY SO45 .... 66 C3
  TOTT SO40 .... 37 F4
Waterloo Rd WSHM SO15 .... 52 A1
Waterloo Ter WSHM SO15 .... 52 D1
Watermans La FAWY SO45 .... 66 C4
Water's Edge HEND SO30 .... 56 B1
Waterside FAWY SO45 .... 60 D5
Waterside Rd ROMY SO51 .... 6 A2
Watkin Rd HEND SO30 .... 44 D2
Watley Cl ROWN SO16 .... 26 D4
Watson Wk TOTT SO40 .... 37 E5
Watton Rd FAWY SO45 .... 72 C5
Watts Cl ROWN SO16 .... 39 E2
Watts Rd HEND SO30.... .... 44 C5
Wavell Rd WEND SO18 .... 42 C5
Waveney Gn ROWN SO16 .... 39 E3
Waverley Av HLER SO31 .... 63 F4
Waverley Cl ROMY SO51 .... 6 B2
Waverley Ct HLER SO31 .... 63 E5
Waverley Rd WSHM SO15 .... 52 B2
Wayfarer Cl HLER SO31 .... 71 F4
Waylands Pl HEND SO30 .... 56 A3
Wayside HLER SO31 .... 64 D2
Weald Cl HLER SO31 .... 71 G1
Weardale Rd CHFD SO53 .... 19 H2
Weavers Pl CHFD SO53 .... 9 F3
Weavills Rd ELGH SO50 .... 22 A4
Webburn Gdns WEND SO18 .... 42 C1
Wedgewood Cl FAWY SO45 .... 72 C4
Welbeck Av PTSW SO17 .... 41 F2
Welch Wy ROWN SO16 .... 27 E4
Welland Gdns WEND SO18 .... 42 D2
Welland Gn ROWN SO16 .... 39 E4
Wellands Rd LYND SO43 .... 58 D5
Wellbrooke Gdns CHFD SO53.... 9 F4
Wellers Cl TOTT SO40 .... 36 D5
Welles Cl CHFD SO53 .... 9 H5
Wellington Av WEND SO18 .... 42 D5
Wellington Cl FAWY SO45 .... 66 B4
Wellington Pk HEND SO30 .... 44 A3
Wellington Rd WEND SO18 .... 41 H2
Well La HLER SO31 .... 70 A3
Wellowbrook Cl CHFD SO53 .... 9 E5
Wellow Cl WEND SO18.... .... 43 E5
Wells Pl ELGH SO50 .... 20 D4
Wentworth Gdns ITCH SO19 .... 62 D1
Wentworth Gv FAWY SO45 .... 72 D5
Wesley Cl ITCH SO19 .... 55 F3
Wessex Gdns ROMY SO51 .... 6 B4
Wessex La WEND SO18 .... 29 H5
Wessex Wy RWIN SO21 .... 12 A3
West Bargate SHAM SO14 .... 2 D5
Westbourne Av FAWY SO45 .... 72 C4
Westbourne Crs PTSW SO17 .... 40 D3
Westbrook Gdns ROMY SO51 .... 5 H2
Westbrook Rd HLER SO31 .... 65 G5
Westbrook Wy WEND SO18 .... 30 A5
Westbury Ct HEND SO30.... .... 56 C2
Westbury Rd WSHM SO15 .... 39 F5
Westcot Rd FAWY SO45 .... 72 B5
West Dr ELGH SO50 .... 21 F2
Westend Rd ITCH SO19 .... 42 C5
West End Rd HEND SO30 .... 43 F3
  HEND SO30 .... 55 H3
  WEND SO18 .... 42 C4
Westering ROMY SO51 .... 6 C2
  ROMY SO51 .... 6 C3
Westerley Cl HLER SO31 .... 71 E4
Western District Cut
  WSHM SO15 .... 40 B5
Western Esp SHAM SO14 .... 2 D4
Western Rd CHFD SO53 .... 10 A2
  HEND SO30 .... 43 F3
Westfield Cl ELGH SO50 .... 32 C2
  HLER SO31 .... 69 G3
Westfield Common
  HLER SO31 .... 69 F3
Westfield Crs CHFD SO53 .... 19 G3
Westfield Rd CHFD SO53 .... 19 G3
  TOTT SO40 .... 37 H4
  WSHM SO15 .... 39 G5
Westgate St SHAM SO14 .... 2 D5
West Hill Dr FAWY SO45 .... 60 D5
West Horton La ELGH SO50 .... 21 H5
West La NBAD SO52 .... 8 B2
West Marlands Rd SHAM SO14 ... 2 D1
Westmorland Wy CHFD SO53 .... 20 A1

Weston Cl *ITCH* SO19 .... **62** B1
Weston Crs *WEND* SO18 .... **43** E5
Weston Grove Rd *ITCH* SO19 ...... **53** H5
Weston La *ITCH* SO19 .... **62** A1
  ROWN SO16 .... **26** A5
Weston Rd *ELGH* SO50 .... **20** C3
Westover Rd *ROWN* SO16 .... **38** B4
West Park Rd *WSHM* SO15 .... **2** C1
West Quay Rd *WSHM* SO15 .... **2** B3
Westridge Rd *PTSW* SO17 .... **41** F3
West Rd *FAWY* SO45 .... **66** B4
  HEND SO30 .... **55** H1
  ITCH SO19 .... **54** A5
  SHAM SO14 .... **2** E6
Westrow Gdns *WSHM* SO15 .... **40** C5
Westrow Rd *WSHM* SO15 .... **40** C5
West St *FAWY* SO45 .... **60** D5
  SHAM SO14 .... **2** D4
Westward Rd *HEND* SO30 .... **44** C4
Westway Cl *ROWN* SO16 .... **26** D3
Westways Cl *ROWN* SO16 .... **26** D4
Westwood Gdns *CHFD* SO53 .... **10** A3
Westwood Rd *HLER* SO31 .... **62** D3
  LYND SO43 .... **58** D4
  PTSW SO17 .... **40** D4
Wetherby Gdns *TOTT* SO40 .... **37** E4
Whaddon La *RWIN* SO21 .... **13** G2
Whalesmead Cl *ELGH* SO50 .... **21** H5
Whalesmead Rd *ELGH* SO50 .... **21** H5
Wharncliffe Rd *ITCH* SO19 .... **53** H4
Whartons La *TOTT* SO40 .... **49** E3
Wheat Cl *NBAD* SO52 .... **8** D5
Wheatcroft Dr *WEND* SO18 ...... **42** D3 🔢
Wheatsheaf Ct *HEND* SO30 .... **56** B1 🔢
Whernside Cl *ROWN* SO16 .... **39** F4 🔢
Whinchat Cl *ROWN* SO16 .... **27** H3
Whinfield Rd *FAWY* SO45 .... **66** C4
Whistler Rd *ITCH* SO19 .... **55** E4
Whitcombe Cl *TOTT* SO40 .... **37** G5 🔢
Whitebeam Cl *RWIN* SO21 .... **12** A3
Whitebeam Rd *HEND* SO30 .... **56** D1
Whitebeam Wy *NBAD* SO52 .... **17** G1
Whitefield Rd *FAWY* SO45 .... **72** C5
White Gates *BPWT* SO32 .... **33** H4
White Hart La *TOTT* SO40 .... **34** D4
White Hart Rd *ELGH* SO50 .... **22** C5
White Heather Ct *FAWY* SO45 ... **61** E5
White House Gdns *WSHM* SO15 .. **51** G1
Whitelaw Rd *WSHM* SO15 .... **39** H5
Whitemoor La *TOTT* SO40 .... **24** A5
Whitenap Cl *ROMY* SO51 .... **6** B5
Whitenap La *ROMY* SO51 .... **6** C5
White Rd *ELGH* SO50 .... **21** F2
Whites La *FAWY* SO45 .... **73** H5 🔢
White's Rd *ITCH* SO19 .... **54** C2
Whitestone Cl *ROWN* SO16 ..... **39** F4 🔢
Whitewater Ri *FAWY* SO45 .... **66** D3
Whithedwood Av *WSHM* SO15 .... **40** B4
Whittington Cl *FAWY* SO45 .... **66** D3
Whitwell *HLER* SO31 .... **63** E3 🔢
Whitworth Crs *WEND* SO18 .... **41** H4
Whitworth Rd *WEND* SO18 .... **41** H4
Whyte Cl *FAWY* SO45 .... **72** B5

Whyteways *ELGH* SO50 .... **20** B2
The Wicket *FAWY* SO45 .... **66** D3
Wicklow Dr *CHFD* SO53 .... **19** E1
Widecombe Dr *FAWY* SO45 .... **66** C1
Wide La *ELGH* SO50 .... **30** B2
  WEND SO18 .... **30** A4
Widgeon Cl *ROWN* SO16 .... **27** H3
Wild Arum Wy *NBAD* SO52 .... **18** D1
Wildburn Cl *TOTT* SO40 .... **37** E2
Wild Cherry Wy *NBAD* SO52 .... **9** E5 🔢
Wilde Cl *TOTT* SO40 .... **37** F5 🔢
Wilderness Hts *WEND* SO18 .... **43** E3
Wildern La *HEND* SO30 .... **44** B4
Wild Rose Crs *HLER* SO31 .... **71** E3
Wilks Cl *ROWN* SO16 .... **26** C4
William Macleod Wy
  ROWN SO16 .... **39** G4
Williams Cl *FAWY* SO45 .... **72** D5
Willis Av *NBAD* SO52 .... **17** H2
Willis Rd *ROWN* SO16 .... **29** H4
Willow Cl *HEND* SO30 .... **43** G2 🔢
  HEND SO30 .... **56** D1
Willow Ct *ROWN* SO16 .... **39** G1
Willow Gdns *NBAD* SO52 .... **17** F1
Willow Gn *RWIN* SO21 .... **12** A3
Willow Gv *ELGH* SO50 .... **22** D4
Willow Herb Cl *HLER* SO31 .... **71** E3
Willow Tree Wk *ITCH* SO19 .... **54** D4
Wills Wy *ROMY* SO51 .... **6** A5
Wilmer Rd *ELGH* SO50 .... **20** C4
Wilmington Cl *WEND* SO18 .... **42** B1
Wilmot Cl *ELGH* SO50 .... **21** G1
Wilton Av *WSHM* SO15 .... **52** C1
Wilton Crs *WSHM* SO15 .... **40** B3
Wilton Gdns *WSHM* SO15 .... **40** B3
Wilton Rd *WSHM* SO15 .... **40** B3
Wiltshire Rd *CHFD* SO53 .... **19** H3
Wimpson Gdns *ROWN* SO16 .... **39** F3
Wimpson La *ROWN* SO16 .... **39** E4
Winchester Hl *ROMY* SO51 .... **6** B3
Winchester Rd *BPWT* SO32 .... **45** E1
  CHFD SO53 .... **9** H5
  ELGH SO50 .... **22** C2
  ROMY SO51 .... **5** H3
  ROMY SO51 .... **6** D2 🔢
  ROWN SO16 .... **28** D5
  ROWN SO16 .... **39** G3
Winchester St *HEND* SO30 .... **45** G4
  WSHM SO15 .... **52** D1
Winchester Wy *TOTT* SO40 ..... **37** E5 🔢
Winchfield Cl *ITCH* SO19 .... **62** C2 🔢
Windbury Rd *ROWN* SO16 .... **39** E2
Windermere Av *ROWN* SO16 ...... **38** D2
Windermere Gdns *TOTT* SO40 ... **37** G4
Windermere Rd *WEND* SO18 ...... **42** D3
Windfield Dr *ROMY* SO51 .... **6** B3 🔢
Windmill Copse *FAWY* SO45 ..... **66** D4 🔢
Windmill La *HLER* SO31 .... **56** A5
Windover Cl *ITCH* SO19 .... **55** E1
Windrush Rd *ROWN* SO16 .... **39** E3
Windrush Wy *FAWY* SO45 .... **67** E2
Windsor Ct *ELGH* SO50 .... **21** F2 🔢

Windsor Ga *ELGH* SO50 .... **10** C5
Winfrith Wy *ROWN* SO16 .... **26** D4
Wingate Dr *ITCH* SO19 .... **54** D2
Wingate Rd *TOTT* SO40 .... **37** F4
Wingrove Rd *TOTT* SO40 .... **49** E4 🔢
Winifred Cl *ELGH* SO50 .... **22** C3 🔢
Winkle St *SHAM* SO14 .... **2** D6
Winnards Pk *HLER* SO31 .... **70** D2
Winn Rd *PTSW* SO17 .... **41** E4
Winsford Av *ELGH* SO50 .... **22** A5
Winsford Cl *ELGH* SO50 .... **22** A5 🔢
Winsford Gdns *ELGH* SO50 ..... **22** A5 🔢
Winsor La *TOTT* SO40 .... **35** H4
Winsor Rd *TOTT* SO40 .... **35** F5
  TOTT SO40 .... **50** A1
Winstanley Rd *ROWN* SO16 .... **26** C4
Winston Cl *ELGH* SO50 .... **20** C2
  ROWN SO16 .... **39** F2
Winstone Crs *NBAD* SO52 .... **17** F1
Winterbourne Rd *ROMY* SO51 ...... **6** C2 🔢
Winters Cl *FAWY* SO45 .... **72** D5
Winton St *SHAM* SO14 .... **3** F1 🔢
Witham *CHFD* SO53 .... **9** E5
Withy Cl *ROMY* SO51 .... **5** H3 🔢
Wittensford La *LYND* SO43 .... **34** A4
Wittering Rd *ROWN* SO16 .... **27** F4
Witt Rd *ELGH* SO50 .... **22** C4
Witts Hl *WEND* SO18 .... **42** C4
Woburn Cl *ELGH* SO50 .... **10** C5
Woburn Rd *ROWN* SO16 .... **27** H3
Wodehouse Rd *ITCH* SO19 .... **54** A3
Wolseley Rd *WSHM* SO15 .... **40** A5
Wolverley Ct *ROWN* SO16 .... **40** B1 🔢
Wolverton Wy *SHAM* SO14 .... **53** F2 🔢
Wolvesey Pl *CHFD* SO53 .... **19** E2 🔢
Wonston Rd *ROWN* SO16 .... **27** H3
Wood Cl *ITCH* SO19 .... **55** E4
Woodcote Rd *PTSW* SO17 .... **41** G1 🔢
Wood End Wy *NBAD* SO52 .... **9** E4
Wooderson Cl *ELGH* SO50 ...... **22** B3 🔢
Woodhouse La *HEND* SO30 .... **45** E4
Woodland Cl *WEND* SO18 .... **43** F5
Woodland Ms *HEND* SO30 .... **43** F3
Woodlands Cl *CHFD* SO53 .... **9** H1
  FAWY SO45 .... **66** C4
  HLER SO31 .... **65** F4
Woodlands Ct *FAWY* SO45 ...... **66** C4 🔢
Woodlands Dr *HLER* SO31 .... **63** F4
Woodlands Dro *TOTT* SO40 .... **48** B4
Woodlands Rd *TOTT* SO40 .... **48** A3
Woodlands Wy *HLER* SO31 .... **63** H2
  NBAD SO52 .... **17** E2
  WSHM SO15 .... **40** D4 🔢
Woodland Vw *HLER* SO31 .... **63** H2
Woodlea Gdns *HEND* SO30 .... **43** G3
Woodlea Wy *ROMY* SO51 .... **8** B3
Woodley Cl *ROMY* SO51 .... **6** C1
Woodley La *ROMY* SO51 .... **6** A2
Woodley Rd *ITCH* SO19 .... **53** H4
Woodley Wy *ROMY* SO51 .... **6** C1 🔢
Wood Ldg *TOTT* SO40 .... **36** D3
Woodmill La *WEND* SO18 .... **41** H1
Woodpecker Copse *HLER* SO31 .. **71** H2

Woodpecker Wy *ELGH* SO50 ..... **19** H4
Wood Rd *TOTT* SO40 .... **48** D5
Woodrush Crs *HLER* SO31 .... **71** E3
Woodside *ROWN* SO16 .... **18** C4
Woodside Av *ELGH* SO50 .... **20** B2
Woodside Crs *ROWN* SO16 ...... **18** B4 🔢
Woodside Gdns *TOTT* SO40 .... **49** E5
Woodside Rd *ELGH* SO50 .... **20** A2
  NBAD SO52 .... **17** F2 🔢
  PTSW SO17 .... **41** F4
Woodside Wy *HEND* SO30 .... **56** A2
Woodstock Cl *HEND* SO30 ...... **56** D2 🔢
Woodstock Dr *PTSW* SO17 ..... **41** E3 🔢
Woodthorpe Gdns *HLER* SO31 .. **65** F4
Woodview Cl *ROWN* SO16 .... **29** E3
Woodville Rd *FAWY* SO45 .... **73** H5
Woolston Rd *HLER* SO31 .... **62** D2
Woolwich Cl *HLER* SO31 .... **55** H5
Wootton *HLER* SO31 .... **63** E3 🔢
Worcester Pl *ITCH* SO19 .... **54** D5
Wordsworth Pl *HLER* SO31 .... **65** H1
Wordsworth Rd *ROWN* SO16 ..... **40** A3
Wren Rd *ELGH* SO50 .... **20** A5
Wright's Hl *ITCH* SO19 .... **54** C5
Wryneck Cl *ROWN* SO16 .... **27** H3
Wychwood Gv *CHFD* SO53 .... **10** A3
Wycliffe Rd *WEND* SO18 .... **42** C3
Wykeham Cl *ROWN* SO16 .... **28** C5 🔢
Wykeham Rd *HLER* SO31 .... **62** D4
Wylye Cl *WEND* SO18 .... **42** D4
Wyndham Pl *WSHM* SO15 .... **52** C2 🔢
Wynter Rd *WEND* SO18 .... **42** D4
Wynyards Gap *NBAD* SO52 .... **17** F2
Wyre Cl *CHFD* SO53 .... **9** H5
Wyvern Cl *CHFD* SO53 .... **9** H5

Y

Yardley Rd *HEND* SO30 .... **56** B2
Yarmouth Gdns *WSHM* SO15 ...... **39** H3
Yarrow Wy *HLER* SO31 .... **71** E3
Yaverland *HLER* SO31 .... **63** E4
Yelverton Av *FAWY* SO45 .... **67** E4
Yeomans Wy *TOTT* SO40 .... **37** H4
Yeovil Cha *WEND* SO18 .... **42** D4
Yew Rd *WEND* SO18. .... **42** C4
Yew Tree Cl *ELGH* SO50 .... **22** C3
  HEND SO30 .... **56** B1 🔢
Yewtree Cl *FAWY* SO45 .... **67** E5
Yew Tree Dr *HLER* SO31 .... **65** H3
Yewtree La *ROWN* SO16 .... **38** C1
Yonge Cl *ELGH* SO50 .... **20** D3
York Buildings *SHAM* SO14 .... **2** E3 🔢
York Cl *ELGH* SO50 .... **32** D2
  NBAD SO52 .... **18** D2
  SHAM SO14. .... **53** G1
  TOTT SO40 .... **38** A4
York Dro *WEND* SO18 .... **42** D5
Yorke Wy *HLER* SO31 .... **69** G2
York Rd *ELGH* SO50 .... **20** C5
  WSHM SO15 .... **40** A5

Index - featured places

Abbey Chiropractic Clinic
  ROMY SO51 .... **5** G4
Abbey Mead Surgery
  ROMY SO51 .... **5** F4
Abbotswood Junior School
  TOTT SO40 .... **37** F5
Alderman Quilley
  Secondary School
  ELGH SO50 .... **20** B5
Aldermoor Health Centre
  ROWN SO16 .... **28** A5
Allington Manor Business Centre
  ELGH SO50 .... **31** G2
Alma Road Surgery
  PTSW SO17 .... **41** E4
Alma Road Surgery
  ROMY SO51 .... **5** H4
The Alpha Business Park
  SHAM SO14 .... **41** F5
A M F Bowling
  ITCH SO19 .... **54** B1
Anchor Business Centre
  CHFD SO53 .... **9** F5
Applemore College
  FAWY SO45 .... **66** A3
Applemore Recreation Centre
  FAWY SO45 .... **66** A2

Associated Football Club
  TOTT SO40 .... **38** A4
Atherley House Surgery
  WSHM SO15 .... **52** B1
The Atherley School
  ROWN SO16 .... **26** B3
Avenue Clinic
  WSHM SO15 .... **52** D1
Baddesley Park Industrial Estate
  NBAD SO52 .... **17** H2
Banister School
  WSHM SO15 .... **40** D5
Bargate Museum
  SHAM SO14 .... **2** E3
Bargate Shopping Centre
  SHAM SO14 .... **2** E3
Bartley C of E Middle School
  TOTT SO40 .... **35** F5
Barton Peveril College
  ELGH SO50 .... **20** B5
Bassett Green Junior School
  ROWN SO16 .... **29** F5
BBC South TV & Radio Solent
  WSHM SO15 .... **52** C2
Beechwood Middle School
  WEND SO18 .... **42** B5

Belgrave Industrial Estate
  PTSW SO17 .... **41** G2
Bellemoor Secondary School
  ROWN SO16 .... **40** B2
Berrywood Primary School
  HEND SO30 .... **44** D3
Bevois Town Primary School
  SHAM SO14 .... **41** E5
Bitterne C of E First School
  ITCH SO19 .... **54** B1
Bitterne C of E Infant School
  ITCH SO19 .... **54** B1
Bitterne Health Centre
  WEND SO18 .... **42** C5
Bitterne Leisure Centre
  WEND SO18 .... **42** C5
Bitterne Manor Primary School
  ITCH SO19 .... **41** H5
Bitterne Middle School
  ITCH SO19 .... **54** B1
Bitterne Park Clinic
  WEND SO18 .... **42** A4
Bitterne Park Junior &
  Infant School
  WEND SO18 .... **41** H2
Bitterne Park Secondary School
  WEND SO18 .... **42** A2

Bitterne Park Surgery
  WEND SO18 .... **42** A4
Botley Junior & Infant School
  HEND SO30 .... **45** G5
Botley Park Hotel & Country Club
  BPWT SO32 .... **45** F2
Boyatt Shopping Centre
  ELGH SO50 .... **20** C1
Boyatt Wood Surgery
  ELGH SO50 .... **20** B1
Brickfield Trading Estate
  CHFD SO53 .... **19** F1
Bridge Gallery
  WSHM SO15. .... **52** D1
Broadlands House
  ROMY SO51 .... **15** G1
Brompton Gallery
  SHAM SO14 .... **3** F1
Brookes Hill Industrial Estate
  TOTT SO40 .... **24** D3
Brookfield Secondary School
  HLER SO31 .... **71** E1
Brookwood Industrial Estate
  ELGH SO50 .... **20** B3
The Brownhill Surgery
  CHFD SO53. .... **9** H4

Burgess Road Surgery
ROWN SO16 .... 29 G5
Burridge Social & Sports Club
HLER SO31 .... 57 H5
Bursledon C of E Junior & Infant
School
HLER SO31 .... 64 A2
Bursledon Windmill Museum
HLER SO31 .... 56 A5
Business Centre
SHAM SO14 .... 3 G6
By Pass Football Club
ROMY SO51 .... 5 H5
Cadnam Surgery
TOTT SO40 .... 35 E5
Calmore County Junior &
Infant School
TOTT SO40 .... 37 E2
Calmore Industrial Estate
TOTT SO40 .... 37 G2
Calmore Sports Club
TOTT SO40 .... 36 C2
Cameleon Theatre
WSHM SO15 .... 52 B1
Cantell Secondary School
ROWN SO16 .... 29 E5
The Canute Surgery
ITCH SO19 .... 54 A4
The Cedar School
ROWN SO16 .... 27 E5
Central Trading Estate
SHAM SO14 .... 3 J2
Centurion Industrial Park
PTSW SO17 .... 41 G5
Chamberlayne Park School
ITCH SO19 .... 62 C1
Chandlers Ford Infant School
CHFD SO53 .... 9 H4
Chevron Business Park
FAWY SO45 .... 72 B2
City Grove Trading Estate
ELGH SO50 .... 20 A2
City Industrial Park
WSHM SO15 .... 2 A3
Clayfields Sports Centre
FAWY SO45 .... 66 B1
The Coast Clinic
FAWY SO45 .... 73 H5
Colden Common Primary School
RWIN SO21 .... 11 H2
Commercial Business Centre
CHFD SO53 .... 9 G5
Copythorne First School
TOTT SO40 .... 35 F2
Crescent Primary School
ELGH SO50 .... 20 C3
The Crestwood
Community School
ELGH SO50 .... 20 B1
Cupernham County
Junior & Infants School
ROMY SO51 .... 6 B2
Deacon Trading Estate
ELGH SO50 .... 21 E4
Deanery Campus
SHAM SO14 .... 3 G4
Discover Bible School
WSHM SO15 .... 52 A1
Dorset Healthcare Nhs Trust
WEND SO18 .... 43 E5
Dorset Medical Centre
SHAM SO14 .... 2 E1
Dorset Medical Centre
WSHM SO15 .... 52 D2
Dr Munroe & Partners
TOTT SO40 .... 37 H4
Durley Primary School
BPWT SO32 .... 33 G3
Eastleigh Borough Council
ELGH SO50 .... 20 B3
Eastleigh College of
Further Education
ELGH SO50 .... 20 C4
Eastleigh Football Club
ELGH SO50 .... 30 A2
Eastleigh Health Centre
ELGH SO50 .... 20 C3
Eastleigh Museum
ELGH SO50 .... 20 C4
Eastleigh Rugby Club
ELGH SO50 .... 21 E3
East Street Shopping Centre
SHAM SO14 .... 3 F5
Eling County Infant School
TOTT SO40 .... 50 A1
Embley Park School
ROMY SO51 .... 4 A5

Fairisle Junior & Infant School
ROWN SO16 .... 27 E5
Fair Oak Junior & Infant School
ELGH SO50 .... 22 D5
Fawley Business Centre
FAWY SO45 .... 73 G5
Fawley County First School
FAWY SO45 .... 73 G5
Fenwick Hospital
LYND SO43 .... 58 C4
Flanders Industrial Park
HEND SO30 .... 44 B4
Fleming Park Leisure Centre
ELGH SO50 .... 20 A3
Forest Edge School
TOTT SO40 .... 37 G5
Forest Gate Surgery
TOTT SO40 .... 37 G5
Forestside Medical Practice
FAWY SO45 .... 66 C5
Foundry Lane Middle &
Primary School
WSHM SO15 .... 39 H4
Foxhills County First School
TOTT SO40 .... 49 F3
Freeground Junior &
Infant School
HEND SO30 .... 56 D1
Freemantle Business Centre
WSHM SO15 .... 52 A2
Frobisher Industrial Centre
ROMY SO51 .... 5 F2
Fryern Junior & Infant School
CHFD SO53 .... 10 A5
The Fryern Surgery
CHFD SO53 .... 10 A4
Gasholders
SHAM SO14 .... 3 H1
Glenfield Infant School
WEND SO18 .... 42 B5
Greatbridge Business Park
ROMY SO51 .... 5 F2
The Gregg School
WEND SO18 .... 42 C1
Greggs School
PTSW SO17 .... 41 E3
Group Surgery
ROWN SO16 .... 29 H5
Grove Medical Practice
WSHM SO15 .... 40 A5
Gurdwara Sikh Temple
SHAM SO14 .... 53 E1
Hall of Aviation
SHAM SO14 .... 3 H5
Halterworth CP School
ROMY SO51 .... 6 C4
Hamble County Primary School
HLER SO31 .... 69 G1
Hamble County
Secondary School
HLER SO31 .... 63 G5
Hampshire County Council
ELGH SO50 .... 20 A3
Hampshire County Council
ELGH SO50 .... 20 D3
Hampshire County Council
TOTT SO40 .... 49 H3
Hampshire County Cricket Club
WSHM SO15 .... 40 D4
Hamwic College
SHAM SO14 .... 3 F3
Hardley School
FAWY SO45 .... 72 C3
Harefield Clinic
WEND SO18 .... 42 C5
Harefield Junior & Infant School
WEND SO18 .... 42 D4
Hazel Wood 1st School
TOTT SO40 .... 37 E5
Heathfield Infant &
Middle School
ITCH SO19 .... 55 E5
Hedge End Business Centre
HEND SO30 .... 44 B4
Hedge End Retail Park
HEND SO30 .... 44 A5
Hedge End Town Council
HEND SO30 .... 56 B1
The Heritage Centre & Museum
TOTT SO40 .... 50 B1
Highfield C of E (a)
Primary School
PTSW SO17 .... 41 E2
Hightown Primary School
ITCH SO19 .... 55 G3
Hill Lane Surgery
WSHM SO15 .... 40 C5

Hiltingbury County Junior &
Infant School
CHFD SO53 .... 9 G2
Hindu Temple
SHAM SO14 .... 53 F1
Holbury County Jmi School
FAWY SO45 .... 72 C5
Hollybrook First School
ROWN SO16 .... 40 B1
Hollybrook Middle School
ROWN SO16 .... 40 B1
Holy Family RC Primary School
ROWN SO16 .... 38 C2
Hook with Warsash
Primary School
HLER SO31 .... 70 D5
Hounsdown School
TOTT SO40 .... 49 H3
Hythe CP School
FAWY SO45 .... 67 E1
Hythe Medical Centre
FAWY SO45 .... 66 D3
Itchen College
ITCH SO19 .... 54 C2
J M L Trading Estate
WSHM SO15 .... 2 A1
J M L Trading Estate
WSHM SO15 .... 52 C2
Kanes Hill Primary School
ITCH SO19 .... 55 G1
King Edward VI School
WSHM SO15 .... 40 C4
Kings Copse Primary School
HEND SO30 .... 56 C2
Kingsland Market
SHAM SO14 .... 3 F2
The Kings Primary School
HEND SO30 .... 43 F1
Kings School
ELGH SO50 .... 22 B5
Knightwood Primary School
NBAD SO52 .... 8 D4
Langdown County
Infants School
FAWY SO45 .... 67 F3
Langdown County Junior School
FAWY SO45 .... 67 F2
Leigh House Hospital
CHFD SO53 .... 9 F3
Leisure Centre
SHAM SO14 .... 53 E1
Liner Industrial Estate
WSHM SO15 .... 52 A1
Locksheath County Infants &
Primary School
HLER SO31 .... 71 G4
Locks Road Surgery
HLER SO31 .... 71 G3
Lockswood Surgery
HLER SO31 .... 71 G2
Longbridge Industrial Park
SHAM SO14 .... 3 H5
Lordshill Health Centre
ROWN SO16 .... 27 F5
L S U College of
Higher Education
WSHM SO15 .... 40 D5
Lucia Foster Welch College
SHAM SO14 .... 3 G5
Ludlow Infant School
ITCH SO19 .... 54 A4
Ludlow Middle School
ITCH SO19 .... 54 A3
Lulworth Business Centre
TOTT SO40 .... 37 G2
Lydlynch County First School
TOTT SO40 .... 37 G5
Lyndhurst Infant School
LYND SO43 .... 58 D5
Lyndhurst Surgery
LYND SO43 .... 58 D5
Malvern Business Centre
ROWN SO16 .... 40 B2
Manor Infant School
FAWY SO45 .... 72 C3
Mansbridge Primary School
WEND SO18 .... 30 A4
Mansel Infant & Junior Schools
ROWN SO16 .... 38 D2
Marlands Shopping Centre
SHAM SO14 .... 2 D2
Marwell Zoological Park
RWIN SO21 .... 13 F3
Mason Manor Primary School
ROWN SO16 .... 39 F4
Mayflower Theatre
WSHM SO15 .... 52 D2

Merdon Junior School
CHFD SO53 .... 9 H4
Meridian TV Studios
SHAM SO14 .... 53 G1
Millbrook Clinic
ROWN SO16 .... 39 E4
Millbrook Community School
ROWN SO16 .... 39 E1
Millbrook Secondary School
ROWN SO16 .... 39 E1
Millbrook Trading Estate
WSHM SO15 .... 39 E5
Millers Dale Surgery
CHFD SO53 .... 9 F3
Millhouse Business Centre
ITCH SO19 .... 53 H3
Monks Brook Industrial Park
CHFD SO53 .... 19 F1
Moorgreen Hospital
HEND SO30 .... 43 H2
Moorlands Infant School
WEND SO18 .... 42 C3
Mortimers Farm
Industrial Estate
ROMY SO51 .... 24 A3
Mountbatten Business Centre
WSHM SO15 .... 52 B2
Mountbatten Secondary School
ROMY SO51 .... 6 C5
The Mount Hospital
ELGH SO50 .... 21 F1
Mount Pleasant Industrial Estate
SHAM SO14 .... 41 F5
Mount Pleasant Junior School
SHAM SO14 .... 41 F5
Nelson Industrial Park
HEND SO30 .... 44 F5
Netley Abbey Infant School
HLER SO31 .... 62 D5
Netley Court School
HLER SO31 .... 62 D5
Netley Marsh C of E
Controlled Infant School
TOTT SO40 .... 36 C5
New Forest Golf Club
LYND SO43 .... 59 F4
New Forest Museum &
Visitors Centre
LYND SO43 .... 59 E5
Newlands Infant &
Middle School
ROWN SO16 .... 39 E3
The Newton Health Clinic
SHAM SO14 .... 53 E1
Nightingale County Junior &
Infant School
ELGH SO50 .... 19 H5
Nightingale Surgery
ROMY SO51 .... 6 A3
Northam Business Centre
SHAM SO14 .... 53 G1
Northam Primary School
SHAM SO14 .... 53 G2
North Baddesley County Infants
School
NBAD SO52 .... 17 H2
North Baddesley Junior School
NBAD SO52 .... 17 H2
Northbrook Industrial Estate
ROWN SO16 .... 40 A2
Northview Gallery
HLER SO31 .... 64 C2
Norwood CP School
ELGH SO50 .... 20 C3
Nuffield Theatre
PTSW SO17 .... 41 E1
Nursling C of E Primary School
ROWN SO16 .... 26 D4
Nursling Industrial Estate
ROWN SO16 .... 26 B5
Nursling Industrial Estate
ROWN SO16 .... 38 B1
Oakfield Primary School
TOTT SO40 .... 37 G4
Oaklands Community School
ROWN SO16 .... 27 F4
Oak Lodge School
FAWY SO45 .... 66 A2
Oakwood First School
ROWN SO16 .... 27 H4
Oakwood Junior School
ROWN SO16 .... 27 H4
Oatlands House Health Clinic
ROWN SO16 .... 40 A2
Oceanographic Centre
SHAM SO14 .... 3 H7
Odeon Cinema
WSHM SO15 .... 2 B3

Oil Refinery
FAWY SO45 .... **73** F4

Old Anchor Inn Surgery
ELGH SO50 .... **21** E3

The Old Fire Station Surgery
ITCH SO19 .... **54** A4

On Line Gallery
WSHM SO15 .... **52** D1

Orchard County Infant &
Junior School
FAWY SO45 .... **66** C3

Orion Business Centre
WEND SO18 .... **30** A4

Otterbourne Primary School
RWIN SO21 .... **10** D1

Park Gate Business Centre
HLER SO31 .... **65** H4

Park Gate Junior School
HLER SO31 .... **65** H5

Peacock Trading Estate
ELGH SO50 .... **20** B1

Phoenix Industrial Park
ELGH SO50 .... **21** E4

Pitmore School
CHFD SO53 .... **10** B3

Plaza Theatre
ROMY SO51 .... **5** H4

Police Station & Courts
SHAM SO14 .... **52** D2

The Polygon School
WSHM SO15 .... **52** C1

Portswood Primary School
PTSW SO17 .... **41** G2

Portswood Road Surgery
PTSW SO17 .... **41** F3

Princess Anne Hospital
ROWN SO16 .... **39** H1

Redbridge Community School
ROWN SO16 .... **38** D4

Redbridge Primary School
ROWN SO16 .... **38** D4

Red Funnel Ferry Terminal
SHAM SO14 .... **2** D6

Red Lodge School
ROWN SO16 .... **28** C5

Regents Park Girls School
ROWN SO16 .... **39** G4

Regents Park Surgery
WSHM SO15 .... **39** H4

Regional Film Theatre
SHAM SO14 .... **3** G7

Rex Industrial Estate
CHFD SO53 .... **19** G1

Ridgeway House Special School
ITCH SO19 .... **54** A2

Romsey Abbey C of E
Primary School
ROMY SO51 .... **5** F4

Romsey County Junior School
ROMY SO51 .... **6** A3

Romsey Cricket Club
ROMY SO51 .... **5** H5

Romsey Hospital
ROMY SO51 .... **6** A4

Romsey Industrial Estate
ROMY SO51 .... **5** H3

Romsey Infant School
ROMY SO51 .... **5** H4

Romsey Rugby Football Club
ROMY SO51 .... **5** H5

The Romsey School
ROMY SO51 .... **5** G3

Romsey Sports Centre
ROMY SO51 .... **5** H5

Rowmans House Industrial Estate
ROWN SO16 .... **27** E3

Royal South Hants Hospital
SHAM SO14 .... **53** E1

Rushington Business Park
TOTT SO40 .... **49** G2

Russell Hicks & Temple
ROMY SO51 .... **5** G4

St Andrews Surgery
ELGH SO50 .... **20** C4

St Catherines Road
Junior School
ELGH SO50 .... **20** C1

St Christophers School
WEND SO18 .... **42** A4

St Denys Primary School
PTSW SO17 .... **41** G3

St Francis Primary School
NBAD SO52 .... **18** D1

St Georges Catholic Boys School
ELGH SO50 .... **29** G3

St James Primary School
HEND SO30 .... **43** H2

St Lukes Surgery
HEND SO30 .... **44** B3

St Marks C of E Junior School
WSHM SO15 .... **40** B5

St Marys C of E Primary School
SHAM SO14 .... **3** G1

St Marys C of E Primary School
SHAM SO14 .... **3** H1

St Marys College
WEND SO18 .... **42** A4

St Marys Surgery
SHAM SO14 .... **3** G2

St Monica Infant School
ITCH SO19 .... **54** C4

St Monica Middle School
ITCH SO19 .... **54** C4

St Patricks RC Primary School
ITCH SO19 .... **54** A4

St Swithun Wells RC
Primary School
CHFD SO53 .... **19** H1

Salterns School
TOTT SO40 .... **38** A4

Sarisbury Green C of E
Primary School
HLER SO31 .... **65** E5

Sarisbury Infant School
HLER SO31 .... **71** E1

Scantabout Primary School
CHFD SO53 .... **10** B4

School
SHAM SO14 .... **2** D5

Shakespeare Business Centre
ELGH SO50 .... **20** D2

Shakespeare County
Infant School
ELGH SO50 .... **20** C2

Shamblehurst CP School
HEND SO30 .... **44** C4

Sherborne House School
CHFD SO53 .... **9** H3

Shirley Business Park
WSHM SO15 .... **40** A5

Shirley First & Middle School
WSHM SO15 .... **40** A3

The Shirley Health Centre
WSHM SO15 .... **40** A5

Shirley Swimming Pool
WSHM SO15 .... **40** A5

Shirley Warren Primary School
ROWN SO16 .... **39** G2

Sholing First School
ITCH SO19 .... **54** C3

Sholing Girls School
ITCH SO19 .... **54** C3

Sholing Infants School
ITCH SO19 .... **54** C2

Sholing Middle School
ITCH SO19 .... **54** C2

Sidings Industrial Estate
HLER SO31 .... **63** F5

Simcoe Clinic
WSHM SO15 .... **40** C5

Sinclair First & Junior School
ROWN SO16 .... **27** G4

Solent Business Centre
WSHM SO15 .... **51** H1

Solent Industrial Centre
WSHM SO15 .... **40** A5

Solent Industrial Estate
HEND SO30 .... **44** B3

Solent Peoples Theatre
ITCH SO19 .... **55** E4

Southampton Airport
Parkway Station
ELGH SO50 .... **30** B3

Southampton Central Mosque
SHAM SO14 .... **53** F1

Southampton City College
SHAM SO14 .... **3** G3

Southampton City Council
PTSW SO17 .... **41** G2

Southampton City Council
ROWN SO16 .... **28** B4

Southampton City Council
ROWN SO16 .... **38** C2

Southampton City Council
ROWN SO16 .... **39** H3

Southampton City Council
SHAM SO14 .... **2** D5

Southampton City Council
SHAM SO14 .... **2** D4

Southampton City Council
SHAM SO14 .... **3** H2

Southampton City Council
SHAM SO14 .... **3** G1

Southampton City Council
WSHM SO15 .... **2** A1

Southampton Football Club
WSHM SO15 .... **52** C1

Southampton General Hospital
ROWN SO16 .... **39** H1

Southampton Institute & Millais
Gallery
WSHM SO15 .... **52** D2

Southampton Magistrates Court
WSHM SO15 .... **53** E1

Southampton & New Forest
Magistrates Courts
WSHM SO15 .... **52** C2

Southampton Sports Centre
ROWN SO16 .... **28** B5

Southampton Sports Club
ROWN SO16 .... **38** C2

Southampton Technical College
SHAM SO15 .... **3** K4

Southampton University
ROWN SO16 .... **18** A5

South West Health Authority
HEND SO30 .... **56** B3

Spitfire Court Surgery
SHAM SO16 .... **3** K5

Springhill RC Primary School
WSHM SO15 .... **52** C1

Stanton Industrial Estate
WSHM SO15 .... **39** G5

Stoke Park County Junior School
ELGH SO50 .... **21** G3

Stoke Park Infant School
ELGH SO50 .... **21** G4

Stokewood Surgery
ELGH SO50 .... **22** A4

Stroud School
ROMY SO51 .... **7** E3

Super Bowl
WSHM SO15 .... **39** F5

Superstore
SHAM SO14 .... **2** C1

Superstore
SHAM SO14 .... **2** C2

Surrey House First School
ITCH SO19 .... **55** E4

Surrey House Health Centre
ITCH SO19 .... **55** E4

Swanwick Business Park
HLER SO31 .... **64** D3

Swaything Clinic
PTSW SO17 .... **41** G1

Swaything Primary School
PTSW SO17 .... **41** F1

The Synagogue
PTSW SO17 .... **40** D5

Talisman Business Centre
HLER SO31 .... **65** H4

Tankerville School
ELGH SO50 .... **20** D3

Tanners Brook Infant School
WSHM SO15 .... **39** F5

Tanners Brook Junior School
ROWN SO16 .... **39** F5

Tatchbury Manor House
TOTT SO40 .... **36** B3

Tatchbury Mount Hospital
TOTT SO40 .... **36** C2

Tauntons College
WSHM SO15 .... **40** C3

Test Vale Surgery
TOTT SO40 .... **37** H4

Test Valley Business Centre
TOTT SO40 .... **38** B2

Testwood School
TOTT SO40 .... **37** H3

Thornden School
CHFD SO53 .... **10** B3

Thornhill Clinic
ITCH SO19 .... **55** F2

Thornhill First School
ITCH SO19 .... **55** E2

Thornhill Junior School
ITCH SO19 .... **55** E2

Thornhill Park Surgery
ITCH SO19 .... **55** F1

Totton College
TOTT SO40 .... **37** F4

Totton College
TOTT SO40 .... **49** G2

Totton Recreation Centre
TOTT SO40 .... **37** F4

Tower Industrial Estate
ELGH SO50 .... **21** E4

Townhill Infant School
WEND SO18 .... **42** C2

Townhill Middle School
WEND SO18 .... **42** C2

Townhill Park Health Clinic
WEND SO18 .... **42** C2

Townhill Surgery
WEND SO18 .... **42** D1

The Toynbee School
CHFD SO53 .... **19** H1

Trinity Business Centre
TOTT SO40 .... **37** G2

Trinity Industrial Estate
WSHM SO15 .... **39** F5

Trojans Sports Club
ELGH SO50 .... **29** G2

Tudor House Museum
SHAM SO14 .... **2** D4

Twyford Surgery
RWIN SO21 .... **11** H2

University of Southampton
PTSW SO17 .... **41** F1

University of Southampton
ROWN SO16 .... **40** D1

Vermont School
ROWN SO16 .... **28** C5

Victor Street Surgery
WSHM SO15 .... **39** H3

Virgin Cinemas
SHAM SO14 .... **3** G6

Waterfront Garden Surgery
FAWY SO45 .... **61** E3

Waterloo Industrial Estate
HEND SO30 .... **44** B3

The Waterside Health Centre
FAWY SO45 .... **67** E3

Wellington Sports Club
ELGH SO50 .... **29** H2

Wessex Nuffield Hospital
CHFD SO53 .... **10** B2

Wessex Nuffield Hospital
ELGH SO50 .... **20** D3

Wessex Regional
Health Authority
HEND SO30 .... **44** B3

West End Surgery
HEND SO30 .... **43** G2

Western Community Hospital
ROWN SO16 .... **39** G3

Weston Park Boys School
ITCH SO19 .... **62** D1

Weston Park First School
ITCH SO19 .... **62** C1

Weston Park Junior School
ITCH SO19 .... **62** C1

Weston Shore First School
ITCH SO19 .... **62** B2

West Quay Retail Park
WSHM SO15 .... **2** B2

West Quay Shopping Centre
SHAM SO14 .... **2** C2

Westwood Business Park
TOTT SO40 .... **37** H2

The Whiteley Surgery
HLER SO31 .... **65** H2

Wildern Clinic
HEND SO30 .... **44** C5

The Wildern School
HEND SO30 .... **44** C5

Wildground County
Infant School
FAWY SO45 .... **66** D4

Wildground County
Junior School
FAWY SO45 .... **66** D4

Willments Industrial Estate
ITCH SO19 .... **53** H2

The Winchester Gallery
ROWN SO16 .... **40** C1

Woodhill Preparatory School
CHFD SO53 .... **9** H4

Woodhills School
HEND SO30 .... **45** F5

Woodlands Community School
WEND SO18 .... **43** H4

Wool House Maritime Museum
SHAM SO14 .... **2** D5

Woolston First School
ITCH SO19 .... **54** A5

Woolston School
ITCH SO19 .... **54** B4

Wordsworth Infant School
WSHM SO15 .... **40** A3

The Wyvern Community
Secondary School
ELGH SO50 .... **22** C5

Yeoman Industrial Park
TOTT SO40 .... **38** B2

Notes

Notes